Gerald Bu

HISTORY IN THE ARAB SKIES:

Aviation's Impact on the Middle East

RIMAL PUBLICATIONS

First published 2011

Rimal Publications
Nicosia, Cyprus
www.rimalbooks.com

ISBN 978-9963-610-73-0

Cover design by Marcus Butt
Book design by Chara Adamidou
Printed and bound by Kailas
Nicosia, Cyprus

For Amelia, Miranda, Marcus – and Edward,
who landed unexpectedly during the writing of this book.

Table of Contents

Introduction

The story of the rapid expansion of aviation during the past century weaves its way in and out of the history of the Middle East. The region provided neither the cradle of flight, nor the birthplace of its early pioneers. Yet aviation played a decisive and fateful role in the shaping of the region – in the colonial years, the era of independence and the modern period. Air power, limited as it was, helped the Arab Revolt achieve success during the First World War. Aerial superiority also gave the British the upper hand in Mesopotamia during the same war after a number of setbacks at the hands of the Ottoman Turks and played a key role in driving Axis powers out of North Africa in World War Two. It gave Britain's special forces the edge in a campaign against Marxist rebels in southern Oman in the 1970s; and it provided a formidable weapon which helped in no small way to hand Israel a number of victories over Arab states in the second half of the 20th century. It is not an exaggeration to say that the shape and the character of the modern Middle East would have been different without the invention of the aeroplane.

The development of civilian aircraft also impacted social and economic patterns in the region, slashing the time taken to travel between towns and cities separated by vast tracts of desert or high mountains. Traditional ways of life were changed overnight by the arrival of the aeroplane. Mecca was suddenly within reach for millions of pilgrims – from within the Middle East and also from around the world. Christian pilgrims, too, began arriving in the Holy Land by air from every corner of the globe. The search for oil and gas in the deserts and seas of the Gulf region throughout the 20th century was accelerated by the arrival of survey and supply aircraft, paving the way for the decades of prosperity. Fresh fruit and vegetables could be flown from Lebanon to the arid Gulf states. And businessmen in droves could fly in to share in the Gulf's prosperity.

That prosperity has been exploited in part to turn what until the 1960s was a remote and barren part of the world into one of the major hubs of international aviation. Today, vast new commercial planes like the Airbus A380, built with the major Gulf airlines in mind, carry businessmen and tourists from one corner of the globe to another and bring in the Asians who provide the labour to construct and maintain the cities. These airlines have names that are familiar in households throughout the world: no football fan alive can fail to tell you that Arsenal – one of the top teams in the English Premier League – play at the Emirates Stadium in London. Similarly, the sight of the Emirates logo on touchline advertising boards at football stadiums in South Africa during the 2010 World Cup is unlikely to have raised eyebrows among the millions of television viewers worldwide. The airlines of the Gulf have international reputations.

The spectacular expansion of the Gulf airlines – Emirates, Etihad and Qatar, in particular – over a relatively short time might give the impression that the development of aviation in the Middle East was no more than a by-product of the oil boom. But this is far from the truth. The roots of the first Arab airlines can be traced back to the 1930s, while the first aeroplanes were seen in the region only six years after the Wright brothers became the first men to break the barrier of powered flight. The Middle East has been steeped in aviation for more than a century – a fact that has been largely neglected by historians. The Arab public, for its part, has developed a cynical mindset in which developments as a whole in the region over the past century are assumed largely to have been manipulated by outside powers to the detriment of the indigenous inhabitants. So the achievement of a century of flying in the region is hardly seen as a cause for celebration. To some extent the cynicism might be justified: the extent to which the Arabs have or have not managed to exploit the opportunities presented to them from the earliest pioneering years of aviation is one of the themes explored in the pages ahead.

Yet I believe there are grounds for commemoration, if not celebration. For the region was fortunate to witness some of the most important pioneering flights across its territories, opening up new routes to India, the Far East, Australia and South Africa. Tiny biplanes, piloted by a lone man or woman, bumped their way through the skies of the Middle East as they headed precariously towards new horizons. Many of the pioneers wrote about their experiences, providing vivid and historically important accounts of the places and people they met along the way. For example, in 1919, Captain Ross Smith made the first flight from England to Australia. In his diary he described the section of his flight from Crete to Cairo: "Weather again bad. Low clouds made crossing Cretan mountains difficult... had to fly through rain at 2,000 ft most of the way across the Mediterranean... struck African coast at Sollum, then flew east to Cairo across desert via Matruh. Hope to reach Damascus or Baghdad tomorrow..." In the 1930s, the French aviator and author Antoine de Saint-Exupéry wrote an exquisitely poetic description of a flight across North Africa that was supposed to set a new record for a flight from Paris to Saigon. He ended up crashing into the desert before he reached Cairo and being rescued by Bedouin. Accounts of this kind establish the connections between the aerial exploits during the various stages of flight development, and the land and people of the region.

For centuries before the Wright brothers' success in achieving powered flight, mankind had looked to the heavens for inspiration. The sky high above was the domain of God and the winged angels. Muslims believe that the Prophet Muhammad flew on a horse with wings from Mecca to Jerusalem for his night journey to heaven. Christians believe that Christ "ascended into heaven" and sing of "Angels from the Realms of Glory". The inhabitants of the Middle East, as much as those everywhere, had a yearning for a more elevated state of spirituality that translated, in part, into an instinctive desire to rise into the sky. In the words of one aviation historian, "human beings have always dreamt of flight... The flight to which humans traditionally aspired was that of the birds, a business of feather and flapping wings. To this the myths and legends of many cultures testify."[1] Over the centuries, many attempts were made to turn such myths into reality.

Muslims from the Middle East were among those who tried to defy the laws of gravity, including Abbas ibn Firnas, an Arab who was born and lived his life in Cordoba in Andalusia (modern-day Spain) during the 9th century. As a successful scientist, he turned his attention to the conundrum of how man might fly through the air. According to sketchy reports from the time, in 875 he attached some feathers to his body and fixed more on a wooden frame that would serve as wings. When he launched himself from the top of a hill he was reportedly seen to fly briefly before crashing to the ground and injuring his back. He never experimented this way again. Abbas ibn Firnas' attempt to fly is believed to have inspired the pioneers of later generations (among them Leonardo da Vinci) who were obsessed by a desire to achieve heavier-than-air flight. There is at least one physical reminder of one of the earliest would-be aviators: an airport north of Baghdad is named after him.

In 1178, a Muslim citizen of Constantinople (today's Istanbul) tried to fly from the top of the Hippodrome in the presence of Emperor Comnenus. The aspiring aviator was clothed in a long and ample white robe, the folds of which had been stiffened by wands of willow with the intention that they should form wings. The story goes that while the crowd urged him to fly, the emperor cautioned him against the attempt. The Muslim waited until he judged that the wind was favourable and then jumped. Not surprisingly, he fell heavily to the ground, breaking a number of bones in the process. He, too, abandoned the search for a means of flying. Constantinople was also the scene, according to Turkish historical accounts, of a successful gliding flight across the Golden Horn waterway. Hezarfen Ahmed Çelebi is said to have attached wings to his body and taken to the air from the top of the Galata Tower, before landing safely on the other side of the Golden Horn. Even if the exact details of the event are hazy, the fact that Çelebi experimented in this way is further proof of mankind's craving to fly. Çelebi is still remembered: Hezarfen airport in Istanbul is named after him.

But surely these early experiments had long faded from the minds of the inhabitants of the Middle East when the first flimsy aeroplanes arrived in the region early in the 20ᵗʰ century. The sense of awe and excitement at seeing for the first time what had previously seemed impossible – a mechanical contraption carrying a man through the air – was as great on the streets of Cairo and Alexandria as it was in Paris and London. The Middle East, in short, was a witness to the development of flight almost from the day of its birth.

I don't remember the first time I was taken on an aeroplane. I was less than two at the time. The year was 1951 and the country was Iran (or Persia, as it was called in those days). My father was a manager of the Imperial Bank of Persia (later becoming the British Bank of the Middle East), and my parents had been living in Tehran since 1938. My two brothers and my sister had been born there. A British Overseas Airways Corporation (BOAC) timetable from 1951 indicates that the Canadair Argonaut airliner would have left Tehran (where I, too, was born) at 7.30 in the morning, headed for Lydda in Israel. After an hour on the ground, it would have continued to Rome for another refuelling stop. The Argonaut was scheduled to reach London airport at 10.30 at night, with passengers arriving finally at the BOAC Air Terminal in Victoria – an elegant art deco building close to the mainline station – just before midnight.

While I have no memory of that first flight it set a pattern that has continued for six decades. Flying and the Middle East are interwoven with my own history and that of my family as much as they are with the history of the region. Old air tickets, BOAC bags (the small zip-up cabin bags that the airline used to issue to passengers), fans, post cards and boarding cards that have survived our many changes of abode evoke memories the way that diaries do. Flying is in our blood. My uncle Frederick lied about his age to join the Royal Flying Corps towards the end of the First World War. He was stationed in Mesopotamia and was awarded the Distinguished Flying Cross medal. A clock my uncle made from the spindle of a wooden propeller taken from a biplane of that era (handed down to me by my mother) is my sole physical connection with him. My two brothers and my sister still talk of the flights they made around the Middle East in the 1940s, 50s and 60s. On at least one occasion, my three siblings came out to Jordan (where my father was working) for the school holidays, because a family photograph shows the four us on the tarmac at Amman airport in front of a BOAC Argonaut. My two brothers and sister are in school uniform ready for the flight back to England. I owe to them my lifelong obsession with flying which led, eventually, to my obtaining a pilot's licence of my own. Carrying on the family tradition, my niece Alison is a First Officer with British Airways. As I write, she is – appropriately – on a stopover in Jeddah.

My early memories of flying and the Middle East are also tainted equally with joy and despondency. Joy at the prospect of the end of term at boarding school, and taking the train to London, the coach from the BOAC terminal to Heathrow and the flight to Beirut or Bahrain – wherever my parents were based at that time. Despondency crept up slowly at the prospect of agonising farewells at the airport before the flight back to London and then the long trek by car and train to the desolation of a town in the Somerset countryside. Life as an exile from aviation and the Middle East was not easy. But the thought that one day I would be at Heathrow again, boarding a plane back to the Middle East, sustained me during those long terms at boarding school. Daydreaming of flying was my escape mechanism – to a ludicrous extent. There was a hymn that we sang frequently in chapel that contained the lines: "Rank on rank the host of heaven, Sent its vanguard on the way." In my imagination, 'vanguard' became Vickers Vanguard, a turbo-prop airliner that was in service in the 1960s.

Flights out to visit my parents for school holidays were recorded in a smart blue, stiff-backed book with the imperial-looking BOAC crest on the cover. This was the personal log book for members of the (at the time) futuristic-sounding 'Junior Jet Club', to which all very young BOAC travellers could belong. After boarding, the log was taken by a member of the cabin crew to the captain to be filled in and signed during the flight.

I also used an old school exercise book to record the flights I took in those early years of my life. I see that on 17 January 1963, I accompanied my father on a business trip from Bahrain to Doha. We flew there on a Kuwait Airways Vickers Viscount (registration G-APOW) and returned on a Gulf Aviation de Havilland Heron (G-APKV). I don't remember how I spent the day while my father was working, but I do recall arriving back at Doha airport to find that the flight was overbooked. But this was not a problem. A seat was found for my father, while I sat on a wooden box at the back of the small cabin for the short flight back to Bahrain.

It was during this period that I first visited Dubai. The plane from Bahrain landed on a tarmac runway – but the airport building still wasn't much more than a single-storey structure. In previous years, when my father flew to Dubai, the facilities had been more basic. As the small Gulf Aviation de Havilland Dove descended he used to sit behind the pilot, and the two of them would peer through the heat haze looking for the two lines of oil drums that marked the landing strip of compacted sand.

Two days after the trip to Doha with my father, the exercise book log shows, I flew back to England to return to boarding school. The Comet 4 jet airliner (G-APDN) stopped at Baghdad, Amman and Rome on the way – landing eventually late at night at Manchester because Heathrow had been closed by snow. I remember that my sister was with me on that flight. At Amman, one of the joining passengers was Crown Prince Hassan, the younger brother of King Hussein. I had attended nursery school with the prince when my parents lived in Jordan. At my sister's insistence I made myself known to Prince Hassan who gave me a photo of himself with the inscription: "It's good to see an old friend again." The prince was returning for the new term at Harrow – one of Britain's most prestigious public schools. I was reminded of the January 1963 flight while conducting research for this book by an entry I discovered in the *Imperial Airways Monthly Bulletin* of August 1927. The link, it turned out, between air travel and Arab royalty's attendance at British public schools extended back many decades. The bulletin said Imperial Airways (the forerunner of BOAC) had had the "distinction of carrying on the Cairo-Basra service HM King Feisal and the Emir Ghazi of Iraq. Earlier in the month, the heir to the throne of Iraq, who was returning from Harrow accompanied by his tutor, travelled in the 'City of Baghdad' [as the aircraft was named] between Cairo and Baghdad."

The Middle East/aviation theme continued for me after school and university. As a young reporter with the *BBC* I relished assignments that in some way involved aviation. It was my luck, therefore, to be sent to Algiers in January 1981 to await the arrival of the 52 Americans who had been held hostage at the US embassy in Tehran. I reported live from the tarmac of Algiers airport (where, for some reason, there was a strong stench of sewage) as the Air Algérie Boeing 727 came to a halt in front of the VIP lounge. Moments later, the hostages came down the steps to freedom after 444 days in captivity. Algeria had played a leading intermediary role to secure their release.

Flying memories from my reporting days do not always have happy associations. During the Israeli siege of West Beirut in 1982, as a *BBC* correspondent I was one of the many thousands of civilians who were terrified by the daily and nightly whine of jets overhead, followed by the thunderous sounds of aerial bombardment. Towards the end of 1983, during a lull in the fighting, Beirut airport was reopened. I decided to take my family to Cyprus for a break. We were just getting off the airport bus to board the Middle East Airlines plane when a shell crashed onto the tarmac. Along with the other passengers we scrambled up the steps. On board, the cabin staff propelled us all to the nearest seats. Faces taut with fear, hearts beating fast. The next explosion rocked the aircraft on its wheels. It was my three-year-old daughter who calmly pointed out the smoke rising from the tarmac a few feet from the left wing-tip. The third explosion was felt, not heard. The sound was drowned by the roar of the jet engines, which were being started even as we were scrambling aboard. The pilots swung the Boeing 707 onto the nearest runway and without stopping or taxiing to the end for maximum length the jet took off, banking and turning out to sea as soon as it was airborne.

Beirut airport has since been rebuilt, with a new runway allowing an approach over the sea instead of the slums of Ouzai. New and bigger airports are being built throughout the Middle East. Low-cost airlines are making air travel affordable to increasing sections of the population, building on a long-established tradition of Middle Eastern air travel. A British aviation writer of the 1940s, with the patronising tone of the day, wrote: "The Arab accepts the idea of flight as part of his life with the same practical philosophy as he accepts the 'jerricans' in the western desert instead of his traditional water-skins. Aeroplanes nowadays are sometimes chartered by air-minded Arabs for their pilgrimages to Mecca."[2] Today, the inhabitants of the Middle East are air-minded as never before – in terms of accepting air travel as a part of daily life. In this respect they join the rest of the world's population in viewing flight as a mundane activity, rather than a spiritually uplifting one. On a recent flight on Etihad Airways I observed two Emirati girls as we made our night-time approach towards Abu Dhabi airport. The eyes of each girl were focused on portable DVD players and they never as much as glimpsed out of the window to see the tracery of lights on the dark backcloth below.

The wonder of flying in the Middle East may be lost. But its long, interesting and influential role in the history of the region should be preserved for posterity.

The pages ahead do not pretend to offer a comprehensive account either of aviation in the Middle East or of the contemporary history of that part of the world. The idea, instead, is to provide a narrative that explores some of the moments when they intersected. Where possible I have incorporated some lengthy descriptions and comments from publications from each particular era to give a sense of the mood at the time. For the sake of authenticity, I have left the original spellings of place names in these quotes and indicated their modern equivalents where necessary. I hope that readers will be tolerant of the inconsistency that results from this.

one

A Right Royal Occasion

The winter of 1909-10 in Cairo was one that Egyptians and foreign residents there would never forget. It was when Egypt took its place alongside just a handful of countries on the aviation map. The map itself had been created only seven years earlier when the Wright brothers achieved the world's first manned, powered and controlled flight by a heavier-than-air craft – at Kitty Hawk, North Carolina in the United States. The focus of flying development then shifted to France. But even there, progress in developing the techniques of flying was slow. Elsewhere in Europe it was slower still: the first officially recognised inaugural flight in Britain did not take place until late in 1908. Only in July 1909, did Frenchman Louis Blériot, in a monoplane he had designed himself called a Blériot XI, beat off a challenge from his compatriot, Hubert Latham, to become the first pilot to achieve what at the time many swore would be impossible: to fly across the English Channel. One major aviation hurdle had been crossed, but countless others had not – such as the first flight between the English cities of London and Manchester. So in the winter of 1909-10, when Egypt was introduced to aviation, flying was still very much in its infancy.

Young and limited though aviation was, the thought that man could now leave the ground and return to it safely – after centuries of failure – captured the public imagination. People longed to witness the spectacle for themselves, particularly after Blériot had demonstrated how flying could conquer the sea as well as the land. In August 1909, shortly after his aerial crossing from France to England, the first international flying competition, La Grande Semaine d'Aviation de la Champagne, was held at Reims in the Champagne district of France. Twenty-three 'aircraft' (the word seems too grand for the wire, wood and canvas contraptions of the day) competed for cash prizes in speed, distance and duration contests throughout the week-long event. The event drew huge crowds. Those who came to Reims to see Blériot, Latham and others compete for the prizes included royalty, society elite from across Europe and thousands of people without rank or privilege. Those who were able to attend the meeting were agog at what they saw. Others followed the event via the awe-struck descriptions in newspapers and magazines. The Reims week was an exceptional success for those interested in promoting aviation; and a resounding commercial bonanza for the businessmen who had sponsored it. Little wonder that others sought to emulate it.

A similar event, held the following October at Juvisy near Paris, attracted a crowd of 200,000 people. The local railway became gridlocked and many arrived too late for the show. When it ended, "mobs unable to return wrecked the stations at Juvisy and Savigny, and also several trains."[1]

The next day, on 13 October 1909, the daily English-language newspaper in Egypt, the *Egyptian Gazette*, carried an article under the headline: "Aviation in Egypt: Heliopolis Meeting – 150,000 Francs in Prize Money." The report said: "Egypt has at last taken a decided step to attract tourists to this country. Judging by the crowds which attended the recent meeting at Juvisy, aviation is the most paying attraction of the present day. No more suitable place could be found than Heliopolis with its miles of rolling desert, plenty of space for the aviators and plenty of space for the spectators." The aviation week would be held in February 1910, the report added, but the location of the aerodrome would not be decided until a French expert had arrived to advise on the matter.[2]

As a group of businessmen in Cairo, including a Belgian

entrepreneur, Baron Édouard Empain, and a former Egyptian prime minister, Boghos Nubar Pasha, started making arrangements with the Automobile Club of Egypt for the Heliopolis meeting, other aviation developments were being recorded elsewhere in North Africa. As early as 1909, *Flight* magazine was reporting the establishment of an aero club in Algeria [an integral part of France at that time] – but the club concentrated on ballooning rather than the flying of fixed-wing aircraft.[3] The first fixed-wing flight in Algeria is credited to Frenchman René Metrot in October 1909. The following month, Metrot and another Frenchman, known only as Monsieur Saurin, gave an exhibition of flying in Algiers before a crowd of 25,000 people, the former on a Voisin, the latter on a Blériot of the cross-Channel type. M Metrot met with the greatest success, and his best flight was two kilometres in length. M Saurin made one or two long jumps of about 200 metres.[4] But there was better to come. In December, Metrot made a 3-kilometre cross-country flight from Algiers to Blida, "where he rounded the clock of St Charles Church, at height of about 150 metres... On the previous Tuesday M Metrot evoked great applause by racing an express train for 7 kilometres. The train of course was badly beaten, and then the aviator flew back without incident."

The go-ahead entrepreneurs of Cairo would, no doubt, have followed all these events with particular interest. As the date of the Heliopolis aviation week approached, excitement – both official and private – grew. Advertisements appeared in the press declaring: "Great Week of Aviation at Heliopolis under the patronage of HH The Khedive [Abbas II, the title adopted by the most senior member of the Egyptian ruling family – but Britain had occupied Egypt in 1882 and was the real power there], 6-13 February 1910. 12 aviators... 18 aeroplanes...50% reduction to soldiers and children. Special trains from Alexandria and back... Special tramcar service from Cairo to Heliopolis." Public curiosity had been heightened by an exhibition in Alexandria the previous November of a Blériot monoplane. In the words of the *Egyptian Gazette*: "On Sunday last there took place in one of the halls of the Jardin Rosette, beautifully decorated for the occasion, and kindly placed at the disposal of the first aviators to come to Egypt by the engineer, Mr Nicolas Paraskevas, the opening of the exhibition of a monoplane of the Blériot Type XI, which has become celebrated throughout the world since the Calais to Dover flight." Members of the Aviation Club of France (under whose auspices the Heliopolis meeting would be held) explained some of the technical aspects of the aircraft, while a French pilot worked the mechanism, the better to explain the movements of this wonderful man-made bird. The crowds who came to see the Blériot XI included many women as well as men – something that seems to have taken the *Egyptian Gazette* reporter by surprise: "Before closing we should like to express our satisfaction at having seen such a large number of ladies present among the spectators, showing that scientific interest in aviation has penetrated even to the drawing room."[5]

But in mid-December 1909, aviation in Egypt was still no more than a theoretical enthusiasm, lacking one key ingredient: no one there had yet witnessed an aeroplane leaving the ground. This state of affairs was rectified by a wealthy and colourful Belgian aristocrat, the first man to fly in Belgium and a keen racer of cars and motor boats. Baron Pierre de Caters intended to enter the record books as the first person to fly in Egypt (as he had just been in Constantinople) and his arrival in Cairo caused a stir. Newspaper readers were told that he would "give Cairo a practical insight into the mysteries of flight". It was even suggested that this "early exhibition of aeroplaning in Cairo will adversely affect the Heliopolis week, but in an interview with our representative, Baron de Caters treated any such idea as being too ridiculous for serious consideration."[6]

On Wednesday 15 December 1909, de Caters left his hotel at 5am "and motored to the scene of his coming triumphs to inspect the progress that is being made in the reconstruction of his Voisin biplane and returned to breakfast at about nine o'clock." Later that day ("a red-letter day in the annals of Egyptian sport", in the view of the *Egyptian Gazette*), de Caters realised his ambition and made the first aeroplane flight in Egypt – but not without some difficulties and delays, not to say moments of farce. A crowd of dignitaries gathered during the afternoon at an area of specially designated open ground at Abbassia, today a crowded district of central Cairo. At 4pm "nearly everything was ready except the wind, which remained a little too persistent for an immediate flight", so de Caters used the time to explain some of the workings of the aeroplane to the awaiting spectators, while "superintending some of the finishing touches which were requisite to put the 'bird' in a condition for successful flight." At 4.30 the biplane was ready, but, much to the regret of the *Gazette's* correspondent, who commented that in the "fickle afterglow of the sunset all ambitions for successful snap-shotting had to be abandoned." The Voisin was then "pointed towards the way it should go and the hinder part of it 'anchored' to a spring balance which was securely attached to a bar of iron driven deep into the ground." When the steel propeller was started it "revolved to such purpose that it raised clouds of dust which for a few moments veiled the rear part of the aeroplane from the spectators. A violent whir of machinery, some vibration, and the impatient striving of the 'bird' to break loose as a grey hound held on a leash."

But the excitement was premature. De Caters discovered a problem with the propeller that would need fixing – his announcement causing murmurs of scepticism among some of the onlookers about the prospects of his being able to fulfil his promise. But after a new propeller had been attached to the plane, the Belgian aviator was ready to give it another try. When the Voisin's engine was restarted the *Egyptian Gazette* reporter's prose became breathless: "With a whirr and a rush like a chased bird the 'thing' with the Baron inside is making a bee track across country while all the world wondered. No time to think, only to watch; not a bit like watching a horse race – just a new sensation, a blend of admiration and expectancy with a touch of excitement; no doubt as to whether it would fly or not – that was a foregone conclusion – only, would it fly all right. At a distance that can only be measured by imagination, but say 200 metres, it swayed to the right and a wing looked like touching the ground. It was travelling at a terrific pace, as though it had a train to catch, and at this time it ran on one wheel, on the right side, the others doing nothing but revolve in the air. Almost immediately the great thing righted itself, de Caters had done something that he ought to have done and as it steadied itself the front wheels left the ground! 'Why it is really rising!' said a lady and at the same moment there was a general exclamation of wonder... and 'it' was seen to have left the earth. No fiasco, but a real flight. Baron de Caters was flying; and he flew two complete circuits (let us guess) of three quarters of a mile each, and then he alighted as gently as a dove. That was all! It took exactly three minutes from start to finish and the impression will last a lifetime to many who had never seen a man fly before. One could go a hundred times to see it!"[7]

With his modest circuits over Abbassia in the fading evening light, Baron de Caters had introduced flying to the biggest and most influential Arab country, setting Egypt on a course that would help to shape its history and identity. Over subsequent days the Belgian conducted more demonstration flights, making history again in Egypt by taking up two women passengers: "Neither of these ladies had been in the air before, but they were both very plucky about it and seemed to be enjoying themselves. [One of them] said she did not experience the least fear and found the whole sensation quite delightful."[8]

The Egyptian public had been given its first taste of aviation, and as de Caters packed up his Voisin and sailed home (having made history himself, the prospect of an aviation week did not interest him), preparations for the Heliopolis meeting moved up a gear. International aviators (mostly French) began arriving by sea in Alexandria. From there, the crates containing their planes were taken by train to Cairo and then by road to Heliopolis for reassembling. These pioneer pilots – the celebrities of their day – were not shy in making boastful predictions of what they would achieve in Egypt. A Briton, Mortimer Singer, announced that he planned to fly his Farman aircraft "in the neighbourhood of and over the Pyramids, which is, of course, a feat quite possible to the practised aviator, for the highest of those amazing monuments is about 452 feet, where [Louis] Paulhan, also on a Farman biplane, has flown very nearly 2,000 feet high." All very well in theory; but whether Singer was cut out physically for this role was another matter. As the *Egyptian Gazette* pointed out rather unkindly: "Mr A Mortimer Singer is not by any means a youth or a featherweight [and] one would never expect that so typical and solid a Britisher would have furnished quite the most remarkable example in the past year of how easily a man may learn to aeroplane."[9]

Having reassembled their flimsy aeroplanes, the pilots then faced the often perilous task of trying them out again in the air. The results were not always happy. Singer suffered two minor accidents to his Farman when he first took to the sky. A subsequent, more serious, misfortune meant that his boast of being able to fly over the pyramids was never put to the test. A fellow pilot had just successfully completed five circuit flights around the aerodrome when it came to Singer's turn to try out his aeroplane. Luck deserted him and his machine fell "heavily to the ground from a height of 20 metres. We understand that the unfortunate gentleman has sustained a fracture of the leg, as well as severe contusions in other parts of the body."[10] Singer was out of the competition. He had planned to represent the Aero Club of the United Kingdom in the event. The club, in an official notice to members, said "this sad occurrence" was "not only a blow to the hopes of the Club at Heliopolis", but was "also a serious loss to England, whose honour he was going to sustain against all the well-known foreign aviators."[11] Aviation was still regarded as a sport – but one in which national pride and honour were already supremely important.

Things were not going well either for Hubert Latham, arguably the star attraction at Heliopolis, having been the first aviator to try, unsuccessfully, to cross the English Channel just ahead of Blériot. During a trial flight at Heliopolis, Latham had reached a height of about 50 metres when "a sudden gust of wind caught the plane and hurled it to the ground", wing first, at an angle of 45 degrees. Latham, who was tied to the seat, was thrown out, fortunately clear of the machine, and sustained "a contused jaw and a slight injury to the leg; the accident will however not prevent him making further ascents. The narrowness of the escape will be appreciated from the fact that Mr Latham informed us that had he been another five metres higher the machine must have turned turtle and inevitably killed him."[12]

With Singer out of contention, just four countries were represented on the opening day of the Heliopolis Aviation Week: France led the way with eight entries, while the Netherlands, Germany and the United States each had one entry. National pride might have been at stake for the competitors and their backers. But for many of the inhabitants of Egypt all that mattered was that they were about to witness history being made and join the comparatively small handful of people across the world who had seen a man flying through the air. The significance of an Arab country hosting an aviation meeting so soon after the birth of flying was commented on widely – and not just in Egypt. In London, the *Pall Mall Gazette* speculated on the impact on the Middle East as a whole: "The whirr of the engine in the air trembling among the ruins of Baalbec [sic] will soon be no stranger than the whistling of a chauffeur in the streets of old Cairo; and the Arab who would now fly as for his life at the sight of an aeroplane will within a year or two be as indifferent to the winged carriages as he is now to the tall, slender sails of the boats that plough the Nile. Soon most of the mystery of life will have disappeared."[13]

Among Egyptians commentators, too, the importance of the upcoming event could not be over-emphasised. A front-page article in *al-Jarida* said: "The dream that we have dreamed in our youth and which every other person has dreamed before us and after us has now come to reality. Is there anyone who has not dreamed that he was flying in the air and then awoke wishing that the dream had come true?.. We live today in a time of marvellous accomplishments, a time of realising our aspirations and dreams... some mathematicians had said that it was virtually absurd and that eagles and vultures were the largest animals that could easily fly. Thus, we are impatient in this country to see the first people to fly, just as others are impatient." Referring to the first flight in Egypt, made the previous December by Baron de Caters, the commentator said: "We could not believe that we saw with our own eyes what people had so much wanted to see for thousands of years."[14] The mood was similar in *al-Mu'ayyad*: "The people of Egypt will see an amazing sight. They will see that humble humans have taken control of the air and have mocked the winds at will. They have begun to move about the kingdom of the air as they move about dry land and on the sea."

Their appetites duly whetted, the comparatively small number of Egyptians who could afford the fare (along with large contingents from the sizeable expatriate community) made their way to Heliopolis on Sunday 6 February 1910 full of hope and expectation. It was, in the end, a right royal occasion, enjoyed on the opening day alone by an estimated 40,000 people. The facilities that had been built for the competition and the spectators "were very impressive and comparable to those at Reims. An aerodrome, an open field with a circumference of five kilometres was staked out at the northern edge of the Oasis of Heliopolis. This served as the course for the competition. A wooden wall encircled the field. Inside the wall on the east was a very large roofed grandstand or tribune for first-class ticket holders. It included sections reserved for women and for the Khedive. On the west side was an area set aside for the general public."[15]

The ever-enthusiastic *Egyptian Gazette* declared that "everything conspired to make the opening day at Heliopolis a success – wind, or rather the absence of it in any appreciable volume, and a veiled sun accorded with the conditions most favourable for the man in the air and the spectator below; and the consequence was... an afternoon's flying well worth watching." By noon a "steady stream of Europeans and natives" were on the move, some in cars, others in "cabs of sorts, and a swarm crowding within and clinging to the tram cars which plied in that direction." Less fortunate visitors took a bus or walked. On approaching the aerodrome "one found every window and the roofs of the houses crowded with eager groups of people gazing into space with eyes fixed on a graceful plane manoeuvring in the distant sight of all and sundry." The cafés and restaurants of Heliopolis along the line of the route had "surpassed themselves in frantic endeavours to cater for and tempt the loiterer and pedestrian and countless tables and chairs spread themselves on either side of the road way and crowding every mound or rise of earth so as better to lend a view of the aerial wonders."

The flying began at 2pm, and almost two hours later the royal party, headed by Khedive Abbas, arrived at Heliopolis accompanied by a cavalry escort. The band of Britain's 7th Dragoon Guards played the Khedival Anthem as the nominal head of state took his place in the tribune, where he was received by state officials.

A variety of cash prizes were on offer. Each day prizes could be won for height, distance and speed. There was a further award for the first aviator to fly from Heliopolis, around the Giza Pyramids and back to the aerodrome. Towards the end of the first afternoon, French aviator Henri Rougier, in a Farman biplane, "made a beautiful series of circles and the masterful control which he exercised over his machine commanded the administration of the beholders and constantly, as he neared the great mass of spectators near the tribune, he was received with applause. It was not until night was beginning to fall and the grayness of dusk made it impossible to distinguish him further that he condescended to come down. That was close upon six o'clock and during his flight he had attained the height of 193 metres and had covered a distance of 65 kilometres and 500 metres."

By the end of the first day, spectators at Heliopolis were aware both of the excitement and danger of flying. Frenchman Jean Gobron took off in his Voisin, "but within five minutes, and while he was on the further side of the course, he had suddenly to descend and a horror-stricken crowd of watchers had the mortification of seeing a mass of flames burst from the graceful machine which only a few moments before had passed them as a thing of beauty." Cars sped over to the spot where Gobron had crashed, finding him, "to the satisfaction of everyone, unharmed and apparently quite amused at the incident."[16]

Over subsequent days, the weather and the performances of pilots and machines varied greatly. But Wednesday 9 February was particularly memorable. "Glorious weather favoured the Heliopolis Aviation Meeting today," a reporter for *The New York Times* wrote. "There was an enormous attendance, which included the Khedive,

Prince Fuad and Prince Ibrahim, who were particularly interested in the flights. Great enthusiasm was shown by the spectators, especially when at one moment there were four aviators in the air, their machines showing up with great clearness against the golden sky... Mr Duray beat the world's five-kilometre record, covering that distance in 4 min, 12 4/5 sec. M Metrot made a continuous flight of 851 kilometres much to the delight of the spectators, who cheered the aviator to the echo when he alighted after this the longest aerial voyage yet made in Egypt... The Egyptian natives were simply stupefied by today's display of flying."[17]

Stupefaction – not just on the part of the "natives", but among everyone in Cairo – turned to disappointment, however, when the event that had been billed as the climax of the week failed to materialise. Former prime minister Boghos Nubar Pasha had offered the prize for the first return flight to the Giza Pyramids. Elaborate preparations were made, with signallers placed on top of high and prominent landmarks along the route – even on the pyramids themselves. Thousands of people converged on Giza to await the aircraft and to witness the sight of planes flying round the pyramids. So, "bitter was the disappointment when it was found there would be no race."[18] No explanation was given for the fact that the competitors failed to take up the challenge. It has subsequently been suggested that "given the 'temperament' of the aircraft, there would have been some risk in flying 50 kilometres, especially over Cairo where there would have been no place to make an emergency landing. Circumventing Cairo would have added considerable distance to the route."[19]

The pyramids contest was, in the end, too ambitious for an aviation industry still in its infancy. But aside from the award of big prizes, two little-known but significant and interesting events also took place during the Heliopolis meeting. The first constituted one of the earliest incidences anywhere in the world of stunt flying. Jan Olieslagers, a Belgian-born European motorcycle champion, had taken up flying just before the Heliopolis meeting and made his first public appearance there in a Blériot monoplane, presenting a programme of what *The New York Times* described as "trick flying... his stunts were of such a daredevil nature as to call forth the plaudits of the thousands of people who were present more to see height, speed and endurance records broken than spectacular performances."[20] The second curiosity was the arrival of a tall and elegant young French actress named Baroness Raymonde de Laroche. She had learned to fly only the previous year, and during the Heliopolis meeting she flew four times around the course, a distance of 12 miles, for which she was granted a licence by the French Aero Club. The total number of female pilots in 1910 was miniscule. So Baroness de Laroche was one of the first in a distinguished line of pioneering aviatrices, and her appearance at Heliopolis represented another feather in the cap for Egypt.

The Heliopolis meeting launched Cairo's reputation as a centre of international aviation – a position that it was to occupy, in different guises, throughout the first half of the 20th century. Above all, Heliopolis acted as a catalyst. In its immediate aftermath, there was a proliferation of attempts to fly longer distances and climb to greater heights – in preparation for still more ambitious journeys across international boundaries and into uncharted territories throughout the Middle East and North Africa.

French-controlled North Africa was one region in particular where attempts at more ambitious distance flights were made. In the spring of 1911, the first major cross-country flight there was recorded when a pilot flew a two-seater aircraft from the town of Oran (on Algeria's northwest coast) to Tielat, a distance of 68 kilometres.[21] In June the same year, the French regional government in Algeria offered a prize worth £10,000 for the first aircraft to cover 500 kilometres without a stop, carrying 1,000 kilograms of "war material". The idea of the prize, the government explained, was to encourage "the designing and building of a useful type of machine"[22] – the first indication that a major European power with vested interests in the Middle East and North Africa saw aviation as potentially much more than just a crowd-pulling spectacle. In another enterprise intended to push the limits of aviation, the town of Oran, in 1912, offered a prize of 5,000 francs "for the first aviator to pilot his machine over the mountain which separates [a part of]

Oran from the Mediterranean sea." The money went to a Frenchman by the name of Servies, who flew at a height of 2,000 metres (6,500 ft) to achieve his goal.[23]

Algeria was not alone in North Africa in becoming a focus for aviation development. In Morocco, in early 1912, the French military authorities announced plans to establish aviation centres at Fez and Casablanca, with two aircraft assigned to each.[24] Around the same time, the residents of Tunis were being treated to aerial displays in the skies over the city by two French pilots, who went on to carry out a circular flight of 60 kilometres, passing over Carthage, Ariana, la Manouba and Tunis.[25] In October 1912 Roland Garros, a French pilot who was to become a hero of World War One and who, today, has a world championship tennis stadium in Paris named after him, travelled by sea to Tunis with the intention of trying to break the world altitude record – apparently attracted by the still, clear skies of North Africa. After initial problems with his oxygen apparatus, he eventually succeeded, flying to a height of 19,000 feet.

The next time Garros returned to Tunisia he arrived by air – becoming, in September 1913, the first person to fly across the Mediterranean Sea. He took off from Fréjus, near Cannes on the French Riviera in a Morane monoplane, with the intention of refuelling at Sardinia. But, according to one report, "he was going so well that he passed this point at a great height... and, after his eight-hour flight, there still remained some 5 litres of petrol."[26] It was a remarkable achievement. *The New York Times* reported how Garros had "contemplated the flight for some time, despite the efforts of his friends to persuade him to abandon the idea. He disdained the offer of the French Admiralty to assist him with a chain of torpedo boats, and, without saying anything to his friends, arranged to make the attempt." He set off at 6am and for a time his friends heard nothing. Then radio reports indicated that he had passed overhead both Corsica and Sardinia, completing the 558-mile flight to Bizerte in Tunisia where there were "scenes of wild enthusiasm when Garros landed. The crews of the warships in the roads joined the townspeople in giving him a magnificent welcome."[27]

The New York Times described the flight as "one of the most notable feats in aviation". It was an apt assessment. The significance of Garros' achievement ranks alongside that of Blériot's cross-channel flight of 1909. The long-term implications went far beyond both the skill and courage of the pilots concerned and the technical achievements of the aircraft designer. Blériot's conquest of the English Channel meant that Britain, "the world's greatest naval power, had been forced to recognize that its navy may no longer be able to defend it against all future forms of attack from abroad."[28] Garros' successful flight across the Mediterranean had similar strategic and political consequences: it meant that henceforth the grip of the European colonial powers over the countries of North Africa and the Middle East would be even tighter. Lines of fast communication and transport could be established between European capitals and colonial outposts; and personnel and equipment could be moved quickly to any spot in the colonies where an insurrection might occur. Conversely, any nationalist movement seeking to challenge colonial rule would now have to take account of the European powers' command of the air.

The idea that aviation would play an important part in strengthening the lines of control reaching out from colonial capitals had taken root several years earlier. Once again, France was beating Britain into second place in this respect. "From the first," wrote *Flight* in September 1910, "it has been quite evident that one direction in which enormous advantages will probably accrue from the perfecting of aerial craft was in the traversing of regions of the Sahara Desert type, and stretches of water which otherwise mean a detour of hundreds of miles to reach the other sides, although only a few miles distant. In this respect all honour is due to the French nation." The magazine pointed out that the Ligue Nationale Aerienne (the world's first school for pilots) had been working with the support of the French ministers of war and public works, and with the governor-general of Algeria, with a view to establishing "a cross-desert service of aircraft between Colomb-Béchar, the terminus station on the South Oran Railway, and Timbuctoo, which will reduce what is at present a four months' journey to a matter of 24 hours... It is hoped then to establish regular trans-Sahara flights, placing Algeria in direct communication with the French African central possessions. The whole scheme is primarily a military one, although it will be open to enormous commercial developments in addition."[29] The last sentence could have been lifted from an imperialist's manifesto. Flying was about to become another instrument in the colonial armoury.

From 1910 until the outbreak of World War One in 1914, the Middle East and North Africa region was the focus of numerous pioneering aviation ambitions, many of which never became a reality. One of the most outlandish ideas of the day was that of French pilot J Mamet, who announced in September 1911 that he intended to fly round the world. Starting from France, it was reported, he would "fly over the Pyrenees, down the East Coast of Spain and across the Mediterranean to Algeria. From there he hopes to fly on to Egypt by way of Tunis and Tripoli. A steamship will then take the aviator to India, and after flying as far as he can there the aviator will visit Australia, South America and West Africa."[30] His ambitions may have been vast, but there is no record to indicate that Mamet's foreign excursions by air took him any further than England.

The small group of men – and a few women – who became so intoxicated by the 'sport' of aviation and its infinite possibilities were unaffected by the numerous accidents that killed many of the early aviators. The desire to reach the furthest outposts of empire provided a powerful incentive for these pioneers, whose horizons were not restricted to French possessions in Africa. The early aviators also looked further east. In late 1912, tentative plans were put forward to establish an aerial connection between Britain and India, the jewel in the imperial crown. For the plan to succeed it would be essential to secure a route through the Middle East. These early hopes of an Anglo-Indian air corridor coalesced around the idea of a long-distance air race. Several Indian princes were said to have raised £666 between them in prize money. The proposed route ran across France, Belgium and Germany, then on to Constantinople, Konya, Adana, Alexandretta (modern-day Iskenderun in Turkey), Meskene (in eastern Turkey), along the Euphrates to Baghdad, following the Tigris to Basra, across the Gulf to Bushehr (in Persia, modern-day Iran) and then to Karachi (which in those days was part of India).[31] While no more was heard of this scheme, it is significant that less than a decade after the Wright brothers' first flight, the Middle East was seen as an integral part of any future air link between Europe and eastern Asia.

French aviators also had ambitions for the Middle East, reflecting in part, no doubt, the French government's desire to check British ambitions in the region – at a time when the Ottoman Empire was on the point of collapse. Towards the end of 1913, a pilot called Seguin crashed in France, forcing the suspension of "arrangements which were being made by the Ligue Nationale Aerienne for him to fly from Paris to the Persian Gulf... supplies have been sent to Tripoli, Aleppo and Baghdad. An attempt is now being made to secure another aviator to make the flight."[32] There is no record of a replacement being found for this particular adventure. But Seguin's accident did nothing to quell the enthusiasm of three other French pilots, who were already making their way eastwards in separate attempts to reach Cairo, chasing a prize of 500,000 francs offered by *Le Matin* newspaper. Pierre Daucourt, in a Borel monoplane, was delayed first by an accident to his plane before leaving France, and again by the Austrian authorities who forbade him from flying over southern Hungary between Budapest and Belgrade. Daucourt eventually reached Constantinople, before crashing in the Taurus Mountains on the subsequent eastwards leg. While his plane was only slightly damaged, the following night, "while the machine was being watched by guards, it was set alight in some way. There was an explosion and the machine was completely destroyed."[33] (Other reports indicate that Daucourt and his mechanic J Roux were killed in the fire that followed the crash.) Daucourt's competitors for the prize money arrived in Constantinople soon after him. Marc Bonnier (with mechanic Joseph Barnier) was followed by a brave and aggressive pilot called Jules Vedrines. The latter flew over the city in his Blériot, flamboyantly dropping a Turkish flag on to the Sultan's palace and a French flag on to the cruiser 'Jeanne Blanche' in the harbour. Bonnier, who is also at Constantinople, and Vedrines have decided to continue their journey to Asia Minor in company, 'for the glory of their country'."[34]

Mechanical problems delayed Bonnier, so, after a two-week rest, Vedrines and his mechanic set off alone on 19 December 1913, making a non-stop 650-kilometre flight over the Taurus Mountains to Konya. Four days later he reached Tripoli on the coast of modern-day Lebanon (landing in al-Tall Square, in front of the Nawfal Palace[35]), and the following morning (25 December) flew the short distance to Beirut, "where he was accorded an enthusiastic reception."[36] So it was Vedrines, landing in a field in the Karantina district (on the eastern side of the city, close to the port), who introduced aviation to Beirut – home in later decades to one of the most important airports in the region. From Beirut, Vedrines flew on to Jaffa (on the Palestine coast) and Kantara (at the northern end of the Suez Canal in Egypt), before reaching Cairo, flying a circuit around the city and landing at Heliopolis. Flushed with success, the aviator's imagination clearly got the better of him. He announced that he would spend two weeks in Cairo before proceeding, by way of Jerusalem, Aleppo, Baghdad, Bombay, Calcutta and Singapore to Australia. From there he would sail to America and fly across the continent. Regrettably, none of these bold plans came to fruition.

Bonnier, meanwhile, had overcome his engine problems and set off for Cairo, following a similar route to that taken by Vedrines. He and his mechanic reached Beirut in their Nieuport monoplane in the late afternoon when the light was fading. Unable to locate Karantina, they landed on sand dunes south of the city near the current Cité Sportive – where Beirut's first airport would eventually be located in the 1930s. Denied the glory of being the first pilot to reach Cairo from Europe, Bonnier decided to earn a place for himself in aviation history in another way – by making a detour on his way to Egypt. On 31 July 1913, he "flew to Jerusalem, where his machine, the first to land at the Holy City, attracted a good deal of attention. The next morning he flew the 250 miles to Port Said and later in the afternoon arrived in Cairo. The French National Aerial League have now asked him to continue his flight from Cairo to the Cape."[37]

On this occasion, the wishful thinking came from Bonnier's French sponsors. A newspaper in South Africa had offered a prize of £500 for the first pilot to fly from Cairo to the Cape before 1 November 1914. But the immediate prospect of this deadline being met seemed remote. Even flying as far as the Sudanese city of Khartoum, on the River Nile 1,000 miles to the south, was seen as an impossible challenge in early 1914. But thanks to the seemingly constant supply of courageous young aviators keen to make their mark, it was one that was taken up by two pilots, Frenchman Marc Pourpe and Briton Francis (Frank) McClean (who in 1912 had famously flown between the two towers of Tower Bridge and under several others on the River Thames in London). Pourpe had acquired the Morane monoplane that Garros had used for his first trans-Mediterranean flight and took off in it from Heliopolis on 11 December 1913. But after only a short time in the air, "probably through being caught in a *remous* [a pocket of unstable air], the machine dived to the ground, and was considerably damaged, the pilot however, escaping unhurt."[38] A few days later, Pourpe took off again, landing at Sohag, on the Nile 240 miles south of Cairo with engine trouble, before continuing to Luxor ("bringing his machine down in the desert, near the Karnak temple"). During the final stages of his flight, he was troubled by a "side-wind which carried a lot of sand"; but he eventually reached Khartoum, to be welcomed by the Sirdar [commander-in-chief of the British-officered Egyptian army in Sudan], Sir Reginald Wingate. Sudan, another remote region under British authority, was also now on the aviation map of the world.

Pourpe had travelled to Khartoum and back in a conventional landplane. His British rival, Frank McClean, flew southward in a Short Brothers floatplane (taking off and landing on water) that had been shipped out to Alexandria in four wooden crates. After reassembling the biplane in a shed on a wharf in Alexandria harbour, McClean flew from there to Cairo, landing on the Nile. Accompanying him on his venture was a co-pilot, Alec Ogilvie, and a four-man support team. McClean's sister, Anna, also tagged along. The aircraft could seat four people and the combination of people on board varied, with the rest of the team travelling overland. One of McClean's passengers early on was Horace Short, who, with his brother Eustace, had designed and built the floatplane.

McClean's progress was smooth until he reached Aswan where "he made some flights to the delight of the great crowd which had gathered to see the machine." But after flying another 130 miles southwards he experienced engine trouble, which resulted in a frustrating one month's wait for new cylinders to arrive from Paris. Leaving McClean to await new parts, Horace Short returned to England, reporting back some of their adventures. He described the Egyptians along the Nile as having been terrified by the sight of the biplane, citing the case of two "native carpenters who were required to do some repairs" refusing "to enter the machine (although the engine was out) lest it should fly away with them."[39] During McClean's flight to Khartoum and back (which took exactly three months), his aircraft's Gnome engine suffered no fewer than 13 breakdowns. In a letter to Short, sent during one of the delays, the normally reticent and patient McClean expressed his exasperation at the technical problems he was encountering, adding that he was "getting tired of this series of happenings."[40] But frustrating though the experience must have been for him personally, McClean's venture would also be important for the development of Egypt's role as an aviation hub for the region. He was the first person to see the civil and military potential of using water as a springboard for flight – and is credited for having been the father of Britain Fleet Air Arm. *Flight* magazine noted in 1914 that he was "possessed of a fair share of the stuff that makes the world go round", and had "probably done more for the advancement of flying than any other individual." By bringing his floatplane to Egypt, McClean planted an idea that would come to fruition in subsequent decades when commercial air routes to southern Africa were eventually opened up through Cairo. So, once again, Egypt played host to a leading pioneer of flight – in this case involving planes taking off from water.

As McClean had been preparing for his Nile venture, a Russian airman, named as M Kouzminsky, claimed the honour of being the first person to fly in Persia. How he transported his Blériot monoplane to Tehran is not recounted. But a correspondent for

The Times reported that the Russian flew from the Palace of Kasr-i-Kajar, four miles north of the capital, to the Cossack parade ground where the shah, the regent, the ministers, and foreign dignitaries had assembled. After three or four circular flights over Tehran "at no very great height he made a rather exciting descent, splintering part of his machine." The correspondent quoted one of the distinguished guests as calling out in excitement: "Maintenant on commence à voler en Perse!"[41] In fact, as will become clear shortly, there is good reason to believe that aircraft were in use before this in the very far south of the country, close to the Gulf. But Kouzminsky's flight was certainly the first in Tehran.

The year 1914 also witnessed the first attempt by a country in the Middle East region, Ottoman Turkey, to join the club of international aviation. The Turkish Minister of War, Enver Pasha, decreed that two Turkish pilots should fly from Constantinople to Alexandria – to boost national morale and prove definitively to their own subjects and to the world at large that Ottoman Muslims could compete with Europeans in modern technological development. Two monoplanes were selected for the task that was given the title the 'Alexandria Expedition' and would involve stops at a number of important Ottoman-ruled cities along the way.[42] Captain Fethi Bey and another officer were deputed to fly a Blériot, and Lieutenant Nuri Bey and companion were assigned a Deperdussin B. Fethi Bey flew successfully across Turkey and reached Syria, stopping in Aleppo and Homs, before arriving in Beirut on 15 February 1914, landing in the Manara district. After making repairs to their aircraft the team flew to Damascus (the first recorded flight there) where, as was the case in every other town they visited, they were greeted enthusiastically. But on the next leg of their flight – to Jerusalem – they ran into trouble over the Galilee hills. It is not clear how this happened, but the bodies of Fethi Bey and his companion, along with the wreckage of their plane, were later found to the east of Lake Tiberias. They were given a hero's burial in Damascus in the courtyard of the Mosque of Salah al-Din al-Ayyubi (the leader of the Arab army that drove the Crusaders out of Jerusalem in 1187, a man who epitomises still the Arabs' yearning to throw off Western dominance). The epitaph on the tombstone of the young Ottoman pilot reads: "This is the tomb of the pilot martyr Yuzbachu Fethi Bey who achieved Martyrdom the day he crashed his aeroplane named Muavenet-i-Miliye near the Lake of Tiberias."[43]

The flight of Nuri Bey and his fellow officer was also to end badly. Their Deperdussin took off from Jaffa on 11 January 1914 en route to Jerusalem. The plane began circling over the sea to gain height before heading eastwards when, for no accountable reason, it crashed into the Mediterranean Sea. Both men were rescued, but the officer accompanying Nuri Bey later died. To try to restore a measure of honour, another plane was shipped to Beirut and a flight from there to Alexandria was completed successfully by a replacement pilot in May 1914.

However, the failure of the first two pioneering flights, undertaken with such high expectations, must have been a crushing blow to Ottoman prestige. If those young Muslim aviators had succeeded in flying from Constantinople, the seat of the Caliphate, to Egypt (still nominally part of the empire, but in practice under British control), then the boost to the development of 'home-grown' aviation in the Middle East – to a sense of entitlement to a place in the modern technological age – would surely have been enormous. The bitter failure of Fethi and Nuri Bey and their engineers merely served to underline the fact that by the middle of 1914 the major colonial powers of the day, France and Britain, were able to reach North Africa, Egypt, Sudan and the Eastern Mediterranean by air. The 'Alexandria Expedition' was planned with great haste and with the concentration more on the expected public relations benefits than on the technical preparations that such an undertaking required. The failure of the venture served to expose the gap that existed between technological capabilities in Europe and the Middle East. A combination of scientific advance, immense personal courage and a great deal of luck meant that France and Britain were able to use aviation to consolidate political control – and economic dominance of the region.

But other scientific and technological developments around this time meant that the global significance of the Middle East was about to change forever. Oil was discovered in Iran (Persia) in 1908. A brief *Flight* report from London Aerodrome in November 1910 recorded the first sale of an aircraft (yet again a Blériot monoplane) "for a purely commercial reason" – in connection with the "laying of oil pipes across a desert in Persia" – a reference to the arid region in southern Iran where the country's first oilfields were located.[44]

But before the potential of flight as an adjunct to the oil industry could be exploited to the full, or before planes could start carrying mail or passengers, aviation in the Middle East would evolve fast – and in a dramatically different direction – in response to the pressures of war. The outbreak of World War One in August 1914 and the decision a few months later by the Ottoman Turkish government to join forces with Germany against Britain and its allies would mark the start of the second stage of aviation's development in the Middle East. By the end of the war, most inhabitants of the region had probably either seen aircraft in the sky or heard about their abilities in conflict. In fact, aircraft were playing an active role in support of military operations in the region more than two years before the outbreak of the Great War. In October 1911, Italy invaded the Ottoman-held territory of Libya, using alleged Ottoman hostility to Italian economic activities there as a *casus belli*. Italian forces occupied the major Libyan coastal cities: Tripoli, Benghazi, Derna, Homs and Tobruq. But all along the way they encountered "a number of small but determined Ottoman garrisons. These had been augmented by the local population who, while not favourable to the sultan [in Constantinople], still considered him as their 'commander of the faithful.'"[45] Italy stationed more than 100,000 troops in Libya to counter these rebellions, in addition to balloons and aircraft. At the close of 1911, more than 20 Italian planes were stationed in areas of the country, nine of them in Tripoli. A number of the pilots were volunteers,[46] and the operations of this fledgling air force appear to have been sporadic, rather than part of a planned strategy. This is the impression gained from one account of action in Libya in early 1912: "Although authentic news of the aeroplane is very difficult to obtain from the reports which have been received, there seems no doubt that the aviators have proved how useful they can be. On the night of January 17th a party of 400 Arabs attacked a blockhouse held by 18 Italians near Benghazi. During the fighting, Lieut Giulio Gavotti ascended on his Farman biplane, and flying over the enemy, dropped some bombs on them, with such effect that they speedily retired, leaving a number of wounded behind."[47]

What this account does not mention is that two months earlier, in November 1911, Lieut Gavotti had been selected as the pilot who would pioneer the practice of using aircraft as means of conveying and dropping bombs. In a letter to his father he wrote: "Today I have decided to throw bombs from the aeroplane. It is the first time that we will try this and if I succeed, I will be really pleased to be the first person to do it." The bombs had been sent out from Italy in two cases, and pilots were told that they were to be dropped over enemy positions. Lieut Gavotti said he and his colleagues had received no instructions from his superiors on how to carry out the new task, so "we are taking the bombs on board with the greatest precaution. It will be very interesting to try them on the Turks." The Italian airman added: "Near the seat, I have fixed a little leather case with padding inside. I have laid the bombs in it very carefully. These are small round bombs, weighing about a kilo-and-a-half each. I put three in the case and another one in the front of my jacket." Later that day, Lieut Gavotti took off with his load and successfully dropped his bombs on Ain Zara oasis, just east of Tripoli.[48]

The Italians' campaign in Libya also presented the first opportunity for aircraft to be used to distribute wartime propaganda. "The aeroplane," *Flight* magazine reported, "has been put to a somewhat novel use by the Italian authorities in Tripoli. A proclamation has been prepared assuring the Arab tribes of Italy's friendly attitude towards them, and stating that her sole desire is to develop the resources of the country. After copies had been made in Arabic a difficulty arose as to how to get them to the Arabs, but this was overcome by the aviators taking them and dropping them into the Arab camps."[49]

Italy was also able to claim a less distinguished 'first' during the campaign against the Ottoman Turkish and Arab forces. A certain Captain Moizo had "the distinction to be the first airman to be captured in actual war... having landed near Janzour [on Libya's coast] in order to adjust the engine of is Nieuport monoplane, [he] was captured by a party of Arabs and taken to the Turkish headquarters."[50]

A few days after the capture of the Italian airman, the Conference of the Inter-Parliamentary Union (founded in 1889 by parliamentarians striving for international understanding and peace) met in Geneva. A motion proposing the prohibition of aerial warfare was passed by a large majority (although the French delegation strongly opposed it). It was highly unlikely that governments and military commanders at the time would have heeded such a resolution – any more than they would today. But in any event the resolution was too late. As the Italian campaign in Libya proved, aviation was already a minor actor in war; and in the four years that followed it was to take on a leading and sometimes decisive role – in the Middle East quite as much as anywhere else.

two

Air War on Several Fronts

The First World War brought flying to Ottoman-controlled Mesopotamia (today's Iraq) for the first time, and aviation later played a key role in the creation of the modern state of Iraq. The region had been beyond the reach of the earlier aviation pioneers, who had made it no further than Egypt in their eastward probes. As a result, air support for the British-led campaign in Mesopotamia was slow to come. In addition, extreme weather conditions that had never before been experienced by aviators (searing heat in summer, devastating floods in winter) hampered operations. The ensuing delays in shipping aircraft, spares and pilots to the front came close to converting one calamitous Allied defeat in Mesopotamia into the failure of the campaign as a whole – and thereby crippling Britain's Royal Navy.

Britain could not afford to lose the war in Mesopotamia. It had recently converted its warships to run on oil instead of coal. The empire's sole source of oil was Iran (Persia) – in particular a major oilfield in the southwest, close to the northern end of the Gulf. Yet less than 100 miles distant from the oil port of Abadan and the vital pipeline running inland to the wells around Ahwaz lay the borders of Ottoman Turkish-controlled Mesopotamia. On 6 November 1914, the day after Turkey's declaration of war, an infantry brigade group from India began to land near Basra; its mission was to protect the Persian oilfields and pipeline.[1] The Allied expeditionary force captured Basra on 21 November, and a subsequent Turkish attempt to retake the city five months later was repelled. The oil supplies were secure. With no detailed strategy of what to do in the rest of Mesopotamia, the British-led force decided to move steadily northwards – their eyes on Baghdad.

Their progress, judged from a military perspective, was easy. Most of the troops they encountered were composed of Arabs who had been forcibly conscripted into the Ottoman army. T E Lawrence (Lawrence of Arabia), a British army officer at the time, was sent to Mesopotamia in 1915 by his commanders in Cairo. He noted that the Arab forces were in the "unenviable predicament of having to fight on behalf of their secular oppressors against a people long envisaged as liberators, but who obstinately refused to play the part. As may be imagined, they fought very badly. Our force won battle after battle till we came to think an Indian army better than a Turkish army."[2] But the real enemy during the opening months of the Mesopotamia campaign was a combination of severe heat and poor lines of supply (the River Tigris was the main thoroughfare for transport) for the front-line Allied troops. A British Royal Flying Corps (RFC)[3] officer, who stopped in India en route by sea to Basra in June 1915, was told about the conditions he could expect in Mesopotamia: 60 per cent of the expeditionary force was sick and 15,000 men had been invalided out in one month alone. Insufficient transport meant that troops were on half rations; and boats intended to serve as new river transport sent from Calcutta had either been sunk in the monsoon or sent back for repairs. All the way up the Gulf to Basra the RFC officer's ship "passed a string of hospital ships bound for India, a testimony of the truth of what they had told us in Bombay."[4]

Airmen assigned to Mesopotamia encountered many of the same difficulties as the troops. But despite the setbacks caused by disease and supply shortages, Allied land forces made swift progress northwards and the RFC was placed under no immediate pressure to go into action. According to official records, the first RFC practice flight in Mesopotamia took place only at the end of June

1915, with the barest details entered into the official log: "Major Reilly flying the Maurice Farman Shorthorn with Major Broke-Smith made a 35 minute flight reaching an altitude of 4,800 feet and ascertaining that the speed of the machine was 55 mph."[5] So the day when the RFC could be an effective part of a front-line attacking force was still far off. The RFC's role during this period, as its fleet of biplanes was gradually reassembled after being unloaded from ships in crates, was mainly to carry out reconnaissance missions for the field force commanded by Major-General Charles Townshend ("a bold general who modelled himself on the young Bonaparte"[6]). Townshend's initial goal was to secure the whole of Basra province up to the Ottoman-held town of Kut al-Amara, about 100 miles south of Baghdad. It was the job of RFC pilots not only to locate and describe enemy positions, but also to give their commanders an idea of the topography of this largely uncharted territory. In June 1915, for example, No 30 Squadron carried out "a notable reconnaissance from Amara to Kut al-Amara, a distance of 123 miles by air... to locate the enemy's dispositions at and below Kut al-Amara... A sketch map made at the time was subsequently used by Major-General Townshend for his plans on the attack on Kut al-Amara."[7]

In August 1915, with Kut al-Amara captured, Townshend felt that Baghdad was within reach. Given the conditions he was facing, this was a curious conclusion to reach. For a start, this was the peak of summer with day-time temperatures of 120° Fahrenheit/49° Celsius. Then the Allied forces were hampered both by a serious supply bottleneck at Basra and the severe difficulty of sustaining transport along a river threading through the desert. Nevertheless, Townshend "pushed rapidly on, gambling on reaching Baghdad before his precarious lines of communications starved him to a halt." The ease with which the expeditionary force had defeated the enemy seems to have made the British commander complacent. He clearly had no knowledge of the gap between the fighting ability of the mainly conscript Arab forces he had defeated in Basra province and the professional Turkish army waiting for him in the town of Ctesiphon (known today as al-Mada'in), 20 miles south of Baghdad. But if he had studied carefully and taken heed of aerial reconnaissance reports, he might have thought twice about attacking Ctesiphon without first seeking troop reinforcements and strengthening his supply lines.

At the end of September 1915, the Allies' front-line airbase was moved northwards to Kut al-Amara. From the air it was easy to see that the advancing army would have a fight on its hands. RFC records show that the "movements of the enemy in retreat up the Tigris from Kut past Aziziya as far as Ctesiphon were observed daily until the 6th of October. On the 3rd October Major Reilly reconnoitred Ctesiphon from Kut al-Amara reporting that the Turks were already strongly entrenched in prepared positions."[8] This last part of the report in particular, speaking of "strongly entrenched" Turkish troops, should have sounded alarm bells in Townshend's brain. Here was an early example of aviation providing raw information that – interpreted correctly – could have saved thousands of lives and averted a disastrous Allied humiliation. Perhaps the British commander, who can have had no experience of working with air support, did not trust the reconnaissance reports. Or maybe he decided to overlook them. Either way, the result was catastrophic for his army.

Given the depleted state of Townshend's men after the long and debilitating summer campaign, the chances are that the Ottoman force at Ctesiphon would have triumphed under any circumstances. But a curious incident involving aerial reconnaissance and the fate of gathered intelligence made Ottoman success certain. During a flight behind enemy lines on 20 November (two days before the battle began) Major Reilly, the officer who had given the warning about the Turks' preparedness for war, was shot down by machine gun fire. A subsequent monograph on the battle of Ctesiphon written by a senior Turkish officer recounted the importance of the shooting down, describing it as having had "an effect out of proportion with reality." The capture of the plane ("this little event") was taken as "a happy omen that the luck of the enemy was about to change. It caused a deeply felt improvement in general morale." This, to no small extent, was because Major Reilly had sketched a map showing

British and Turkish military dispositions that was intended for the eyes of his military commanders. Having fallen into enemy hands it provided the Ottoman army with "priceless information" ahead of the battle. Even more important for the Ottoman commanders than knowledge of the military dispositions was the map itself: "Major Reilly's greatest gift to us was the sketch showing the course of the Tigris from Diala to Aziziya. This little sketch, probably of small account to the enemy [the Allies], was an important map in the eyes of the Iraq command. For at HQ and with the troops there was no such thing as a map."[9]

Unaware of the significance of Reilly's capture, Townshend still believed that he alone had the advantage of surprise. His plan was to hold the Turks with a frontal attack while he hooked round their left flank. Unfortunately his available force was not large enough to carry out the strategy. Turkish artillery and machine guns "took a fearful toll of British and Indian troops advancing across ground as flat and devoid of cover as a table; Townshend's attacking infantry division lost more than half its effectives killed and wounded." Some 4,600 Allied troops and more than 6,000 Ottoman soldiers lost their lives in the battle of Ctesiphon. The defeated army retreated, pursued by Ottoman forces, into Kut, where Townshend was ordered to "stand fast pending the arrival of fresh forces. Soon he and his army were cut off and under siege."[10] Lawrence described eloquently the folly that led to the Allied defeat, speaking of "our rush advance to Ctesiphon, where we met native Turkish troops whose full heart was in the game, and we were abruptly checked. We fell back, dazed; and the long misery of Kut began."[11]

As vain attempts were made by under-resourced Allied military units to relieve the "long misery" of the siege of Kut, thousands of Allied troops were killed or wounded. The RFC, too, was limited in its resources – most of its equipment was either war-damaged or unserviceable, its pilots afflicted by the heat-related illnesses that ravaged the ranks of the Allied army. At times, the RFC was emasculated. For example, so few serviceable planes remained by the time the battle of Ctesiphon began that when one aircraft was forced to land behind enemy lines only one other remained active and in working order. A report from a senior British officer, General Sir John Nixon, on air operations in Mesopotamia during 1915 acknowledged that "during the actual period of the battle at Ctesiphon, a series of accidents deprived the RFC of several officers and machines."[12] Even in early December 1915, with Kut under siege, "there were no machines available for reconnaissance work, all being under repair."[13] To make matters worse, a month later, growing Ottoman air power presented the Allies with a new challenge. At the start of the war, the Ottomans had few aircraft or competent pilots, and it was only after the Germans began training Turkish aviators and providing modern aircraft that the Ottoman air force began to make its presence felt. German airfields had been established, first along the length of Palestine, and then in Syria and northern and central Iraq.[14] In February 1916, Townshend reported the advent of the "first hostile aeroplane over Kut apparently engaged in reconnaissance work. A few days later, he heard from a Turkish deserter that four Turkish aeroplanes had landed in Baghdad." Soon, unchallenged, Turkish planes were dropping bombs on Kut, adding to the suffering of the besieged troops.

The RFC and the Royal Naval Air Service (RNAS), meanwhile, were also receiving fresh equipment and were soon in a position to drop supplies into the besieged town. The RFC's No 30 Squadron reported that during February 1916 "in addition to reconnaissance and artillery observation work, frequent flights were made to Kut al-Amara for the purpose of dropping stores, spare parts for wireless plant, medical comforts and money both in cash and notes."[15] Despite the arrival of supplies, many hundreds of British and Indian soldiers fell ill and died of disease and malnourishment. The officer corps, by contrast, appears to have suffered little. Townshend in particular continued to call on RFC pilots to drop creature comforts and equipment to help him pursue his leisure-time pursuits with greater ease. A London *Daily Telegraph* correspondent in Basra in February 1916 wrote: "Cheery messages come through from General Townshend (at Kut). He is sowing vegetable seeds, and has asked for gramophone needles. These and other light requisites are dropped to his camp by aeroplane. He reports sufficient supplies for a long period to come." The British commander was deluding himself. In reality, conditions were becoming desperate – to an extent that in early April, an urgent appeal for extra food for the starving troops was sent out. The RFC was told to drop "as much food as possible into Kut". Bomb frames were removed from all machines and replaced by hastily devised dropping gear. Each machine carried 150 pounds of food per journey. Some 61 food dropping flights were made from 17 to 28 April and, combined with the RNAS Squadron, "19,000 pounds of food were dropped of which Kut acknowledged receipt of 16,800 pounds... While returning from a food dropping flight on the 25th, Lieutenant Davidson was attacked by a hostile monoplane and wounded in the shoulder. The machine was hit in thirty two places. Escorts in future were provided."[16]

But even this emergency food relief mission was not enough. After successive military attempts to relieve the siege had come to nothing, the Allied force in Kut al-Amara surrendered on 29 April 1916. No fewer than 13,000 Allied troops were taken prisoner by the Turks. It was "a disaster to British arms that made the same kind of impact on British and world opinion as the fall of Tobruk in the Second World War."[17]

The pioneering role of aviation in this bleak episode in British military history was significant. The potential benefit of solid information garnered from military reconnaissance – and the dangers of not acting on it – were clearly seen. Also demonstrated was the vulnerability of small, slow and low-flying aircraft to being shot down – with the potential hazard of military intelligence acquired in the air falling into enemy hands. One unforeseen consequence of the siege of Kut itself had been the deployment of British planes in the first ever airborne humanitarian aid supply mission. Above all, the Ctesiphon/Kut experience showed how crucial it was, just over a decade after the Wright brothers' first successful powered flight, to have an air force in command of the skies above an advancing army. A despatch from Sir Percy Lake, a senior commander of the British Indian Army, written towards the end of 1916, made this clear: "The superiority of certain of the hostile aeroplanes over any of our machines in the matter of speed, combined with a large reduction in the number of our pilots (due to sickness partly attributable to overwork), enabled the enemy in May and June to establish [in Mesopotamia] what was very nearly a mastery of the air." That final phrase, used there probably for the first time ever – in the context of a war in the Middle East – was henceforth the concern of military planners and strategists throughout the world. Mastery of the air remains Israel's abiding obsession. Conversely, the Arabs' constant inability to match or even dent Israel's air superiority has contributed in a major way to their failure to defeat or even contain the Jewish state.

An interesting footnote in any debate about the impact that air superiority might have had in the battles for Mesopotamia in 1915-16 comes from an observation by T E Lawrence. He had been sent to Mesopotamia to see if he could help "by indirect means" to help end the siege of Kut – presumably by organising a guerrilla force to penetrate enemy positions, or some such unconventional tactic. His mission was not well received by British army officers in Mesopotamia, who regarded him as an unwelcome interloper. In any event, Lawrence later recalled, "it was too late for action, with Kut just dying; and in consequence I did nothing of what it was in my mind and power to do." Nevertheless, despite Lawrence's image of being something of a mystic, seduced by the simplicity of desert life, he clearly understood before many of his contemporaries in the British military establishment the value of air power. "Had British headquarters in Mesopotamia obtained from the War Office eight more aeroplanes to increase the daily carriage of food to the garrison of Kut," he wrote, "Townshend's resistance might have been indefinitely prolonged."[18]

Lawrence also suggested that the British should have done more to encourage the Arabs of Mesopotamia to rise up against the occupying Ottoman power. Britain had arrived in Mesopotamia with the aim of conquering the enemy, rather than seeking Arab support for a campaign against their Ottoman overlords – the object of British policy in Arabia and Palestine. While Lawrence was not well received in Mesopotamia, it is possible that at least some of the officers he met there listened to his advice. No 30 Squadron records mention that on 27 June 1916, pamphlets were dropped, "informing the Arabs of the Declaration of War on the Turks by the Sharif of Mecca."[19]

The "declaration of war" was the start of the Arab Revolt announced by Sharif Hussein, whose family traced their descent to the grandfather of the Prophet Muhammad, Hashim ibn Abdel-Manaf. As such they were known as Hashemites, and they governed the western (Hejaz) district of the Arabian Peninsula (including the sacred Islamic cities of Mecca and Medina) on behalf of the Ottomans. In return for a British promise of independence in the post-Ottoman world, the Arabs agreed to take up arms against the German-backed Turkish forces. The Arab Revolt, starting on the Arabian Peninsula, was part of a broad Allied military front that extended westward to the Suez Canal. Its aim was to drive the Turkish army northwards by a series of offensives launched at different points along the front.

Just as Basra was a vital asset for Britain to hold in order to ensure the supply of Iranian oil for Royal Navy ships, so control of the Suez Canal was vital to safeguard the route to and from India. British commanders surmised correctly that the Ottoman army would try to seize the canal and occupy Egypt. This would have the effect not only of stripping Britain of its line of communication to the subcontinent, but might also stir up an Islamic rebellion against the infidel British and French presence in the region, or at very least encourage the emerging anti-British nationalist movement in Egypt. Reinforcing the Suez Canal defences was, therefore, a top priority. An RFC detachment was dispatched by sea from England to Egypt in November 1914, within months of war being declared, to help in the defence efforts. It was not a detachment that would strike immediate fear into the enemy, consisting of just three flimsy Maurice Farman Shorthorn biplanes, two spare engines, two tent hangars and six months' supply of petrol and oil. But the Shorthorn had space in front of the engine (the plane was known as a 'pusher' – the propeller pushed it from behind) for both a pilot and an observer/bomber. It was the reconnaissance capability of this type of aircraft and others acquired later by the RFC that gave the Allies in Egypt the edge over the Ottoman forces. For most of the time, intelligence supplied by RFC pilots meant that British commanders knew where the enemy was and what kind of attack to expect. Without this capacity, the British task of holding a line at Suez and preventing an Ottoman occupation of Egypt was by no means guaranteed.

The most reliable type of intelligence was extracted from photographs, showing not just the disposition of enemy positions, but also the lie of the land. But taking clear pictures from a shuddering biplane, with the pilot and observer exposed not only to the elements but also to the possibility of attack from the ground (as Major Reilly discovered in Mesopotamia) was not easy. Author C S Lewis served as an RFC pilot in France during World War One and described the difficulties in carrying out this "somewhat amateurish" process. For a start an observer "could not operate the camera from his seat because of the plane directly below him, so it was clamped on outside the fuselage, beside the pilot; a big, square, shiny mahogany box with a handle to change the plates... To make an exposure you pulled a ring on the end of the cord. To sight it, you leaned over the side and looked through a ball and crosswire finder." The pilot then had to fly the plane accurately over the spot to be photographed, not always an easy task in windy or turbulent conditions. One hand was on the controls, while the other was needed to "push the camera handle back and forward to change the plates, pulling the string between each operation."[20] Under these circumstances it seems remarkable that any accurate information was collected.

Throughout January 1915, the fragile RFC planes, cameras at the ready, took off from makeshift airstrips close to the Suez Canal and flew eastwards out over the Sinai desert to observe the Turkish army positions. The commander of the British army in Egypt, Sir John Maxwell, described later how the RFC pilots were "much handicapped by inferior types of machines", but "notwithstanding these drawbacks, they furnished me regularly with all information regarding the movements of the enemy."[21] Such information enabled Britain's Minister of War, Lord Kitchener, to announce towards the middle of January that "the much talked of advance of the Turkish forces against Egypt has up to the present failed to materialise. Certain bodies of Turkish troops under German officers have been observed by our aircraft to be attempting to penetrate the country east of the Suez Canal, but no large force has yet appeared, and there has been scarcely any contact with our troops guarding the Canal."[22] Later in the month, Turkish forces advanced along the Mediterranean coast, through al-Arish, towards the northern end of the Suez Canal. RFC and RNAS observers (the latter in seaplanes) monitored the advance and carried out bombing missions to impede the army's progress. At the end of January, *The Times* of London reported that "the Turkish advance on Egypt has begun. It is not yet probable that the Turks have penetrated the Peninsula of Sinai, but a column has reached Bir Muhadat, less than 30 miles from the Suez Canal... a British seaplane has dropped bombs on the column, inflicting losses."[23]

Aircraft were also in action as the Turkish assault on the canal began on 27 January. British airmen "succeeded in dropping bombs, to the disgust of the Bedouin, on hostile bodies advancing westwards. One of our aeroplanes had a narrow escape of being obliged to descend in the neighbourhood of the enemy, darting away again when almost in their clutches amid heavy fire."[24] By the end of the first week of February, the Turkish army had been driven back, without being able to use its specially designed pontoons to cross the canal. A correspondent for the London *Daily Mail* described the important intelligence-gathering role played by British aircraft in the defeat of the Ottoman force. He spoke of how "the Turks steadily went on dragging their fated pontoons across the sand [towards the canal]. There could be no question of surprise. Sooner or later they were bound to debouch into the range of hostile aeroplanes." The correspondent added that until the day before the attack on the canal began, British airmen "almost convoyed the Turkish troops like policemen... there is no doubt that, for all his [the enemy's] determination, our aeroplanes (in which are included the waterplanes) harassed the enemy considerably... there have been some exploits here which it would be unjust to let pass unmentioned. One of our airmen scored a bull's-eye with a bomb from a height of 7,000 ft, and destroyed a full score of the enemy in close order, at the lowest counting... The enemy have for the present retired far out of the reach of our aeroplanes. Whether they will come back or not is a question everyone puts in Egypt."[25]

From Turkey's perspective, the opportunity of inflicting a quick and decisive defeat on the Allies and capturing the Suez Canal had been missed. So this was one of the key moments in the war in the Middle East, and one in which aircraft played a decisive part. Another Ottoman attack was launched on the canal in April 1916. But by then the Allied defences – ground and air – were impenetrable. The focus of British commanders, meanwhile, was on preparation for the day when they could push the Turkish army northwards, out of Sinai and into Palestine. Air power once more gave the Allied forces the advantage of watching and probing areas far behind enemy lines. One key British objective was to oust the Turks from al-Arish (sometimes spelt El Arish), a town on the Mediterranean coast that for many centuries had served as gatekeeper for both Egypt and Palestine. As early as the spring of 1915, "three aeroplanes made a flight from the Canal to El Sirr, some 25 miles south of El Arish, dropping nine bombs, which were effective. About 150 to 200 tents were seen. The distance flown was more than 170 miles. No other enemy troops were seen this side of El Sirr, though one or two small posts of about 20 men are known to exist."[26] At around the same time, seaplanes flown by French pilots (under British command), were taking off from the waters of the Eastern Mediterranean on reconnaissance missions over Palestine itself (the planes were kept on ships then lowered into the water for take-off). The Turks' main command centre in southern Palestine was at Bir Saba (known these days outside the Arab world as Beersheba), north of al-Arish, where the Germans had established a landing ground. French airmen joined the British in these operations. One French pilot, Louis Cintré, was awarded the (British) Distinguished Flying Cross medal for his services as a seaplane pilot. The citation for his award said he had "displayed great skill and intrepidity in a reconnaissance over Bir Saba in April 11th, 1915, when his plane was subjected to heavy shrapnel and musketry fire, and was hit in more than one place. With consummate coolness, [Cintré] circled over Bir Saba again and again until the number and position of the enemy were observed. He then turned his plane towards the ship, and, though the engine was damaged, succeeded by very skilful handling in traversing the distance of 35 miles to the coastline in safety."[27]

The remaining Turkish positions throughout Sinai came under intense pressure in the early months of 1916. In addition to the positions themselves, the vital supply lines (especially those carrying water to remote outposts in the Sinai desert) were also targeted by British and French pilots. Six RFC aircraft carried out a raid against Bir al-Hassana, the Turks' advance base in central Sinai in March 1916, destroying the facility that the troops depended on for survival: the main water reservoir. The airmen dropped 40 bombs "on the reservoir, buildings and trenches with great effect and, according to the description of one observer, the camp presented the appearance of a volcano in eruption."[28] One can only try to imagine the horror felt by soldiers and civilians alike, many of whom would never before have seen an aircraft, let alone the destruction caused by aerial bombing.

By the following summer the RFC had resumed its assault on al-Arish: aeroplanes were given orders to "engage any hostile machines and to devote special attention to enemy troops and camps. A column of troops about 1,000 strong were seen south of the town on the march, and three bombs exploded among them. All camps were effectively bombarded."[29] The noose was now tightening: a Turkish airfield just five miles south of the town came under air attack. Two planes on the ground were destroyed, two hangars set on fire, and eight others badly damaged. "It is assumed," an official communiqué said, "that these hangars contained aeroplanes, and in all probability at least five, possibly more, were put out of action... We lost three machines in the course of the action."[30] Britain was determined not to lose mastery of the air over the Sinai and southern Palestine, as it had so nearly done in Mesopotamia.

But just when all seemed to be going well for the Allies, the Ottoman forces surprised the British commanders by launching another thrust in the direction of the Suez Canal. Once again, the RFC pilots played a crucial role in spotting the enemy advance – their action applauded by General Sir Archibald Murray, head of the Egyptian Expeditionary Force that was preparing to advance northwards into Palestine. "A reconnaissance by the Royal Flying Corps," he wrote later, "revealed the fact that a large enemy force had moved westwards from El Arish... I cannot speak too highly of the work of the RFC during the whole period. Their work was extremely arduous and exhausting. The average total daily reconnaissances during this period amounted to 23¼ hours, and during the first five days of August to as much as 31½ hours. Many pilots and observers were out two or three times a day for several consecutive days under very accurate anti-aircraft fire and were frequently engaged in air combats with enemy machines of superior power."[31] For once, the RFC was facing serious opposition in the sky – resulting from the training and equipping programme organised by the Germans. In the summer of 1916 General Kress von Kressenstein, the German officer commanding the Ottoman army in Egypt and Palestine "received reinforcements from [Turkish Defence Minister] Enver Pasha in Constantinople; a squadron of German aircraft also arrived and proceeded to make regular air raids on Port Said which intimidated the civilian population. One German plane even reached Cairo and dropped a few bombs."[32] In the end, the Turkish attack was repulsed, with many Turks killed and 4,000 taken prisoner. Murray decided the moment had come to drive the remaining Ottoman forces out of Sinai and begin the advance into Palestine. As his troops were moving in on al-Arish (captured on 22 December 1916) he used the RFC once again to soften up Beersheba further to the north. At dawn on 11 November, five BE2 biplanes and one Martinsyde took off from an advanced refuelling airfield at Mustabig (half way between the Suez Canal and al-Arish) and launched a raid on Maghdaba (in the Sinai desert) and Beersheba. At the former, "the enemy's camp and store sheds were bombed, and a number of direct hits caused much damage. At Bir Saba a 100-lb bomb hit the aerodrome; an Aviatik [German biplane] whilst being brought from the hangar was directly hit, the hangar also being damaged... Two hostile Fokkers [German biplanes that enjoyed great success over France] were driven down in a damaged condition."[33]

As important as it was to capture the Turks' railhead and other facilities at Beersheba, Murray also needed to take the well-fortified city of Gaza which, in early 1917 (after the capture of al-Arish and Rafah – at the southern end of the modern-day Gaza Strip, on the border with Egypt), was now the southernmost Ottoman position. His attack on the city, launched at the end of March, lasted only two days and ended in failure for the Allies because supplies of water and ammunition were insufficient.[34] A second attempt, made the following month, was an even greater military failure, with around 6,000 British and Allied troops killed. As a result, Murray was relieved of his command. His replacement, General Edmund Allenby, was also ordered to capture Gaza, but he took time to prepare for his assault on the city, building a railway to bring water and other supplies to his front-line troops. By November, he was ready. Allenby's assault on Gaza was assisted by what must have been one of the earliest instances of air/sea collaboration in war. Aircraft were used not only conventionally to acquire intelligence and drop bombs, but also to direct fire from ships onto targets on land and then to cut the lines of retreat. An RNAS officer recalled how "the bombardment of these lines of retreat was undertaken by battleships which, lying fairly close inshore, could range on them with the greatest ease, though their targets were generally invisible. It was here that the seaplanes came in. They were employed in spotting; that is to say, they circled above the targets, and the observers, noting where the shots fell, corrected the aim of the gunners by wireless signals."[35] Within days, Gaza was in Allied hands, with the Turks in retreat northwards.

In the weeks before and after the capture of Gaza, seaplanes (British and French) had also been in action against Ottoman and German targets along the coast of Palestine to the north. For example, in August 1916, 10 British seaplanes took part in a raid on the port city of Haifa – a major rail terminus. The city was strong defended, with Mount Carmel to its rear providing a natural defence and an obstacle to low-flying seaplanes. The railway facilities also proved to be a more difficult target than the pilots had expected: "The reconnaissance of the previous week had encountered no anti-aircraft fire, but the Turks had been busy in the interval and had got two gun positions between the town and the railway station. All the seaplanes were hit, but not seriously enough to hinder them, and the orders were carried out. Station buildings, store sheds, rolling stock, tents, were effectively bombed."[36]

Beirut was the next strategically important target to be neutralised as a result of Allied air power. Goods unloaded at the port were taken by railway eastwards over the mountains to Damascus, from where they were sent south by train to Ottoman outposts in the Hejaz. But in 1917, the Allies learned that the port was also being used as a refuelling base for German submarines. It was bombed three times during that year, on each occasion with greater intensity. A detailed account of the second bombing raid – which began at 4.30am one August morning – vividly conveys the impact that the Allied planes had, both on their targets and on the astonished inhabitants of Beirut. The lead aircraft "began the operations by firing two trays from its Lewis gun at the extremity of the long arm of the harbour where there was a watchtower. That the attack was a surprise seemed evident, because it was only after the machines had been engaged for some time that a flag, doubtless intended as a warning to ships not to approach, was seen to have been hoisted on the tower. The first and second machines had orders to look out for submarines." None was spotted, but the port area was bombed extensively. Before the operation finished, "the whole of the harbour was veiled with smoke... Not a single bomb fell in any part of the residential quarters, and it may be noted with interest that the inhabitants of Beirut evidently realised that there was little danger in the attack excepting at points of military importance, for many of them were assembled on the roofs and verandahs of their houses watching the proceedings. By ten minutes to seven the last machine had returned to its ship."[37]

British air superiority undoubtedly played a vital role in overcoming German-backed Ottoman forces in the Middle East, and 1917 proved to be a turning point for the Allies. By the end of the year, not only were enemy positions along the whole Mediterranean coast being harassed, but also the strategically important towns of Gaza and Beersheba were finally in Allied hands. Rushdi Sa'id al-Shawwa was a young Palestinian from Gaza (later to become mayor of the city) who had been conscripted as an officer in the Ottoman army. He remembered in later life the chaos that ensued after the Turks had been defeated at Beersheba on 31 October. Ottoman forces "fled, surrendered or were killed," he wrote. Shawwa was detained by Allied troops as he made his way towards Hebron and held prisoner by the Australian cavalry. But on "the morning of Friday 2 November 1917 at 11am planes of the Turkish army came overhead in some number and the Turkish army attacked us. We were all taken prisoner by the Ottomans, but because I was an Ottoman officer they let me go."[38]

On 11 December 1917, Allenby entered Jerusalem, which had been captured by the Allies a few days earlier. But before the expeditionary force could move northwards towards Damascus, the last major city in Ottoman hands, it needed to remove the Turkish presence on the eastern flank – a line stretching from Medina northwards up the Jordan Valley to Jericho, with Amman to the east. This task was assigned to the Arab army that had committed itself to helping the Allies in the war against the Ottomans. Although the flag of the Arab Revolt had been raised by the elderly Sharif Hussein, command of the force was given to his third son, Feisal. The young Arab leader was advised and supported by T E Lawrence – sent by the British authorities in Cairo to assist with the revolt.

The Arab forces of the insurgency operated in isolated groups, often with vast expanses of desert between them. The logistics involved in Lawrence's role as adviser to Arab military leaders were, therefore, immensely complicated. He needed to be in frequent communications with his superiors for such practical matters as collecting cash to pay the Arab soldiers and liaising with Allenby and other British commanders in Palestine and Egypt. Without long-distance radios and with ground transport in the desert so difficult, it is fair to say that Lawrence's task would have been almost impossible without aircraft being available to pick him up from remote locations and whisk him off to Cairo or elsewhere for meetings. It is remarkable how often, in the course of *Seven Pillars of Wisdom*, his account of the revolt, Lawrence mentions in passing that he flew to a particular place. Indeed, early in 1918, when trying to convince his superiors to relieve him of his duties, a weary and dispirited Lawrence said he was tired not only of "riding a thousand miles each month upon camels" but also of "added nervous hours in crazy aeroplanes". The aircraft were old, rickety and unreliable; and the heat rising from the desert sometimes made flying conditions uncomfortable, as he hopped from place to place in Palestine: "At Guweira, Siddons had an aeroplane waiting. Nuri Shaalan and Feisal wanted me at once in Jefer. The air was thin and bumpy, so that we hardly scraped over the crest of Shtar. I sat wondering if we would crash, almost hoping it."[39]

Lawrence may have felt ambivalent about his frequent flights in British military aircraft, but they played an invaluable role in supporting the military goals of the Arab Revolt. On numerous occasions, the successful intervention of British aircraft turned the tide for the Arab force. In July 1917, for example, with Aqaba having fallen, the Turks began to take up new defensive positions further north. For the Arabs to uproot these defences, decisive action was needed. Lawrence decided to "prick the Turks into discomfort by asking General Salmond [the senior RFC commander in the region] for his promised long-distance air raid on Maan [a town north of Aqaba in modern-day Jordan]." Salmond chose his best pilots for the difficult task, ones who "had experience of forced landings on desert surfaces and could pick out an unknown destination across unmapped hills... On this occasion he ordered low flying, to make sure the aim; and profited by reaching Maan, and dropping 32 bombs in and about the unprepared station. Two bombs into the barracks killed 35 men and wounded 50. Eight struck the engine-shed, heavily damaging the plant and stock... Four fell on the aerodrome. Despite the shrapnel our pilots and engines returned safely to their temporary landing ground at Kuntilla above Akaba."[40] By the final stages of the war, Lawrence and the men of the Arab Revolt were able to benefit from the support of modern, well-equipped aircraft. But for much of the conflict the Allies had been forced to rely on obsolete models dating from 1913-14. Lawrence described a land battle at Deraa, north of Amman (in modern-day Syria), where the Ottomans had command of the sky and were harassing the Arab force below. Then a British BE12 biplane, piloted by a man named only as Junor, "suddenly sailed into the circus. We watched with mixed feelings, for his hopelessly old-fashioned machine made him cold meat for any one of the enemy scouts or two-seaters; but at first he astonished them, as he rattled in with his two guns."[41] Junor was out-numbered and out-gunned, but managed to hold his own until he ran out of fuel, eventually making a crash landing.

By the autumn of 1918, Lawrence was shrewd enough to realise that without more robust air support to face the newly trained Ottoman air force, supplied with modern German planes, his force would be unable to link up with Allenby's army to capture Damascus. So he decided to seek help, flying to Ramleh in Palestine, and then driving up to Allenby's headquarters in Jerusalem. Lawrence explained how he viewed the prospects for the Arab army "and how everything was being wrecked by air impotence." He was promised immediate support, including the use of a huge (by 1918 standards) Handley Page 0/400 biplane bomber that had recently been flown out to Egypt from England. From Cairo it had been sent immediately to Palestine, where it played a decisive role in the Battle of Megiddo, in September 1918, when Allenby's army finally broke the Turks' last defensive line west of Damascus. Lawrence was referring to that battle when he wrote that "the co-operation of the air with his [Allenby's] unfolding scheme had been so ready and so elastic, the liaison so complete and informed and quick. It was the RAF, which had converted the Turkish retreat into a rout, which had abolished their telephone and telegraph connections, had blocked their lorry columns, scattered their infantry units."[42] Allenby was as good as his word, and the Handley Page 0/400 was subsequently used to ferry supplies to a makeshift desert strip where other aircraft were lined up to support the Arab army's advance on Damascus. The man chosen to fly the bomber was an Australian, Ross Smith, who had frequently been Lawrence's pilot during the years of the Arab Revolt. It was in the skies over Palestine that Smith acquired the skills and experience that he would put to good use after the war when he became an internationally renowned aviator.

Smith is undoubtedly one of the relatively small number of men who, through his role as a pilot, helped to shape the outcome of the First World War in the Middle East. Without air power, the success of the Arab Revolt and even Allenby's sweep northwards into Palestine would have been significantly more difficult, perhaps impossible. It was the work of pilots and observers, too, which ensured that the Allied commanders knew the size and disposition of the Turkish army advancing on the Suez Canal in early 1915. And it was at a time when Britain had almost lost the mastery of the air in Mesopotamia that the Allies suffered their ignominious defeat at Ctesiphon and endured the subsequent siege of Kut. The shaping of the post-World War One Middle East, it is true, was the fruit of secret connivance between France and Britain – with the Sykes-Picot agreement of 1916 dividing the region into French and British territories, thus rendering Britain's promise of Arab independence worthless. By the end of the First World War, too, Britain, through Foreign Secretary Arthur Balfour, had promised the Jews that it would work for the establishment of a Jewish homeland in Palestine. The stage was set for the Middle East conflict that continues in the second decade of the 21st century. Today, the defeat of the Ottomans and the underhand scheming of Sykes-Picot and Balfour are taken for granted as part of the historical landscape. But if it had not been for a handful of decisive actions involving aircraft across the Middle East during the First World War, then Britain and France might not have been able to impose their strategies on the region and a very different map might have emerged.

The First World War not only redrew the political face of the Middle East, but it also helped to change the outlook of its inhabitants. By the end of the conflict, millions of people who had lived under the heavy hand of Ottoman rule had been rudely introduced to some of the scientific and technological developments of the 21st century – not least that of aviation. The war resulted in the bombardment of towns in Egypt, Iraq, Palestine, Syria. But it also brought about the birth of aerodromes – in Cairo, Basra, Baghdad, Amman, Beirut and elsewhere. When the war ended, these became available for civilian use. A grid of potential air links had been established by military flights that set the pattern for the emergence of commercial flying.

The particular climatic challenges posed by flying in the Middle East also contributed to the development of aviation itself. Before the outbreak of war, a few young and courageous aviators from Europe had made brief forays into the region. But the arrival of those three RFC Maurice Farman Shorthorns at Alexandria in November 1914 had marked the start of a new chapter in aviation, one in which the technology of the early 20th century would be pushed to its limits. Flying was only 11 years old. Overnight, it had to adapt not only to the demands of war, but equally importantly to the rigours of a climate that no European pilots and engineers had encountered before. Aviators had to learn fast how to cope with heat and sand, and what effect these had on airframes, struts and engines. There were no manuals to consult, no experts to call on. Their experience of hot-weather flying and the means of overcoming the difficulties associated with it was unique. The knowledge they acquired was passed on subsequently to others seeking to establish aviation in all regions of the world where high temperatures are normal. Without the lessons learned in the Middle East during the First World War, the development of commercial flying across arid and desert regions would undoubtedly have been delayed by some years.

Much valuable experience was gained in Mesopotamia. RFC Air Commodore Robert Brooke-Popham, mangling the English language as he did so, thought that Mesopotamia was "very nearly as much worse than Egypt, as regards to climatic conditions, as Egypt is worse than England." He added that the heat caused the laminated wooden propellers to warp and split, tyres were frequently punctured by camel thorn, and sand fouled up hinges and moving parts on the tail.[43] Lt-Col J E Tennant served with the RFC in Mesopotamia for two years from just after the surrender of Kut in 1916 and flew in the subsequent campaigns that saw the

Ottomans lose control of Baghdad and the remainder of modern-day Iraq. In a memoir, he wrote in detail about the difficulties of the weather. During the hot months, "aerial work during the day was limited to the early hours, for the late afternoon was as hot as midday till the sun went down; then it was dark. Cooler air was not to be found under an altitude of 3,000 feet, and little difference could be felt under 5,000 feet. Flying in the night one would start in fairly cool atmosphere, but on reaching 500 feet one entered the hot air of the day... Flying in the hot weather was a great strain, and, after service in France, it was odd to see a pilot going off for a long flight dressed only in shorts, stockings, and shirt, with a helmet bound down on to his head, for at 5,000 feet the sun's rays are as fierce as on the ground." [44]

The aircraft themselves had difficulty standing up to the heat: the skin of their fuselages and wings consisted of canvas stretched over wooden frames, with dope (varnish) applied to the fabric to keep it taut. Tennant recalled at one point how, "owing to the continual and almost daily movement of flights, it had been impossible for the last two months to put machines under hangars, and in order to protect them from the sun during the day they were covered with 'chattai' (palm-leaf mats). It afforded good protection and kept the fabric cool. The main object was to keep the light off the doped fabric; heat had small deteriorating effect compared to the light of the sun's rays. Tent hangars being unable to withstand the frequent violent squalls were useless in that country; they also had no ventilation when closed, and the temperature inside became terrific and destructive to the woodwork." Engines were also vulnerable to the effects of weather. Tennant described how a two-day dust storm choked carburettors and bearings with sand and almost tore the aircraft away from the pegs and ropes with which they were tethered to the desert.

The harsh Middle Eastern climate continued to pose a challenge to even the newest of most up-to-date aircraft. When a consignment of French-built Spad biplanes arrived in Mesopotamia, "every engine had to be taken down and overhauled [to check for rust that might have formed during the sea journey out]; the aeroplane wooden parts had shrunk in the heat, necessitating the rebuilding of many machines." When Tennant took the first completed Spad for a test flight he discovered that the water-cooling system devised for a European climate was "inadequate, and the water started boiling as I left the ground. I shoved her up to try to get into cooler atmosphere. At 6,000 feet over the harbour I was suddenly aware of the whole top plane warping into wave-like contortions and steam scalding my face. The auxiliary water-tank in the plane had exploded and flooded the wood and fabric. It was very gingerly that I glided down, expecting the wings to carry away; my next breath was taken when the wheels touched the ground."

The 1914-18 war forced infant aviation into adulthood. As one of today's historians has written, during the first major conflict of the century, "aircraft found their first practical use as instruments of war" and aviation "matured under the stress of combat. For the first time, aircraft were operated on a daily basis, with all that implies of regular servicing and a focus on reliability." For planes operating in the Middle East, added to "stress of combat" was the enormous stress of extreme weather conditions. In this way, the region provided a vital testing ground where pilots and engineers learnt a lot about hot-weather flying – lessons that would be invaluable in the post-war world, when bombers would be converted into airliners, operating across the deserts where aircraft in the Middle East had found their "first practical use".[45] This was a contribution that has never, until now, been fully acknowledged.

As the First World War drew to a close, it was clear to some that aviation would play a role in subsequent years that could not have been imagined in 1914. In his *Practical Flying: Complete Course of Flying Instruction* published in early 1918, Royal Navy Flight Commander W G McMinnies anticipated a world where the aeroplane would "compete successfully with the motorcar or train over long distances, hence the wonderful opportunity for the younger generation to make use of the opportunities it will offer when the war comes to an end."[46] There was no shortage, furthermore, of young men and women who were eager to exploit those opportunities.

three

Breaking Boundaries

A British victory in the First World War had seemed far from certain at the beginning of 1917. But even then, some visionary individuals were able to look beyond the conflict to a day when the nature of aviation would inevitably change. The aircraft had proved itself a powerful, adaptable – and sometimes decisive – instrument of war. Why should it not perform a range of civilian roles in peacetime – and not just in competition with road and rail transport? The prominent British industrialist and aviation pioneer George Holt Thomas believed, for example, that the development of commercial aviation services would be of enormous benefit to business – where "speed was everything". The aeroplane would enable a businessman to leave London in the morning, go to Paris for meetings and be home again for dinner. In a similar way, a plane could take him to Baghdad in a day and a half.[1] The proposals might not seem particularly far-sighted to the modern-day reader, but until the outbreak of war, aviation had been primarily a public spectacle and a hobby for the very wealthy. The names of those who flew in Egypt before the war – Baron de Caters, Baroness de Laroche, and so on – are some indication that it was an elitist pastime.

Some in Britain saw post-war aviation prospects opening up across the British Empire. A senior adviser to Britain's Government of India expressed the view that the establishment of an air route –

for passengers and mail – linking the colony with London should be a peacetime priority. Lord Montagu of Beaulieu's vision, coloured – literally – by the imperial thinking of the day, was for an "All Red" route, on account of its "being nearly all over British territory". The five-day journey would start at Karachi (a city in India at that time). The traveller would spend five nights on the ground – at Basra, Alexandria, Malta, Gibraltar and Land's End (at the extreme south-western tip of England). The voyage over the sea "would be done by seaplane. Mails would be flown continuously by day and night, the landing places being illuminated and the route indicated by miniature lighthouses."[2] Lord Montagu gradually refined his vision, describing in some detail a proposed air corridor from Egypt to India: "Starting from Kantara, [it] proceeds across the Sinai desert through Palestine to Damascus, a considerable amount of difficult and hilly country being covered in the flight." Then an easterly course would be flown to Baghdad, "whence, under conditions of little geographical difficulty, a south-easterly course, more or less following the River Tigris, brings us to Basra." The route thereafter would proceed down the Gulf to Bushehr [spelt Bushire at the time] and Bandar Abbas (both in Iran), but it would be "necessary to skirt the shore, as the mountainous nature of the country, and scarcity of landing-grounds, render a direct course undesirable."[3] Lord Montagu's predictions did not receive universal approval. Indeed, a newspaper report two years later recalled that, at the time, "there were many who jeered, as people had always jeered at prophets at all times and in all countries."[4]

A few days after the ending of the First World War (in November 1918), the ideas of Lord Montagu and others were put to the test. The Handley Page 0/400 bomber that took part in the closing stages of the Allied campaign in Palestine and came to the aid of T E Lawrence and his Arab army had been flown out to Cairo at the beginning of August 1918 by Brigadier-General Amyas Borton. He convinced the authorities in London that, in future, instead of the long and laborious process of sending out aircraft in crates by sea to Alexandria and reassembling them in Cairo, it would be easier and much quicker to fly them there. This he proceeded to do, establishing the precedent of new aircraft being ferried to their bases of operations. Captain Ross Smith (Lawrence's Australian pilot) served under Borton. On 20 November, Borton and Smith – with Major-General John Salmond, RAF Commander of the Middle East, as a passenger – set off from Cairo to Baghdad, with an overnight stop in Damascus en route. This was a journey of around 1,000 miles, across mountains as well as deserts that had never been attempted before. As well as a seven-day supply of food and water, the general carried a letter signed by Feisal, the son of Sharif Hussein, asking Arabs to "render all assistance in case of a forced landing". No such help was needed because the aircraft landed safely in Baghdad. The flight was an historic achievement, generating widespread coverage in the British press. But more was to come. The Handley Page biplane was then flown on to Delhi, achieving the world's first flight from Egypt to India. As was often the case in the early days of flying, it was circumstances on the ground – rather than detailed advanced planning – that determined whether or not to carry on. Salmond said his original destination had been Mesopotamia, "but the weather conditions being favourable, the Air Ministry decided that the flight should continue to India." He added that while the journey had been made in a military aircraft, the possibility existed "for machines now being specially designed for commercial work." In the view of *The Times*, the successful first flight from Egypt to India represented "a notable achievement in the history of British aeronautics."[5] But the significance was infinitely greater than this: it had proved, as Salmond and Montagu had suggested, that a smooth transition from military flying to passenger-carrying civil aviation was possible. It was also now clear that the Middle East – where hot-weather-flying techniques had been pioneered – would be one of the first regions to be involved in the new development. Before the end of December a second Handley Page 0/400 had taken off from England on a flight to Cairo, from where it would follow Salmond's route to India. The aircraft encountered a number of delays en route, finally reaching its destination a month later, in mid-January 1919 – a year that would see aviation breaking boundaries as never before. If military flying had come of age through the 1914-18 conflict, then it was equally true to say – to quote Major-General F H Sykes, Chief of Britain's Air Staff – that civil aviation was "a child of war".[6] By March 1919 the RAF had prepared a string of landing grounds that began at Basra and extended southwards down the Gulf to Bushehr and Bandar Abbas, and Charbar and Karachi in India. The route for future civil flights to India had been charted, to await the day when long-distance air travel would come of age.

Perhaps the most outstanding long-distance flight achievement of 1919 was the first non-stop crossing of the Atlantic Ocean by air – achieved in June by two British pilots, Captain John Alcock and Lieutenant Arthur Brown. The men took off in Newfoundland and fought their way through appalling weather over the ocean, before bringing down their Vickers Vimy biplane, unceremoniously but safely, in an Irish bog. Within a decade, aviators had navigated their way over three increasingly large stretches of open sea: the English Channel (Blériot in 1909); the Mediterranean (Garros in 1913); and now the Atlantic. Alcock and Brown joined the growing list of internationally celebrated aviators. The name of the Australian First World War pilot, Ross Smith, would be added to it before the year was out.

The publicity surrounding Alcock and Brown's triumph, coupled with the success of the pioneering flights from Egypt to India, whetted the appetites of the British and Australian governments for a service that would connect the seat of empire with its most distant possession. Yet it was recognised that more exploratory work would still be needed to find a suitable route eastwards from India – virgin skies still in 1919. Aviators would have to be found to blaze the trail. Britain's Air Ministry thought immediately about Borton and Smith. Conveniently, both men were still in India after their flight from Egypt. More importantly, the skill and courage they had demonstrated as pilots in Palestine during the First World War made them well qualified to explore a possible route eastwards to India – and this is what they were asked to do, travelling by sea in search of possible landing grounds.

The incentive to reach Australia by air from Britain increased considerably when the Australian government offered a prize of

£10,000 for the first pilot to complete the 11,500-mile trip in 30 days. An official announcement about the contest from the British Air Ministry highlighted some of the daunting challenges that would be faced in such an epic flight – at a time when only a handful of aircraft had successfully completed journeys from England to India. "It has always been recognised in official quarters," the Ministry said, "that a flight between England and Australia would be a performance of very great difficulty in the present state of ground organisation, and that considerable time must necessarily elapse before the project could mature. Since little information was available on the proposed line of route beyond Calcutta, it was decided... that no competitor should start until the Air Ministry had been able to obtain reliable data concerning the section of the route between Calcutta and Port Darwin." The completion of Borton and Smith's survey and their ability to provide "detailed information regarding their investigations" enabled the contest to go ahead. However, the Ministry went on to warn that while the route as far as North Africa was relatively straightforward, thereafter hazards could be expected – even on sections that had been opened up by pioneer aviators: "From Cairo to India the difficulties to be faced are greater and vast stretches of uncivilised country have to be traversed. Although more than one flight has been made over this portion of the route, it cannot be said to be in regular operation."[7]

Despite the potential difficulties, several crews registered as official entrants. Among them was a team consisting of Ross Smith as first pilot, his brother Keith as second pilot, and two mechanics. As Australians, the Smiths clearly had an added spur to win the race. Participating aircraft took off from Hounslow, a village (in those days) to the west of London, in November. In the end, five planes had been entered for the race – although one had a fatal accident over a London suburb only a few minutes after take-off. But the official competitors were not the only people heading for Australia by air. Hoping to steal the thunder of the teams setting off from London, a French pilot, Etienne Poulet, and his mechanic Jean Benoist, had left Paris two months earlier. The pair made slow progress eastwards, eventually arriving in Rangoon, in Burma.

Shortly after that, engine trouble precipitated a forced landing in a mountainous region that wrecked the Frenchmen's plane. Their flight to Australia ended there.

The Smith brothers, meanwhile, continued with their own preparations to fly their twin-engined Vickers Vimy. Curiously there was a physical link between their pioneering journey and the previous epic flight earlier in the year: the Smiths' Vimy was fitted out with some of the mechanical parts from that flown by Alcock and Brown across the Atlantic earlier in the year.[8] The Smith brothers may have taken this as a good omen – but if so, they are likely to have changed their minds the moment they took off from Hounslow. All across Europe they encountered wet and misty flying conditions. Even on the island of Crete in the Eastern Mediterranean the weather was unsettled, as Ross Smith's diary entry makes clear: "Low clouds made crossing Cretan mountains difficult. Wind slightly favourable, steered south course after leaving, but had to fly through rain at 2,000 ft most of the way across the Mediterranean. Passed two steamers half-way; checked ground speed and drift on them. Crossing took 2½ hours. Struck African coast at Sollum [on Egypt's north-west Mediterranean shore, close to the Libyan border], then flew east to Cairo across desert via [Mersa] Matruh. Hope to reach Damascus or Baghdad tomorrow... So far have taken 30 hours... Vimy going perfectly."

The following morning, when the Vimy was ready to take off from Cairo, the crew were told that heavy rain was falling in Palestine, "but we decided to go ahead as I knew the country pretty well, having flown over it during the war... Crossed Canal at Kantara, then over Romani under thick cloud to Gaza. Turned inland to Ramleh... [where] we ran into a very heavy rain and had to descend to about 500 ft to see through it and see the ground... flew low to Jordan over Sea of Galilee, thence to Damascus... It was only by knowing the country so well that we were able to get through... Interesting seeing old places again, recalling memories of the war. Landed, Damascus 3pm. Met many old RAF friends."

The Smith brothers went to bed believing that they had now passed successfully through the bad weather. But they woke to yet more heavy rain, eventually taking off mid-morning during a break in the downpour. Once again, low cloud forced them to fly low over the desert towards Baghdad. But worse followed when they "encountered a head wind after striking the River Euphrates. This retarded our progress so much that we could not get into Baghdad before dark." They landed at Ramadi, west of the Iraqi capital, where soldiers of the 10th Indian Lancers helped to tie down their aircraft facing the wind. But late in the evening a gale blew up, "with the result that we had to turn out and hang onto the machine. Before we reached the machine the wind had broken one of the control wires, but with the assistance of the men from the camp we turned the machine into the wind and tied her down more securely." The following morning, after mending the control wire, the Smith brothers flew to Basra, "passing over Kut and other battlefields of the Mesopotamian campaign. This was the first good flying day we had had since we left England." The Smiths and their mechanics took a day of rest in Basra and carried out work on their aircraft, before continuing southwards to Bandar Abbas. Their luck held across India and the Far East, and the Vimy eventually became the first aircraft in the race to reach Australia, its crew sharing the £10,000 prize.[9]

News of this epic journey stunned the world. *Flight* magazine, in an editorial, said: "The seemingly impossible has been accomplished... their achievement is one of those things which leaves the ordinary person spell-bound and incapable of adequately expressing his thoughts... What Captain Ross Smith and his companions have done is to give the world the most striking demonstration we have yet had of the fact that the aeroplane with its engine is a practical vehicle, and neither a toy nor an instrument of warfare alone... It opens up new vistas of travel."[10]

By the end of 1919 it was therefore abundantly clear that Lord Montagu's predictions had been correct, and that the Middle East would play an important role in the development of long-distance commercial air travel. But at this early stage, all the amenities required for safe commercial flying in the region still had to be established: navigation aids, maps and ground services were needed. A way also had to be found to overcome the extremes of temperature experienced in the Middle East before passengers could be expected to welcome the idea of flying with safety over mountains and across large expanses of desert.

While many issues required attention, aviation officials concerned with expanding the Middle East concentrated on two: the development of Cairo as a regional aviation hub; and the start of regular services linking the Egyptian capital with Baghdad and Basra. Major-General Sykes, speaking in early 1919, observed that Britain was situated "at the western edge of the flying world, with the remoter Dominions at the circumference and with India and Egypt near the centre... Egypt is likely to become one of the most important flying centres. It is on the direct route to India, to Australia, to New Zealand, while the most practicable route to the Cape and Central Africa is via Egypt."[11] Lord Montagu came to a similar conclusion, declaring: "I consider that Heliopolis (Cairo) will be the most important single centre of air transport for the Old World – Europe, Asia and Africa."[12]

Heliopolis was, by the standards of the day, already a busy airfield. All the pioneering flights to Palestine, Mesopotamia, India and Australia had passed through it, and the number of planes arriving from Britain was rising steadily – it had also been the RFC's main base during the First World War. A British journalist, who visited the aerodrome at the start of 1920, remarked on the changes that had occurred in the 10 years since the Heliopolis aviation week – the event that put Egypt on the world's flying map. The correspondent recalled how, during the Heliopolis week, "ascents were made to what today would be considered as laughably small heights, and then only when the weather was perfect... On that occasion, though all the best-known airmen of the day were present, not one of them ventured to attempt to fly over Cairo to the Pyramids and back, although a valuable prize was offered for the feat. That was in 1910. In 1920 Heliopolis has become the Clapham Junction [a famously busy London railway junction] of the great Empire air-routes." The airbase, the correspondent wrote, consists of two aerodromes, "one on either side of the old Suez road, along

which caravans passed before the construction of the railways...
It possesses complete workshop facilities, and a good supply of
petrol and water... At present there are several brick hangars for
smaller machines, while for the larger, such as the Handley Page
and Vickers Vimy, emergency canvas hangars have been erected."
The latter were prone to being blown away by strong winds, so
permanent hangars for the bigger aircraft were planned, after
which "Heliopolis aerodrome will be one of the finest of the kind
in the world." Looking to the future, the correspondent predicted a
huge growth in passenger and freight traffic, with air routes to the
four continents.[13]

As for the route from Heliopolis to Baghdad and Basra, British
army and air force officers – with the assistance of air and road
transport – were marking out emergency landing grounds across
the Syrian desert from Damascus to Baghdad. The opening of what
would eventually be an Egypt-Mesopotamia-India air corridor
for military use was the subject of discussion in a November 1919
report by an Advisory Committee on Civil Aviation to the British
government. The committee members said they had been informed
of a decision "for purely Service purposes to establish and maintain
aerodromes and landing grounds for the transit of machines to
India... It appears that this scheme, while meeting Service needs,
will also be a starting point for the civil development of the air
route from Egypt to India; they are advised that the civil air route,
at all events at the outset, will best follow the route laid down for
Service machines. They strongly urge, therefore, that the Service
proposals for joining India and Egypt by air should be put into
effect as soon as possible." The committee also recommended that
a tender be drawn up for a contract to carry mail between Cairo
and Karachi.[14] The recommendations were presented to Winston
Churchill, Secretary of State for Air, and acted upon. Heliopolis'
future expansion was guaranteed.

Throughout 1920, work on securing the Egypt-India route
continued with, for example, Cairo and Bushehr being linked by
wireless/telephone, and intermediate connections established
at Ramleh, Baghdad and Basra. The whole enterprise received a

significant boost when Churchill chaired a meeting in Egypt with senior officials in March 1921 that became known as the Cairo Conference. The main aim was to decide the terms of Britain's mandate for Iraq – granted after the First World War when the Ottoman Empire had collapsed. These were momentous days that would set the shape of the modern Middle East. Britain had a number of geopolitical loose ends from the war years that it wanted to tie up. Prominent among them was fate of Feisal and Abdullah, the sons of the Sharif of Mecca who had proclaimed the Arab Revolt against the Ottoman army. Both men had fought against the Ottoman forces. The British had betrayed the sharif and his family by failing to honour their commitment to support Arab independence, instead making a secret deal with France to divide up the region between them. They had also done nothing to reward Feisal and Abdullah for the parts they played in the Allied campaign. Abdullah had proclaimed himself king of the Arab Kingdom of Syria, but four months later his supporters were defeated by the French in a battle outside Damascus and he fled. Both men felt bitter and abandoned. During the Cairo Conference a partial solution to Britain's awkward predicament was found: it was decided that Feisal would be proclaimed King of Iraq. A short time later, during a visit to Jerusalem, Churchill decreed that Abdullah should become emir of Transjordan (modern-day Jordan).

So Britain was in control, in one guise or another, in three key territories in the Middle East: Egypt, Palestine and Iraq. It was essential, the Cairo Conference decided, that communications linking the three should be strengthened. This meant, in part, making it easier for the RAF to move men and equipment by air. On his return, Churchill announced that plans were being made "for aeroplanes to fly regularly to and fro across the desert between Baghdad and Cairo." At the time, moving a squadron between these cities took a minimum of three months, because the aircraft had to be packed into crates and sent by sea. "Once this route across the desert has been marked out," Churchill continued, "and it was possible for it to be flown in the regular course of affairs, the whole Air Force in Mesopotamia could be speedily transported to Palestine or Egypt. Arrangements could also be made to fly a certain number of commercial aeroplanes carrying mails, and possibly passengers."[15] The RAF, meanwhile, was given the task of peacekeeping in Iraq and Jordan, in the belief that the use of aircraft would be cheaper and more effective than deploying thousands of troops over such large areas of land.

Churchill's reference to the route across the desert being "marked out" refers to the creation of a unique navigation scheme to stop pilots getting lost when crossing the 500 miles of featureless desert. Even though some emergency landing grounds had been established, pilots could still easily stray off course between them. Those who had flown across the desert "saw how unmistakeable were the wheel tracks of lorries used near military camps. Therefore Sir Hugh Trenchard, Chief of Staff, decided that the best guide for aircraft would be a double furrow ploughed the whole length of the route, with fuel reserves stored in drums at suitable points."[16] So, teams were assembled to carry out this extraordinary project: "The navigation track was constructed by survey parties sent out from Cairo on the one side and Baghdad on the other, and to render the track as conspicuous as possible, the wheel marks of heavy Crossley Desert tenders and Rolls Royce tenders were employed. Auxiliary markings in the form of ploughed furrows added to the visibility of the track. By April, 1922, a series of landing grounds had also been prepared along the track at average intervals of twenty miles. All these grounds were conspicuously lettered in the Cairo zone [A-R] and numbered in the Baghdad zone [I-X]."[17] Arrows indicated the direction of approach. The teams ploughed a total of some 310 miles, and "the remainder of the route, which lay over scattered black basalt rock, they marked in white paint. The task took eight weeks." Fuel was made available at two landing strips, "protected from theft and attack by a heavy bronze dome. The depot's locking system was ingeniously designed to function also as a double lock on the aircraft cabin doors, so that an aircraft could not take off either with its door open or with the depot key left at the fuel tank."[18] Another team set up meteorological stations and rest houses. Pilots landing at Rutbah Wells, an oasis on a high plateau halfway between

Damascus and Baghdad, were even able to stay at a complete fort, which offered protection against possible raids by Bedouin.[19]

But the day when the first civilian passenger would fly into Rutbah Wells was still far off. At this stage only the RAF used the navigation aid – particularly useful for those air force pilots flying the regular mail service between Cairo and Baghdad that had begun in June 1921. Civilians wanting to reach Baghdad from Cairo, Beirut or Damascus still travelled overland. But after 1922 the furrow helped to prevent motor vehicles, as well as planes, getting lost in the desert. The 1925 edition of *Cook's Traveller's Handbook: Palestine and Syria* says that at a particular spot east of Damascus "the route meets the Cairo-Baghdad airmail track leading from Amman."[20] The new and safer route, following the furrow, resulted in a significant increase in passenger and freight traffic between Mediterranean ports and Iraq – a little-acknowledged side-effect of the arrival and expansion of aviation in the Middle East.

The RAF's desert airmail route, 590 miles long, ran from Cairo to Ramleh, "which is the main RAF aerodrome in Palestine, passes through Amman in Transjordania and Kasrazrak [Azraq, on the Iraqi border] where landing-grounds have been prepared, and proceeds thence in an almost straight line across the Arabian desert to Ramadie, on the Euphrates, and on to Baghdad."[21] Mail from London was taken by sea to Egypt, "the bags handed over at Port Said by the captain of the steamer to a representative of the Royal Air Force. These, together with the mails from Cairo, will be forwarded by air from the aerodrome at Heliopolis."[22]

Forwarding by air was a more arduous and dangerous task than those few words imply. Crews not only had to navigate the desert route between Damascus and Baghdad ('flying the furrow', as pilots referred to it), but they also needed to have a range of skills and be on full alert all the time. For a start, the aircraft generally flew at an altitude of no more than 9,000 feet, "which meant that engine failure would give them only a few minutes to glide – often steeply – down to an impromptu landing. Passengers often literally pulled their weight, too, irrespective of social status, by joining in to handle the gasoline cans should more fuel be needed. Fuelling en route was a slow job at best, as the fuel had to be filtered through chamois to remove water and grit. Given the unwelcome local attention a landing aircraft could attract, visible for many kilometres in the treeless landscape and with another noisily circling overhead, there was ample incentive to get back into the air and away, for there were Bedouin along the route who resented the aircraft as intruders that frightened their herds."[23]

A correspondent of *The Times* described the experience of flying as a passenger in one of the Cairo-Baghdad mail planes – a de Havilland DH10 twin-engined biplane – in early 1922. His seat, in the front of the aircraft, "was comparatively comfortable, the wind protection, due to the shape of the nose, being so good that the use of goggles is unnecessary, except when looking out over the side." The mails, limited amounts of luggage and "10 days' provisions and water are carried in lockers arranged under the wings of the machine." The DH10 travelled in convoy with two other aircraft, following the Suez Canal to Ismailia. "On approaching the aerodrome at Abu Sueir, near Ismailia, the starboard engine cut out and a signal was made to the other machines, and a good landing made on the edge of the aerodrome. The other machines, seeing that a good landing had been made, continued their flight to Amman. The passenger, not being an airman, had not noticed anything wrong, and was surprised to be told what had happened, and that he had experienced his first forced landing, luckily on an aerodrome and not in the desert." Some three-and-a-half hours later, the DH10 was safely on the ground at the Amman airstrip ("not a very interesting place, being a narrow neck of flat ground between two deep ravines. On the adjoining spur was a large camp occupied by King Abdullah of Transjordan, with Colonel [T E] Lawrence in attendance"). The flight to Ramadi was over largely featureless desert, but "large arrows have been made in the soil to indicate to the airman a coming change of direction. Twenty suitable areas for a landing have been marked with large circles in the course of the 500 miles. Some of these landing grounds are of a gravelly nature, and some are mud flats... About 100 miles from Amman the character of the desert changes, and for about 50 miles there is an uninviting stretch of rugged country in which basaltic rocks with boulders come to the surface, among which it would apparently be very difficult to make a good landing in case of engine trouble, except on the mud flats which Nature appears to have provided for this purpose." The mail flight continued without further incident to Baghdad.[24]

As the Cairo-Baghdad/Basra air connection improved, the British government began thinking about inaugurating routes across Africa. As British air officials had already pointed out, Cairo was seen as the logical hub for routes both eastwards (to Mesopotamia, India and Australia), and southwards (to South Africa). Back in late 1918, Britain's Air Ministry had "despatched to Central Africa two parties with machines and equipment to prospect and survey an aerial route from Cairo to Cape Town."[25] One year later, the Ministry announced that an "all-British" air route from Cairo to the Cape was available for traffic, with a string of landing grounds prepared up and down the route. Sudan, due south of Egypt, was about to become yet another Arab country opened up to international air traffic, the initial route having been pioneered by Marc Pourpe and Frank McClean before the First World War.

The announcement that preparations for a Cairo-Cape service were now complete ignored the fact that no aircraft had as yet flown the full distance. With the Atlantic Ocean crossed by plane, and with Australia within reach by air, South Africa represented the newest challenge. As ever, young aviators stepped forward to take it on. Within weeks, four aircraft were on their way from northern Europe to Cairo with the aim of being the first to complete the long journey to the southern tip of Africa. One of the planes (a Vickers Vimy) was sponsored by *The Times* and carried "a scientific observer" who joined the two pilots in Cairo. The paper devoted many pages to the venture both before and during the flight. The scientist said his first priority was to "report on it with the cold eye of middle age, to ascertain if it be a practical link of Empire, a 'live-wire' of Imperial federation."[26] As the date of the departure neared, the coverage in *The Times* became almost hysterical, playing down the serious challenges and potential dangers ahead, and revealing a naive, schoolboy-like relish for the adventure ahead ("the supply of petrol will be irregular after Khartoum, and we do not expect a rapid trip... [but] we have great hopes of success"[27]). After the aircraft had taken off from Cairo to follow the Nile southwards, an editorial in the paper hailed the event in gushing, hyperbolic prose: "In their day the Pyramids have looked down on many wonderful events. Now it is the turn of man to look down on them, and there is a world of romance in the thought that the first stage of this expedition, in itself a practical proof of man's greatest and latest victory over the forces of nature, should lie along the valley of the Nile, the cradle of civilization, set amidst the sources of the earliest historical knowledge we have of the struggles and triumphs of the human race."[28] The flight itself was ultimately a disappointment. On the initial Cairo-Aswan-Khartoum leg the plane had to make two forced landings because of engine trouble. It then crashed at Tabora (in modern-day Tanzania), and although the three men on board escaped without injury, the aircraft was written off. But despite the failure to reach Cape Town the flight nevertheless made one modest contribution to the Imperial cause: the framework and cabin of the wrecked Vickers Vimy were taken over by the Tabora Sporting Club for use as a cricket pavilion.[29]

In the end, the accolade of being the first aircraft to fly from Cairo to the Cape went to a South African team. The government of South Africa purchased a Vickers Vimy and selected two air force officers for the venture. Lieutenant-Colonel Pierre van Ryneveld and Captain Christopher Quintin Brand took off from Brooklands airfield southwest of London for the initial flight to Cairo. The difficulties they faced then and on the later stages of their journey served to underline the challenges still faced by those eager to see regular commercial air transport linking continents. When their Vimy (named 'Silver Queen') left southern Italy and headed across the Mediterranean to North Africa "the atmosphere became bumpy and the wind grew stronger, the aeroplane rising and falling 500 ft in a few seconds. Little headway was made against the gale. Indeed, the machine was blown back for an hour and a half at one point." At 4am, van Ryneveld took over the controls of the plane from Brand, always a tricky operation, but "particularly so on this night. In the midst of the storm the machine indulged in most disconcerting movements." Then there was the problem of fatigue. Van Ryneveld slapped his face with his gloves to prevent himself from falling asleep, while shining "the electric torch on to Captain Brand's face to keep him awake." The Vimy crossed Crete at 9,000 feet, the undercarriage "just skimming the clouds. Frightful storms were encountered to the south of Crete, and Colonel van Ryneveld said he could not possibly imagine worse weather. Both men longingly awaited the dawn in the hope of sighting land." But as daylight came, there was still no land in sight, only a limitless expanse of sea, and the men flew for an hour and a half before spotting a distant shoreline. They finally reached the coast and landed in a field – at which point "a patrol of native Italian policemen galloped up and surrounded the machine." The pilots were told that they had landed at Derna, in Italian-controlled Libya, after their 11-hour flight. The Vimy was allowed to continue to Sollum and Cairo – where the plane touched down in yet another storm. Those waiting at Heliopolis did not hear the aircraft until it was practically overhead, at which point they fired a flare. When the airmen saw this they celebrated in an unexpected way: they were so relieved "that they opened a tin of bully beef to celebrate the occasion and enjoyed it thoroughly, as they were dreadfully hungry."[30]

The South African pilots were nothing if not dogged in their efforts to reach Cape Town. On the flight from Cairo to Khartoum the Vimy crashed at Wadi Halfa. The plane was wrecked, but the engines were salvaged. The airmen returned to the Egyptian capital where the engines were attached to another machine (Silver Queen 2). On their second attempt to reach Khartoum, the airmen encountered a strong headwind and were forced to come down again – this time safely – at Wadi Halfa. The plane then suffered engine problems that had to be fixed in Khartoum. The pilots' fortunes picked up for a while thereafter – Silver Queen 2 reached modern-day Zambia safely. But there it crashed, and the two airmen completed their journey in a third aircraft – sent from South Africa. So a pioneering air corridor of sorts from Cairo to the Cape had been established, but the journey remained a difficult and dangerous one – hardly yet suitable for commercial traffic.

Van Ryneveld and Brand's journey may have been hazardous, but the hope it created that Britain's African possessions could one day be reached by air was enough to enhance the strategic value of the Heliopolis airbase. British forces had invaded and occupied Egypt in 1882 because the government in London feared that a nationalist uprising might threaten the free passage of ships through the Suez Canal to India. But having taken control of the country, Britain faced a dilemma: it knew that the "acquisition of Egypt and its incorporation into the empire was out of the question. For one thing it would almost certainly have provoked a Middle East war."[31] Yet it could not risk pulling its forces out. So the nature of British rule remained unspecified until Egypt became a formal Protectorate in 1914. Under pressure from a burgeoning nationalist movement in the post-war years Britain published a declaration in 1922 recognising Egypt as "an independent sovereign state". But it was only nominal independence. Britain retained control of, among a number of things, the security of communications of the British Empire in Egypt. Air communications eastwards and southwards were now quite as important as the Suez Canal and the sea route to India. The role of the air force in World War One and the progress made by post-war pioneering flights through Cairo meant that holding onto Egypt, by whatever political stratagem, was more important than ever.

News of all the major pioneering flights – to the Cape and elsewhere – was followed eagerly in the British newspapers. The reports gave colourful accounts of failures as well as successes. The evident dangers and difficulties involved provided fuel to the many sceptics who said that flying would never attract the travelling public. But for every sceptic there was at least one person fanatical about flying and convinced of its commercial value in the future. Few were more fanatical than Alan Cobham who had been an RFC pilot in the First World War. In peacetime he became Britain's best-known airman, dedicating himself to bringing a greater awareness of flying to the government and the public.[32] He was also a leading pioneer of long-distance flights. In November 1924 he piloted a de Havilland DH50 biplane on a flight from England to India and back. His passenger was Air Vice-Marshal Sir Sefton Brancker, Britain's Director of Civil Aviation. The purpose of the flight was to survey a possible air route to India using airships. Cobham was a straightforward, no-nonsense kind of man. He wrote on his return of how necessary it had been for Brancker to see for himself both the "great airship route... which will eventually run to Australia, with possible branch aeroplane lines running off the main airship route... [so] the flight to India was not intended to be a stunt flight, but one in which an aeroplane was used as a business proposition to carry out a certain purpose because the ordinary means of transport could not effectually do the job."

Cobham's flight differed from previous ones in that it did not transit Cairo, instead tracking over Turkey to Syria and Iraq. This route also threw up potential dangers, not least in the need to cross the Taurus Mountains in southern Turkey. Cobham wrote: "I crossed them by the one and only pass and got over at 5,000 ft, and then followed the long flight through the gorge. The bottom of the ravine was 5,000 ft below us, and the mountains, whose summits were in the clouds, were 5,000 ft above us, and it was raining heavily all the time." The aircraft landed in Aleppo in French-controlled Syria. After being entertained for lunch by the French military, "about 50 men pushed our machine through the mud to a dry strip of land [and] we took off for the French outpost aerodrome of Rakka (al-Raqqa, today in northern Syria) on the River Euphrates. The country in this part of the world is perfect for flying, and aerial services should be easy to maintain." After stops at Ramadi and Baghdad, the DH50 continued southwards along the Gulf to India. On the return journey, Cobham noted some of the dangers that planes faced on the route along the Gulf: "Our flight from Karachi to Baghdad was more or less a detailed survey of the proposed air route, and throughout the flight data was collected regarding possible landing-grounds, wireless and telegraph possibilities, and those things needed for a commercial air line." He noted that "in a good many parts it is possible to go for hundreds of miles and be able to force land anywhere, and yet there are other parts of 30 and 50-mile stretches where it is not even possible to crash a plane respectably. So bad is the country in these patches that it would not be possible, even regardless of expense, to make any sort of land-ground. It is quite clear from these remarks that the question of engine failure must be totally eliminated. How it is to be done is for the experts to say."

But engine failure was very far from being eliminated in the 1920s – the heavy, water-cooled motors were notoriously prone to fail. Despite this, commercial flying had been inaugurated almost as soon as the Great War ended and pressure was growing to expand intercontinental air travel – especially from European capitals to the colonies. In early February 1919, the first sustained daily passenger service was established – between Berlin and Weimar in Germany. The following month passengers could fly from Paris to Brussels. During the summer, a service between London and Paris began.[33] These early services, as one aviation historian describes them, "required a sturdy breed of customer... the passengers travelled in open cockpits and wore protective clothing against the weather." Services from London to Paris "frequently failed to complete the three-hour journey non-stop, making a forced landing in farmers' fields for repairs or refuelling."[34]

The difficulties presented by the weather and the dangers of mechanical failure did not stop the expansion of commercial air transport in the Middle East and North Africa either. As early as September 1919 Morocco (a French protectorate at this time) became the first Arab country to be connected to Europe by regular airline service: Lignes Aériennes Latecoère inaugurated flights from Toulouse to Rabat and Casablanca, via Barcelona, Alicante and Malaga.[35] At the beginning of 1921, the French authorities acquired 130 hectares of land at Maison Blanche (on the site of today's Houari Boumediene airport), some 11 miles from Algiers to build an airport for the advent of commercial flights.[36] France's trailblazing services to North Africa raised concern in Britain – to the extent that, towards the end of 1921, an air minister faced questions on the subject in parliament. An MP asked if the minister was aware that "France has six international air routes in operation;

that next year France proposes to create air connections between France and her colonial possessions, communication between Corsica and Tunis being carried out by a seaplane service, and from Marseilles or Toulon to Algiers by airship, as well as aeroplane connections between Oran and Morocco, and between Toulouse and Morocco via Spain; and that British aerial transport today, from leading the world in 1919, has dropped behind both France and Germany...?" The MP followed up with another question: "May I ask my right honourable friend, who, as we know, has the interests of aviation greatly at heart, whether he will agree to discuss with me the possibility of organising an Imperial Air Service?" The minister declined. It was an awkward question for him to address. For there was no avoiding the fact that while pioneering flights had been carried out successfully through the Middle East to reach British colonial possessions as far away as Australia, no airline existed to operate these new routes. The previous summer, industrialist George Holt Thomas had also pointed out that two years had now passed since the inauguration of commercial flights between Britain and continental Europe, yet the 'airways' still went no further. He believed that an "Imperial airway" to Australia, "passing through vitally important areas of the British Empire" was "certain to come. The only question is: 'When?'"[37]

In the shadow of these momentous, but slow-moving, plans for imperial air routes some tender shoots of aviation were already springing up in the Middle East itself. In French-governed Lebanon a military air-strip ('Champ d'Aviation') was established in the Dora district of Beirut, and another at Sidon to the south. In 1922 an Aero-Club of Syria and Lebanon was formed, operating from Rayak in the Beqa'a Valley and Damascus. The instructors were French – as were many of the members. But in 1924 Joseph Elias Akar from Deir al-Qamar in the Chouf Mountain became the first Lebanese citizen to learn to fly – making him surely one of the first Arabs to qualify as a pilot.[38] Lebanon had taken an important first step towards playing a role in Middle Eastern aviation – but the day when Beirut would rival and then outshine Cairo as the main aerial hub for the region was still far off.

four

Imperial in Reality

The post-World War One years had seen a new Middle East emerge, one where Ottoman imperial power deployed over vast areas of land without boundaries had been replaced by French and British colonial rule over newly parcelled nation states. Britain was already the dominant power in Egypt. It now held sway, too, over newly-created Iraq and Jordan, and had been given a United Nations mandate to govern Palestine. The French flag flew over Syria and Lebanon. From the perspective of Britain, the major imperial power of the day, the new state of affairs was satisfactory: sea and air routes across the Middle East to India were secure. Only Persia lay outside the dominion of the two European colonial powers, and Britain was aware of Soviet and German attempts to secure influence there. Nevertheless, the government in London was confident that its long-standing political and commercial ties (recently strengthened by British exploitation of Persian oil reserves) would ensure that the authorities in Tehran viewed favourably any requests for co-operation in securing lines of communications between Cairo and Karachi.

So the imperial routes were in place. What remained still was the need to form a company that could operate along them. At the beginning of 1924 the British government announced plans for the "formation of a heavier than air transport company to be called

The Imperial Air Transport Co Ltd."[1] The plan was that four small existing British air companies would be amalgamated to create the country's first national airline. On 31 March, this came into being with the name Imperial Airways. Operations did not begin for several weeks because of a strike by pilots, but by the end of April the new airline was operating a regular London-Paris operation.

The obstacles the new airline faced in the Middle East related in large measure to geography and climate, as well as to the establishment of landing grounds and installation of equipment. Above all, Imperial Airways still had to find a role to play in a part of the world where the RAF dominated aviation. In March 1925, it seemed that this last issue had been resolved. The aeronautical correspondent of *The Times* wrote enthusiastically: "There is a possibility that the Imperial Airways will become Imperial in reality and not merely in name, as at present, for a proposal has been lain before the Air Ministry to take over the desert airmail services between Cairo and Baghdad on terms which, of course, must involve some sort of State subsidy." The article noted that, if successful, the venture would involve a huge leap forward for the new airline, adding that this was not "a scheme to be lightly enterprised by Imperial Airways, for it means setting up a complete operation plant far from the home base and working under entirely different conditions so far as the personnel are concerned. Obviously, a form of organization very different to that prevailing at present in the Royal Air Force will have to be set up, for the present airmail is admittedly not run on commercial lines." The correspondent concluded that before the airline could expect to charge for mail and passenger services it would have to prove that it could operate a regular and reliable service, and carry out "a large amount of preliminary ground organization".[2]

This is precisely what senior officials of Imperial Airways and the Air Ministry set about doing. A preliminary tour of the region was undertaken by Leo Amery, Secretary of State for the Colonies, and Sir Samuel Hoare, Secretary of State for Air. The whole mission lasted two months. The eight-man team travelled by train and ship to Egypt and then flew, in two aircraft, to Iraq, Jordan and Palestine.

The journey covered 3,500 air miles around the Middle East and involved 50 flying hours. Hoare, on the team's return to Britain, was ecstatic about the prospects for air travel in the region: "That the air will become a great Imperial highway was shown by the fact that in a few weeks we made a journey which would otherwise have taken twelve months, traversing Iraq from end to end and visiting the mountains of Kurdistan and the Persian plains through which the British pipeline brings oil for use of the Fleet. We stayed in Transjordania [Jordan], Palestine and Egypt, and inspected every British activity, military and civil, in those distant and largely inaccessible countries." Hoare predicted that the new highway in the sky would "enable ministers and traders and travellers to pass swiftly and easily as a matter of ordinary routine from one end [of the Middle East] to another, united by an aerial line of closer and quicker intercourse."³ The relative ease with which two British cabinet ministers could fly around the region is an indication of the colonial power's domination of it – brought about, in no small part, by the decisive role played by aviation itself: the defence of the Suez Canal in 1914, the ultimately successful air campaign in Mesopotamia after the fall of Kut, and the involvement of aircraft in Palestine. As well as helping to win battles, air power had given British and Allied airmen experience of the particular challenges facing aviation in the Middle East. That experience was now to be put to civilian use.

The task of fixing the fine details of the Cairo-Karachi route was given to a team that included H Burchall, Assistant General Manager of Imperial Airways, and was supervised by the Director of Civil Aviation, Air Vice-Marshal Sir Sefton Brancker. They carried out a detailed survey of the whole route. But the optimism of their early statements camouflaged the reality: the route was both difficult and dangerous. Despite the fact that some progress had been made in improving the reliability of aircraft engines, failure and breakdown continued to be common. When Brancker and his team set off from Baghdad to Bushehr, "the two machines conveying the party had to make forced landings – Sir Sefton's machine about two miles from Zubair, and the other machine at Mohammerah. Sir Sefton had to walk to Zubair, whence he proceeded by car to the RAF station at Shaibah."[4]

Despite the hiccups, the surveys thus far were successful. Just before the close of 1925, the Air Ministry awarded Imperial Airways a five-year contract (subsidized by the government) to operate the Cairo-Karachi service. Imperial Airways Chairman Sir Eric Geddes, in an address to the company's first ordinary General Meeting, said: "We confidently hope that the first aeroplane will leave Cairo for India not later than January 1, 1927." He went on to tell shareholders, perhaps with the memory of Brancker's unfortunate experience in Iraq earlier in the year still fresh in his mind: "The service is to be run with three-engined machines [de Havilland DH66 Hercules] capable of maintaining their requisite height in flying on any two engines, thus materially increasing the reliability of the service... The route has been surveyed by an officer of your company... We believe we will be able to demonstrate to our own Government and to the Indian Government that reliability and regularity over these long desert tracks can be attained. The board hopes that before the five-year period has expired public confidence in the route will be based upon business reasons, thus bringing greatly increased support to the undertaking."[5]

During 1926, the company pressed ahead and invested in Hercules aircraft – partly because their engines were more safely and efficiently cooled by air rather than water – for the service that was set to begin in January of the following year. The idea was that for the first three months, Imperial Airways planes would operate only between Cairo and Basra, with the final leg to India beginning in April. But work was being carried out at airports and emergency landing grounds the length of the entire route. For the passengers, "rest houses are being provided at all the stages where accommodation does not exist, and these will be staffed by Imperial Airways to provide a quick service of food during the day and comfortable sleeping quarters at night." Each Hercules was being fitted out to carry 12 passengers, "with baggage and a certain amount of mail matter, with one pilot, a mechanic-pilot, and a wireless operator. From Basra to Karachi the passenger load will be reduced to eight, and, as the landing places will not have full ground staff, the machine will carry a second pilot and two mechanics, in addition to the wireless operator."[6]

In the weeks leading up to the inauguration of the Cairo-Karachi service, public attention in Britain was caught by another aviation event – once again involving pioneering long-distance pilot Alan Cobham. Having successfully completed a flight to India and back in 1925, a year later he set off to survey a route to Australia. Inevitably his air passage took him across the Middle East. His experience passing through this region on the outward journey was enough to dispel any complacency that might have infected those planning the first regular commercial service. Cobham was accompanied on his DH50 biplane (fitted with floats to convert it into a seaplane) by a mechanic, Arthur Elliott, and all initially went well. Late one afternoon, the plane reached Ramadi in Iraq, and Cobham set course for the River Tigris, wondering if they would reach Baghdad before dark. He "sent a message through to Elliott, because in my cockpit behind the cabin I am all alone and unable to seek the advice of a second person, and so in order to verify my own ideas on the subject I asked him how much daylight we could reckon on. Elliott, with a very knowing air and a quizzing look at the sun, estimated it at an hour and a half, which was comforting although I knew it to be very optimistic, but it certainly lessened my worries for the time being regarding our safe arrival before dark." With Baghdad, at last, in sight, the plane began gliding downwards, an experience Cobham likened to "sinking into an oven, or suddenly diving from the cool atmosphere of the open sea, into the hottest room of a Turkish bath... the fumes from the engine on the glide seemed to radiate back, if one put one's head over the side of the cockpit, like flames in one's face." The following morning, en route southwards to Basra, the pair confronted their first major challenge – frightening, but not entirely unexpected in the region – bad weather conditions. Cobham described how he "noticed we were getting into a sandstorm region, and a little later we were forced to descend from a comfortable altitude, lower and lower, owing to the thickening sandstorm, until we were flying but a few feet above the river bank, in order to find our way in the blinding dust. From my experience I knew that these sandstorms rise to a great altitude, and even if one could fly above them it would be impossible to see the ground beneath and equally impossible to find one's way over a more or less trackless desert." Cobham decided that the best course of action was to land on the river and wait for the sandstorm to clear. After the two men had spent a night ashore, the DH50 took off and headed once more for Basra, this time following the Euphrates River. Around the marshy areas north of Basra they encountered another sandstorm and were again forced to fly very low. Gradually the marshes "began to give way to the irregular sandy coastline, and I was just congratulating myself that we should soon be out of our worst difficulties and flying at an altitude of not more than forty feet in order to get the maximum visibility ahead, when suddenly there was a violent explosion which appeared to come from the cabin. Instantly I shouted through the connecting window to Elliott asking him what had happened and if we were on fire... Elliott shouted back in a very feeble voice that a petrol pipe had burst." When Cobham landed the plane he saw that his mechanic was bleeding profusely. Elliott had a wound in his side, caused not by a burst pipe but by a bullet fired from the ground. A bullet hole was later found in the side of the cabin. Elliott died that night. Cobham wanted to abandon his mission, but was urged by Sir Samuel Hoare, Sir Sefton Brancker and others in London to continue. He did so, taking with him a replacement engineer from the RAF in Basra.[7] Some weeks later, the Arab who had fired at Cobham's plane and killed Elliott was identified and arrested. He confessed his guilt. But by this time, Cobham was in Australia and preparing to set out from Sydney for the long flight home.

Cobham received a hero's welcome when he returned to England, landing his biplane on the River Thames alongside the Houses of Parliament on 1 October – exactly three months before Imperial Airways was scheduled to launch its Cairo-Karachi service. But several legal issues still had to be addressed before the route could be inaugurated. Even though Britain was the ultimate power in all the territory to be crossed as far as Persia, the law in each country had to be respected. This presented a problem in Egypt because an aviation law had still not been introduced. The correspondent of *The Times* pointed out that "airmen crossing Egyptian territory are always given permission to land as a matter of course, but the use of Egyptian territory as the starting point for an air service is a somewhat different matter, which would normally be regulated by legislation."[8] But in December 1927 the government of Egypt solved the problem when it told the British high commissioner in Cairo that it agreed to the initiation of the air service to Karachi, adding that "its consent is provisional without prejudice to legislation which may eventually be introduced to regulate aviation in Egypt."

Given that the new service would be operating entirely outside Britain, the last task before its inauguration was to position the aircraft along the route – at Heliopolis and Basra. The list of those travelling on the inaugural flights read like something from a P G Wodehouse novel. They included "the indefatigable, monocled" Sefton Brancker. The second aircraft to leave London was "piloted by one-eyed Capt Hinchliffe".[9] The third Hercules, which took off on 27 December, carried Sir Samuel and Lady Hoare. Their plane flew over the whole route to India, landing on schedule and without mishap. Sir Samuel carried a letter from King George to the Viceroy of India, Lord Irwin – the first time that such a missive had been delivered by air. It was also, in the opinion of *Flight*, "probably the first time in the history of flying that a flight of this distance has been attempted following a fixed timetable."[10]

With the route having been inaugurated formally by the minister, the moment arrived for the regular service to begin. On 7 January, a Hercules left Basra carrying one passenger and mail and arrived safely in Cairo. Five days later a Hercules took off from Heliopolis bound for Basra, via Gaza, Rutbah Wells and Baghdad. With him in the cockpit, the captain would have had his copy of *Pilots' Handbook of the Cairo-Baghdad Route*.[11] This 53-page hardback book was intended as an encyclopaedia for pilots, telling them everything possible about what they might encounter on the way, based on the experience gained by RAF airmen. "Every effort has been made," the preface concludes, "to foresee the more probable misadventures which may arise, but it is realised that it is not possible, or even desirable, to try to provide against every possible contingency." The clear message was that ultimate responsibility for safety lay with the pilots: "Where such contingencies are encountered, pilots may rest assured that if they act in accordance with the spirit of these instructions, and if they display initiative and resolution, their action will always be supported. The success of the route rests more in the hands of pilots operating on it than in the hands of those who are responsible for its inauguration and maintenance." The handbook then dealt with a number of topographical and climatic features of the route. For example, Amman "was originally intended as an intermediate port and refuelling base but, although the landing ground is big enough for all types, the nature of the surrounding country makes it inadvisable to use it with large aircraft heavily loaded." Then, if a forced landing could not be avoided over the desert, the handbook said, "flat gravel is safer than bush-covered ground and usually the darker the flints are in colour, the better is the surface; but care should be taken in the air not to mistake dark basalt boulders for dark flint gravel. Fortunately, the basalt country, indicated by special markings on the map, is confined to a well-marked region extending for about one-eighth of the whole journey from Amman to Baghdad."

Weather conditions, as ever, were also highlighted. The book warned that "broken clouds throw dark shadows which often closely resemble land formations or dark pools. At times they completely obliterate some landmarks, and the entire desert assumes a different appearance." It went on to advise that to counter the heat, "the head and neck should be adequately protected from the sun during flights over the desert... glare glasses are recommended to be worn on long desert flights."

Under a section of the handbook entitled "General Notes and Precautions" the airmen of Imperial Airways would have found a paragraph on "Treatment of natives". Experience has proved, the handbook explained, "that individuals or bodies of Arabs encountered on the desert between Amman and Baghdad generally display a friendly attitude, especially to British personnel. This friendly attitude should be cultivated, and all chances of untoward incidents should be rigorously avoided. Pilots who are thrown into contact with Arabs should make every effort to converse with them in friendly fashion, even if conversation is of a most elementary kind. A cigarette, or some small present of food, is a conciliatory introduction, but the Arab likes you to share the present of food with him. No offer of food from Arabs should be refused, as such refusal is considered unmannerly." A code of signals to other aircraft to be marked out in the desert after a forced landing included the letter 'F', meaning "Arabs friendly", and 'H', "Arabs hostile". To help the stranded airman converse with Arabs as he awaited rescue, the handbook provided a list of Arabic phrases phonetically spelt. With a bit of practice the pilot would be able to say such sentences as: "I want you to take me to your Chief"; "In the meanwhile place a guard on the machine"; "By no means let anyone touch it"; "It explodes and hurts people"; and "Oh, be careful".

A vital element of the Cairo-Baghdad handbook was the large-scale map of the route (called "Dr Balls map"[12]) and the very detailed accompanying notes. So, for example, when the pilot reached point 'H' in the desert on his journey eastward he would learn from the notes that "Landing ground 'H' is located between two very large mud flats. All-weather landing ground at 'H' is found on the south-western side of mud flats marked with a circle enclosing letter 'H'." The map showed that to fly from point 'H' to 'J', the pilot should set a course of 74° for 15½ miles. The plane will pass over "nearly level ground with some shrub". On crossing 'J', a small turn to the left is made, to a heading of 69°, towards 'K' – and so on.

The instructions, advice and warnings were well heeded. The Imperial Airways Hercules aircraft plied the route successfully in the first three months of 1927, allowing pilots to build up experience and ground staff to complete facilities along the route in Persia (two regular landing grounds and one for emergencies) ready for the extension of the service to India at the beginning of April. It was with shock, then, that the British government and Imperial Airways executives received word from Tehran at the last minute that the authorities there had decided not to ratify an agreement signed in 1925 to allow flights to cross Persian territory. The new airline may have inaugurated its first empire route, but it was being prevented from providing a full service to Britain's most treasured imperial possession. Imperial Airways was now placed in an awkward position, having signed an agreement with the British government to operate the India service, but being prevented by the Iranian authorities from implementing it. In the words of Geddes, the airline had agreed to launch the service because it had faith in the agreement signed by the British and Persian governments. As a result, the hold-up was a matter for which the British government "must accept full responsibility *vis-à-vis* the company, who were assured before completing the agreement that all political questions had been settled with Persia." By way of compensation, the airline was given permission to operate a weekly – rather than fortnightly – Cairo-Basra-Cairo service. Geddes described this as "a satisfactory palliative of a temporary nature", adding that the delay had "put a serious brake upon the company's activities". This was the start of a period of tension between Imperial Airways and the government – as well as the government and Iran – over the route through the Gulf. Geddes welcomed the fact that the Air Ministry was "proceeding with the preliminaries to diverting the route along the Arabian side [of the Gulf] as an alternative." [13] But this option was not attractive. According to *Flight*, "considerable data relating to this region was collected during the war, but it is not a promising line, for it is along a deserted coast with no regular ports of call and is much longer than the northern route. Sea crossings are involved, and probably a range of mountains along the projecting spur of Arabia at the entrance to the Gulf." [14] By contrast, facilities along the Persian coast were at an advanced stage of preparation and could be brought into use at a moment's notice. The tone of documents from this period indicates that Imperial Airways and the British government never seriously considered switching the route to the southern Gulf coast. They seemed confident that the delay in receiving authorisation from Iran was temporary and further talks with Tehran would soon enable the airline to proceed with its originally planned route.

On the positive side, as the uncertainty continued, the Cairo-

Basra service was proving to be a success. Throughout most of the first year, it operated with 100 per cent efficiency: every scheduled flight was carried out without interruption. The only glitch happened in late December, a few days before the first anniversary of the service, and full adherence to the instructions in the pilots' handbook meant that the incident ended happily. The captain of one of the Hercules aircraft (named City of Cairo – the other three were City of Basra, City of Baghdad, City of Delhi and City of Jerusalem) sent a wireless message to say that strong headwinds across the desert had forced him down short of petrol between landing grounds Nos 5 and 6, 200 miles west of Baghdad. The plane was "missing for some time. Many machines, including those of the Air Force, made continuous searches in the desert and it was found eventually by Capt Warner, an Imperial Airways pilot, who had been flying all night. It was surrounded by Arabs who were very friendly and had assisted the pilot, Mr D Travers, and his passengers, among whom was Mrs Warner, wife of Capt Warner. Sufficient petrol was transferred to the stranded machine to enable it to reach Rutbah post, while the passengers and mail were conveyed to Baghdad in Capt Warner's machine. Wireless messages from the lost machine were not picked up owing to jamming caused by messages sent out between stations enquiring for information."[15]

This single, casualty-free incident did not affect passenger confidence. The number of people travelling by air between Egypt and Iraq rose steadily – as did the volume of mail. The departures from Basra were coordinated with the arrival of fast steamers bringing the mail from India. Likewise, the flights in and out of Egypt linked up with the P&O steamship service from Britain. The postal service to Iraq was later linked up by air services into Persia which had the first internal commercial aviation network in the Middle East. Throughout the second half of the 1920s and into the early 1930s, Iran was the country in the region that seemed poised to take over from Egypt as the aviation hub; had it not been for subsequent disastrous decisions by the Iranian leadership, Iran's role in the region during the 20th century – and not just in the sphere of aviation – would undoubtedly have been much greater.

Persia's much admired internal air service in Persia was operated by a German company, Junkers – at the time one of the world's leading manufacturers of aircraft of the same name. It had won a concession in 1924 to establish an air link from Baku in the Soviet Union to Pahlavi (on the Iranian shore of the Caspian Sea) and Tehran. But disagreement between the company and the government meant it lasted only a few months. Then in January 1927 the Junkers Company was given the monopoly of the postal air service in the country for five years. A passenger/mail network expanded fast, offering regular overseas flights from Tehran to Baku, and internal ones to Pahlavi, Hamadan, Kermanshah, Mashhad, Isfahan, Shiraz and Bushehr. Junkers endeared itself even more to the Iranian government when it responded swiftly to a serious outbreak of cholera in the south of the country by transporting by air a large consignment of serum from Dessau in Germany.

Despite Britain's political difficulties with Iran over the air route to India, it co-operated with the Junkers Company, arranging for mail destined for Tehran to be picked up by the German aircraft in Baku. In 1929 Junkers extended its Tehran-Hamadan-Kermanshah service to Baghdad. Mail then began to reach Iran even faster than before, arriving by sea in Egypt, carried by the regular Hercules flights to Baghdad and then transferred to a Junkers Company plane bound for Tehran. Plans were later drawn up to link Tehran with both Bushehr and Bandar Abbas on Iran's Gulf coast – two possible stopover points on Imperial Airways' planned Cairo-Karachi route.

The Junkers operation in Iran represented an outstanding achievement on the part of the German pilots and ground staff, operating efficiently in a country with huge challenges posed by great variations in climate and geography, and with no radio navigation aids. Even more remarkable is that a proportion of the Iranian population had the opportunity to experience air travel – many decades before the people of other countries in the region. By October 1929 the company's planes had flown 621,000 miles and "carried 10,000 passengers without serious mishap. It is interesting to note that whereas only 10 per cent of the passengers carried in 1927 were Persians, as many as 75 per cent were Persians in 1929."[16]

The development of aviation reflected the policies and outlook of Iran's leader at the time. By the late 1920s the country was being governed by the Pahlavi Dynasty. Its founder, Reza Shah, was a resolute moderniser, determined to build "a new nation to his personal specifications – a revitalized Iran freed from the rapacious hands of foreign powers."[17] The encouragement of a flourishing internal airline networks fitted exactly into the agenda of a man committed to modernise – and therefore Westernise – Iran.

While Imperial Airways and Junkers co-operated in the carriage of post into Iran, the latter was still off-limits to the British airline's planes at the beginning of 1928; but diplomatic contacts were intensifying. With the exception of those directly involved in the talks, few could understand why the government in Tehran had refused to ratify the 1925 agreement. British members of parliament questioned Sir Samuel Hoare several times on the matter. The following reply from the minister was typical of many: "Negotiations through the normal diplomatic channels are still proceeding, and accordingly I should prefer not to make any statement at this stage."[18] Some people suggested it was a case of Iranian retaliation against Britain's initial refusal to allow planes from Tehran to land in Baghdad. Others said Tehran was coming under Soviet pressure to ban the flights. For decades, Russia and Britain had vied for influence in Iran. Russia craved access to the sea on the Gulf coast. Yet Britain could not afford to see another country take control of territory on India's doorstep. During the final decades of the 19th century and into the 20th, "imperial Britain and imperial Russia, each in pursuit of its own interests, stalked Iran. Yet because neither power could significantly advance without risking a major war with the other, feeble Iran hung on to life, a pawn to the ambitions of Russia and the concerns of Britain."[19] In the end, Britain and Russia, for very different reasons, decided to sink their differences. The British government was becoming suspicious of growing German involvement in Iran. Russia, for its part, continuing to seek access to a Gulf port. An Anglo-Russian agreement of 1907 split Iran in two, with a Russian sphere of influence in the north and a British one in the south. But in the aftermath of the Russian Revolution, and with Britain hugely dependent on Iranian oil, some "prominent Persians" living in Iraq were reported as saying the Soviet Union was urging the Tehran government to deny access to British planes. They believed the Soviet government was "endeavouring to disturb relations between Great Britain and Persia by pointing out to Persia that Cairo, the starting point for the aircraft [on the route to India], is in British suzerainty, that Iraq, the second stage, is under British mandate, and that Karachi, the terminus in British territory. Therefore, they say that it is inevitable that Persia will become a British possession or sphere of influence if aeroplanes are allowed access."[20]

This is a possible explanation, but not the most convincing one. Iran could point to several issues where it felt wronged and believed that Britain could help right matters. For a start, Iran had long felt aggrieved by Iraq's control of the Shatt al-Arab waterway at the northern end of the Gulf. Secondly, it objected to an Iraqi nationality law that forced Iranians in Iraq to take out that country's nationality; and thirdly it still claimed sovereignty over the island of Bahrain. There is no doubt that in negotiating air rights with Britain, Iran was using some of these issues as bargaining cards.

But surely, one could argue, a forward-looking leader like Reza Shah would also realise the political and economic value of seeing his country lie on a new air route that would one day connect northern Europe with India, the Far East and Australia. The fact is he did, but not in the way the British government or Imperial Airways wanted him to. Nevertheless, diplomatic contacts continued, and relations between London and Tehran improved markedly in the spring of 1928, culminating in the signing of a broad-ranging Anglo-Persian agreement. The Tehran authorities then said they would, after all, agree in principle to allow Imperial Airways flights to transit airports on Iran's southern Gulf coast, but wanted an airline to send a representative to Tehran to negotiate the details. Imperial Airways' General Manager George Woods Humphery was despatched there in June to begin negotiations.

Imperial Airways, for its part, was far from euphoric. Woods Humphery had discovered when he reached Tehran that the draft authorisation, as a subsequent memorandum from the airline to the secretary of state for air explained, "could only be for three years and that no extension could be expected. There were many controversial points and trying difficulties in the course of these negotiations, during which the [Iranian] Minister of Court made it clear that the Persian Government did not favour the Persian Littoral route but preferred a route through Central Persia. In fact the draft of the authorisation as agreed at Tehran placed an obligation upon the Company to study the possibilities of a Central Persian route during the three year period." Not surprisingly, the Imperial Airways board was perturbed by "the insecurity of foundation" and the "precarious position of the Company by reason of the provisions of the authorisation". The board members had "grave doubts" about whether they could accept either the agreement with the government to operate the route or the Iranian authorisation. In the end, the board "reluctantly acquiesced in the mission on account of the Official [ie British government] view that the Persian Government would extend the authorisation after the three years had expired."[21]

What Reza Shah wanted was a service to India that would put some of Iran's major cities on the air route – rather than having the service stop merely at Bushehr, Jask and Lengeh on the country's sparsely inhabited south coast. His idea, too, was that the Junkers Company should continue to operate between Tehran and Baghdad. The shah was clearly confident that Britain wanted to set up the air link strongly enough to agree to the rerouting. The British government, on the other hand, felt equally confident that Iran would back down and agree to extend the coastal route beyond the three-year authorisation period. Evidence of this emerged in Hoare's reply to a question in parliament about the progress of negotiations with Arab leaders for a possible route along the southern shore of the Gulf. "The recent settlement of the questions which had been outstanding with the Persian Government," he said, "has rendered it unnecessary at the present time to seek for any alternative route for the Imperial Airways service to India." Imperial Airways, caught in the middle, had no option but to prepare for the long-delayed start of the Basra-Karachi service, hoping that the government's confidence was well founded.

Civil aviation, then, for the first time in the history of the Middle East, had become caught up in an international political and diplomatic dispute. The form of its resolution would alter Iran's destiny and change the face of the Gulf.

If Iran constituted a diplomatic problem for Britain, its westerly neighbour, Iraq, did not. Britain had occupied Iraq during the First World War – when its air force had played a key role in defeating the Ottoman army. After the war, its conquering forces remained in Iraq and the country became a British Mandate. Feisal, the son of Sharif Ali of Mecca, one of the leaders of the Arab Revolt, was subsequently chosen at the Cairo Conference as the first king of Iraq. In 1930, Britain and Iraq signed a treaty of alliance – an accord heavily weighted in favour of the British, allowing, among other things, the free use of airbases in the country. Iraq might have taken a tiny step towards independence, but the real power still lay in British hands. A key sector on the route to the east was secure. Sir Samuel Hoare said Iraq was "vital for security of our Imperial communications, and particularly our air communications. Iraq is a member of the International Air Convention and therefore under obligation to allow free passage of civil airlines."[22] Significantly, as Imperial Airways had found to its cost, Iran had not signed the convention.

five

Blot on the Landscape

The dream of opening up an air route from Britain across the Middle East and the Gulf to India dated back to the pre-war years. But despite the heroic efforts of those individual pilots who pioneered the way eastwards, attempts to operate further than Basra in southern Iraq had failed – first because of technical challenges and then for political reasons. By early 1929, it seemed possible at last that passenger flights on the London-India 'Empire Route' were about to begin. Imperial Airways presented the imminent start of the service as a momentous step forward in the development both of the airline and aviation itself. The staff were told in their company newsletter, *Imperial Gazette*, that "the stage is being set for the dawn of aviation's real métier – the establishment of world-spanning air routes, reducing by more than one half the time taken in reaching the four corners of the earth." With no flying possible during the night, the weekly journey to India would take nearly seven days, with "opportunities for sightseeing" at the various stopovers along the way. The actual flying time would be around 57 hours, averaging seven hours a day; and not every leg of the journey would be by air. Passengers would leave London on a three-engined Armstrong Argosy (cruising speed of 90-95 mph) for Basle. There they would take the night express train through the Alps (the mountain range "forming a barrier too difficult to surmount by air at present") to

Genoa. Then they would board "the giant all-metal Short Calcutta flying boat" (a biplane with three engines, capable of cruising at around 100 mph cruise speed) to Suda Bay in Crete via Rome, Naples, Corfu and Athens, before crossing the Mediterranean to Tobruk in Italian-administered Libya and flying from there to Alexandria. Here, passengers would be transferred to the nearby Abukir aerodrome where a Hercules aircraft (a biplane of wood and metal) would follow the desert route established in 1927 as far as Basra. Finally, the air travellers would continue along the most politically contentious stage of the journey when, thanks to a recently signed agreement with the government in Tehran, they would touch down at the airfields of Bushehr, Lengeh and Jask on the Iranian coast of the Gulf.

But not all the blame for the delay in opening up the Empire Route can be placed on the Iranian authorities. There were still many political difficulties facing the new airline in Europe – a hangover from alliances formed during the war. Some states refused Imperial Airways permission to fly over or land on their territory. In 1919, a Convention Relating to the Regulation of Aerial Navigation was signed by the Allies – having been drawn up in such a way that, in the words of H Burchall, Assistant General Manager of Imperial Airways in the 1920s and 30s, "the Allies had a predominating voice in the regulation of air traffic, a feature that did not appeal to neutral and enemy states."[1] This prompted Germany and Italy ('enemy states') to place a ban on British aircraft, creating difficulties not only for European services, but also for those that might seek to extend to the Middle East and further. For example, while it was true that the Alps formed a physical barrier for any aircraft seeking to enter Italy directly from the north, even approaching the country from another direction was not an option for a British aircraft. According to Burchall, the night-train journey to Genoa was necessary because the Italian authorities still "had not agreed to our aircraft entering Italy from France, although the French were using the route we wished to follow." The issue became still more complicated. The agreement with Italy stipulated that an Italian company should operate a mid-week service between Genoa and

Alexandria, complementing the weekend flight of Imperial Airways. The Italians later proposed pooling the route – a proposal that Imperial rejected. As a result, the Italians withdrew permission for the British airline to overfly Italy or land there, forcing it to switch to a longer and more difficult route through Eastern Europe. After much wrangling, agreement was finally reached between Imperial Airways and the Italian government, and the latter restored the original arrangement.

It was against this uncertain background of politics and diplomacy that plans for the inauguration of the Empire Route were completed. Relations with Iran had improved to the extent that Iranian wireless operators, to be stationed at Bushehr and Jask, had received training in Britain. The Egyptian government, for its part, had authorised the construction of a joint marine and land airport close to Alexandria. In the meantime, the Imperial Airways Calcutta-class flying boats would use Alexandria harbour as an airport. [2]

On 30 March 1929, the passengers (all senior airline or government officials) invited to travel on the first flight to Karachi checked in at Croydon airport, south of London, Imperial Airways' base. Each passenger was permitted a total weight, including his or her own, of 221lb (100 kilos). A report in *The Times* explained that the "average person weighs some 166lb, luggage to the amount of about 55lb will be carried free. Children in arms will be weighed with and carried under the same tickets as their mothers or nurses. Other children will be charged at full fare. Unless forbidden by Government regulations, smoking or lighting matches in aeroplanes is permitted, but only if all passengers have agreed to it."[3] The Argosy left Croydon on time, all the connections worked as planned, and the Hercules from Abukir reached Karachi on schedule. Fifteen days later, the first return flight from India was completed successfully. Britain's Secretary of State for Air, Sir Samuel Hoare, judged the fortnight as "a very important one in the history of civil aviation".[4] It was also an important one for the development of aviation in the Middle East, which was now being exposed on a daily basis to the latest innovations both in civil flight and its essential ancillary services, such as navigation, radio-telephony, meteorology and other support systems required to run an international airline successfully.

Imperial Airways was pleased with its new service. Most of the delays encountered on the Middle Eastern sector resulted – yet again – from weather problems. Some months after the route was opened, for example, *Imperial Gazette* readers were told that "one of the worst sandstorms the district has known was responsible for a delay of some thirty hours on the sector between Baghdad and Basra a few weeks ago. A representative of the London *Daily Mail*, who was a passenger on this particular service, reported that the storm was at times so dense that it was difficult to see even a few yards and that passengers, machines and crew were quickly smothered in fine white dust. These sandstorms are, of course, as much responsible for irregularities in an air service as are the fogs which are encountered in more northerly countries."[5]

But political turmoil in the Middle East also caused its fair share of disruptions to the new London-Karachi service. The efforts of Britain and France to establish new nation states there after the First World War had backfired: the region was far from stable – nowhere more so than Palestine. Britain had occupied the territory after defeating the German-backed Turkish army. In 1922, the League of Nations approved a British Mandate for Palestine. But the British administrators soon realised that it would be extremely difficult to reconcile the promises made in the 1917 Balfour Declaration – to back the idea of establishing a Jewish state, without prejudicing the rights of the non-Jewish population living there. Tension erupted into violence in August 1929 when Arabs in Jerusalem accused the Jewish community of violating the sanctity of the Haram al-Sharif (the noble sanctuary, site of the Dome of the Rock and al-Aqsa Mosque) by erecting a screen to separate male and female worshippers at the Western Wall. The rioting spread to cities across Palestine, including Gaza – one of the overnight stops on the Imperial Airways service to India. The *Imperial Gazette* reported that although the "Palestine disorders" had caused "a certain amount of anxiety", they had also provided a "wonderful instance of the 'elasticity' of an Air Way, in comparison with surface transport. Imperial Airways' Aerodrome at Gaza was threatened early in the dispute. At one period, for about 36 hours, it was deserted, the staff having been called in to assist the local police in quelling the disturbance. Detachments of police and machines of the RAF were hastily drafted to the spot and regained possession. Meanwhile, in order to maintain the regularity of the England-India Air Mails, traffic was temporarily diverted over an alternative route via Kantara and Amman. Trouble when it occurs on an Air Route may often be 'flown around' so to speak, and a service maintained."[6]

Technical difficulties could not be side-stepped quite so neatly. Given the relatively unsophisticated design and construction of airframes and engines during this period, it would not have been surprising to learn of many disruptions caused by mechanical problems or by accidents. But the passage of the Hercules aeroplanes across the Middle East was remarkably smooth. Only one fatal accident occurred – at Jask in September 1929. The pilot was Captain Albert Woodbridge, who had achieved fame in the First World War when flying with Donald Cunnell by shooting down and seriously wounding Manfred von Richthofen, the legendary German fighter ace known as the 'Red Baron'. Approaching Jask after dark, his Hercules (City of Jerusalem) crashed and burst into flames. He was killed, along with his mechanic and one passenger. A senior Imperial Airways executive at the time said the airline had been "working at high pressure in the heat of summer, with short staff. This accident was not caused through engine or aircraft failure, but no doubt through an error of judgement by a tired pilot after a long day's flying." Woodbridge had been thrown out of the plane when it crashed, but went back through the flames to try to rescue passengers. He died soon after, expressing remorse – as he saw it – for his failure to save all on board.[7]

That accident apart, the Britain-India air route soon proved to be a successful venture. While Imperial Airways was pleased to boast publicly about this achievement, in private senior executives were concerned: the Iranian authorities had granted the airline only a three-year licence to operate a route along its Gulf coastline, pending the establishment of facilities for a service that would pass from Baghdad and Basra through the centre of the country. Imperial Airways' priority was to survey that route. A senior pilot was despatched to Iran in a single-engined three-seater de Havilland Puss Moth monoplane. His subsequent report was far from encouraging. The first 150 miles of the proposed air corridor, he wrote, "is at right angles to a series of mountain ranges rising to 10,000 ft – a type of country that continues North West and South West for many hundred miles. It is a type of country that would be avoided, if at all possible, for the operation of any air service. Mountainous country limits the opportunities of making forced landings safely where there are no prepared landing grounds and renders their preparation difficult or impossible." As if this was not discouraging enough, he went on to say that mountains "always produce disturbed air conditions... the presence of low cloud and fog in such country introduces a very serious risk of running into the side of a mountain, and snow in winter may lead to errors in navigation, owing to the difficulty of identifying land-marks on the route." The survey pilot acknowledged that the German Junkers Company operated a Tehran-Baghdad service, but "they have an easier passage through the mountains, and on both routes they at least follow a road and telegraph line and are able before the commencement of a flight to ascertain the weather conditions at their destination." His conclusion, in summary, was: "It appears to be entirely impracticable to maintain a regular weekly commercial air service by this route."[8]

These unequivocal findings left Imperial Airways in an extremely uncomfortable position: the licence to operate the Gulf route would expire on 31 March 1932, and the Iranian authorities were adamant that it would not be renewed. At the same time, the corridor Iran wanted the airline to use was not a practical option. The Empire Route was under threat almost as soon as it opened. As the company's Chairman, Sir Eric Geddes, said, there remained "a blot on the political landscape".[9] *Flight* magazine pointed out that the euphoria surrounding the start of the Karachi service had distracted attention away from the terms of the agreement underpinning it. The opening of the England-India route had been greeted "by cheering and shouting"; but after that had died down "it was realised that the Persian government had not given permission for Imperial Airways to make regular use of the aerodromes down the Persian shore of the Gulf. Great Britain was left high and dry, and looked considerably foolish."[10] Imperial Airways made a number of representations to the British government, reminding it of the airline's reluctance to accept the three-year agreement with Iran in the first place. A memorandum presented to the Imperial Airways board in the spring of 1932, recounting how the airline had told the government bluntly a year earlier: "The insecurity of tenure in the Persian authorisation renders it of no value to the Company as one of the foundations of the air route to India." Geddes had also written to the Air Ministry at the time saying the company "was still unable to make plans for the future". He had added that there was "still time to make arrangements, though not of a very satisfactory nature, to operate temporarily down the Arabian side of the Gulf, but that it was essential, if the position was to be safeguarded, that no time should be lost in taking the necessary action."[11] Geddes' arguments could not be ignored, and Imperial Airways received permission from the Air Ministry to look at the possibility of operating a seaplane service along the Arabian coast of the Gulf and sent a representative there in December 1931.

Despite authorising this arrangement, the British government persisted in its conviction that Iran was bluffing, in the hope of wringing out of Britain concessions on a number of regional issues, and that the Iranian authorities would ultimately extend Imperial Airways' licence. Diplomats in London adopted the imperial 'more-in-sadness-than-anger' attitude in its communications with Tehran. After meeting a visiting Iranian minister and failing to secure a commitment to extend the concession, British Foreign Secretary Sir John Simon wrote the following to his envoy in Tehran: "I said that I should regard it as a grave and serious matter if his Government found a difficulty, or refused to co-operate in a service which was international and for civil purposes and was necessary for postal communication. I added that it would, I felt, make a very disagreeable impression if it became known that such an attitude was adopted." The Iranians, for their part, said that if Imperial Airways rejected the cross-country option, then Iran would require "some other advantages" to "counterbalance this loss" and renew the licence for the coastal route. Settlement of the "present case therefore depends on the solution of other questions."[12] But Britain was not prepared to make concessions on the sovereignty of Bahrain or any of the other Iranian demands that the shah sought to link to the aviation question.

Even as the Foreign Office continued to believe that Iran would, in time, capitulate, it encouraged Imperial Airways to explore an alternative route along the Gulf – partly in an attempt to call the Iranians' bluff. A memo of October 1931 said that "preparations for the Arab route, as our second string, should be put in hand at once. So far as preparations on the political side are concerned, the best idea will probably be to give [Britain's top diplomat in the Gulf, Political Resident[13] Sir Hugh] Biscoe a free hand to negotiate as he deems best with any Sheikhs concerned with a view to securing the requisite facilities... We understand that the service will be by flying boats from Basra to Bahrein (where there will be no difficulty) and thence to Gwadar [at that time in India, today in Pakistan] via an intermediate place on the Trucial Coast [modern-day United Arab Emirates], the choice of which lies between Ras al-Khaimah and Umm al-Quwain." Two weeks later, the Foreign Office suggested that "active preparation might well help to bring the Persians to a more reasonable frame of mind."

RAF seaplanes had been operating from Basra along the Arabian coast of the Gulf since the First World War, mainly with the aim of combating piracy (the Trucial Coast was popularly known as the Pirate Coast). But initial soundings indicated that the ruling families in the region were unhappy at the idea of civilian aircraft operating there. Cash might have to be offered to help convince them of the merits of allowing an international air route to operate through their territory. The Foreign Office decided that Sir Hugh Biscoe should be authorised to spend £3,000 a year, adding in a memo to the Air Ministry: "We may get off more cheaply, but it is very desirable that he should have a fairly generous margin so that he may not be hampered in his negotiations by having to refer home for further sanction... There is in general a strong objection among the Trucial Coast Arabs to the advent of the civil air route and it would take a good deal to overcome it." The objection was "very much stronger than it was to the military air route, because a regular civil air route, involving as it does regular visits and more organisation, is regarded by the Arabs as a far more serious threat to their independence. In the second place, not all the money would go to the Sheikh, who is not an absolute ruler but merely the representative of the ruling clan. It would have to be divided among a large number of relatives, possibly amounting to 200 persons." Thirdly, the Foreign Office memo continued, "the money is not simply in the nature of a bribe but also of payment for value received. Biscoe hopes to enter an agreement which would secure the good will of the Sheikh and by which in return for the allowance he would undertake certain responsibilities: these might extend to the payment by him of native guards. Lastly, Biscoe suggests that the sum involved is trifling compared with the cost of any permanent measures of protection, such as stationing troops, which otherwise might be necessary."

In December 1931 Biscoe visited a number of the Trucial Coast sheikhdoms, discussing the possibility of establishing seaplane bases for Imperial Airways. The Foreign Office was optimistic: "Col Biscoe's negotiations seem to be making good progress up to date. He has sounded Ras al-Khaimah (who asked for two days to discuss the matter with his relations) and Dibai [Dubai] (who was friendly and very helpful) and is now going back to Ras al-Khaimah. Umm al-Quwain is technically unsuitable, Dibai feasible, but Ras al-Khaimah much better from the technical point of view."

Ten days later Biscoe reported back in triumph. The Ruler of Dubai, Sheikh Saeed bin Maktoum, had agreed in principle to offer Imperial Airways the facilities they needed: its aircraft would be entitled to land in Dubai Creek; a rest house would be built on its bank, away from the town; the company could base its employees at the rest house and use it to accommodate transiting passengers; and Sheikh Saeed would accept full responsibility for the safety of the aircraft, company personnel, passengers and equipment.

Biscoe returned to Dubai in early 1932 to sign the agreement with Sheikh Saeed, only to find a different state of affairs. The ruler had been taken ill and was recuperating in a house some miles from the town. The British diplomat noticed, too, that the mood had changed. Rumours were flying around, he said, to the effect that Sheikh Saeed was "entering into secret engagements with the British etc" and these had gained credence "encouraged by a stupid article in an Arab newspaper". The balance of power had changed and the ailing ruler faced opposition from a faction "strong enough almost to force the Sheikh's abduction and whose views he can hardly ignore." Biscoe's pessimistic assessment turned out to be correct. He reported to his superiors that he had subsequently received a letter from the ruler saying "he is unable to obtain acquiescence of his relatives to the establishment of an air station and asking it should not be established." Biscoe's suggestion was that the Imperial Airways flying boats should have a night-stop in Bahrain, "and fly thence to Gwadar, using Ras al-Khaimah as a refuelling point in extreme emergency... While nothing short of armed forces can guarantee absolute safety on the Trucial Coast, I do not think that if the Airways used Ras al-Khaimah for refuelling, as the RAF constantly do at present, they would meet with any opposition." The British diplomat added that Imperial Airways had inquired about the possibility of operating landplanes on the route, but he had ruled out this option: "Flying boats would land in front of the Residency Agent's house and near the shore. Land craft would have to land some way inland on an exposed plain. I regard their use beyond Bahrain as out of the question at present." Taking heed of at least part of Biscoe's advice, the British government proposed that the Imperial Airways seaplane service should include a night-stop at Yas Island, a small island off Abu Dhabi, before flying on to Gwadar. Petrol and oil tanks "have already been placed on the island in connection with the Military air route. The Sheikh did not give his consent to this but was informed by Colonel Biscoe in November 1930 that we should have to go ahead with the installation of the tanks... The flying boats would have to use Ras al-Khaimah for refuelling; there is, of course, already a petrol barge at that place in connection with the Military Route."

The prospects for Imperial Airways seemed bleak in early 1932, with the expiry date of the route licence through Iran only a matter of months away. But temporary relief came in February when the Iranian government agreed to extend the concession by two months – to 31 May – while "general negotiations" were in progress. The Foreign Office seized on this development, interpreting it as a sign – as it had believed all along – that Iran would ultimately back down. A memo exclaimed triumphantly: "It looks as if we should not have to worry about an Arab Coast Route except in the event of treaty negotiations being completely broken off."

Nevertheless, Biscoe continued his mission to try to persuade one of the Trucial Coast rulers to allow Imperial Airways to set up a base there. All of a sudden there was a breakthrough. In early March he reported back to his masters to say he had received an unexpected message from the Ruler of Sharjah, Sheikh Sultan bin Saqr al-Qasimi "offering to grant facilities for aircraft, either flying boats or land machines. I understand that the creek at Sharjah has not been considered suitable in the past, but I suggest that a detailed survey be carried out and also the possibility of using it for land machines be examined." This communication from Sheikh Sultan set in train a process that helped to transform the fortune of the Arab Gulf states.

The communication was welcomed enthusiastically by Imperial Airways, which was enthusiastic about the suggestion of landplanes being used on the route. All depended on Biscoe's negotiations with Sheikh Sultan. Any delay would make a switch of the air route to the Arabian coast by the end of May impossible. The British government sought from Iran, and was granted, a second extension of the contested licence – until 1 October. The RAF, meanwhile, identified two possible locations for a landing ground some way from Sharjah town.

Sheikh Sultan continued to favour the idea of Imperial Airways coming to Sharjah; but as was the case elsewhere, not all his relatives agreed with him – fearing that the move would strip the sheikhdom of its independence. The talks continued into the summer. Possibly the extreme heat of the lower Gulf and the strain of the negotiations proved too much for Biscoe: he suffered a heart attack and died on board a British naval vessel in July.

Sheikh Sultan had demanded a number of changes to a draft agreement with the British government – in particular an assurance that the presence of an Imperial Airways base would not prejudice Sharjah's independence. On 22 July, a final accord was signed – the first of its kind in the region, and one that set the pattern for subsequent arrangements with other sheikhdoms during the 1930s. Such agreements represented the first tentative preparatory steps for the day when the Trucial States and, more spectacularly after its creation in 1971, the United Arab Emirates, would become a major centre of international aviation. While the discovery of oil would inevitably have seen the expansion of commercial flying in the Arab Gulf states, the region's decades of involvement in aviation – beginning in 1932 – meant that there was already a solid base on which to build.

In the agreement signed with Britain, Sheikh Sultan gave Imperial Airways the right to select a landing ground and "put on it such marks as are necessary, and their aeroplanes may land on that ground. I will construct a rest house for the passengers and staff of the Company." The airline was given permission to import, free of duty, petrol and spare parts for aircraft and other provisions. Sheikh Sultan further accepted "full responsibility for the protection of the Staff and passengers of the Company and their aircraft, so far as my dependents, relatives and subjects are concerned, and further for their protection as far as possible against marauders from outside of my jurisdiction. I will supply 35 guards and two head guards." Britain agreed to pay the guards' salaries and rent for the "Air Station" and rest house. Sheikh Sultan was to receive a monthly personal subsidy of 500 rupees[14]. Civilian aircraft would pay a landing fee of 5 rupees, but RAF planes would be exempted. The rent for the "Air Station" was 800 rupees a month, "payment to commence from the date the first commercial aeroplane lands." The duration of the agreement was 11 years.

Because of the death of Biscoe, the document was signed for

Britain by H R P Dickson, the Political Agent to the ruler of Kuwait. Dickson also wrote and signed an annex to the agreement, addressing some of the concerns raised by Sheikh Sultan. He informed the Sharjah ruler that "the British Government will respect your and your successors' independence, complete freedom and authority over your subjects and properties and will do nothing to take away your lands from you, and will not interfere in your internal affairs or with your servants, male or female, or your divers, and if any of the Coastal Shaiks [sic] attempt to threaten you owing to the Agreement which we have come to, the British Government will support you. Further, the representatives of the Company residing in Sharjah will have no official position, but will be representatives of a commercial firm. And no evil-doers shall be allowed to take refuge in the rest house." Britain also agreed to another of Sheikh Sultan's demands: that the British-India mail steamer should call at Sharjah, instead of Dubai.[15] Burchall of Imperial Airways, in a lecture a few months later, alluded to Dubai's refusal to offer facilities to Imperial Airways, adding that the change in the mail steamer route was "doubtless to the chagrin of the inhabitants of Dubai, who will realise too late what a chance has been missed."

Burchall went on to say that Sharjah had never been Imperial Airways' first choice for a base in the Trucial States because it was on the western side of the peninsula, "and we would have liked our night stop to be on the east, say at Dibah [in modern-day Oman – at the time it was part of British-administered Trucial Oman]. The advantage of Dibah over Sharjah is that it is 60 miles nearer to Gwadar, the first aerodrome east of the Persian eastern frontier, and therefore its use would allow us to carry less petrol and more paying loads. Dibah, unfortunately, does not meet our technical requirements." Burchall added that the search was continuing for an additional refuelling station on the east coast of the peninsula. To the north of Dibah, there was no possibility of one, because the mountains rose out of the sea. To the south lay Khor Fakhan, Kalba and Fujairah. But the further south the "occasional fuelling station is situated, the less use it will be. An aircraft captain would generally take a short sea crossing against a head wind and then follow the coast south to the emergency station. There is no satisfactory landing ground whatever at Khor Fakkan, which is surrounded by mountains, but just north of Fujairah the mountains recede from the coast. At Fujairah and Kalba are stretches of hard flat ground, the best being at Kalba." Burchall added that negotiations for occasional landing grounds had begun with the rulers of Abu Dhabi and Qatar.[16]

The route had still not, therefore, been finalised, but the unexpected co-operation of the ruler of Sharjah meant that, as far as Imperial Airways was concerned, the air corridor to India would henceforth pass along the Arab side of the Gulf. It was an expensive move – abandoning facilities that had been established at considerable cost over a number of years on one side of the waterway and setting up new ones on the other with the pressure of an approaching deadline. But in the process, Iran had thrown away an opportunity to have a monopoly on the major east-west route, along with the revenue and prestige accruing from it. Traffic between Europe and the Far East was clearly certain to expand: Royal Dutch Airlines – KLM – was already transiting the Iran and, to the annoyance of Imperial Airways, was still being allowed to operate its Amsterdam-Jakarta service that began in 1929 along the Gulf route. Air France, too, was later allowed to do the same for its flights to Saigon. But thanks to British diplomacy and determination to maintain the route to India airlines now had another option – the new Imperial Airways route along the southern coast of the Gulf – thus devaluing greatly Iran's political bargaining card.

About the same time, Iran took another decision that contributed further to its demise as a major international aviation centre: it decided not to renew its five-year contract with the Junkers Company that had been operating a successful internal air service, along with flights to Baku and Baghdad. The Iranians accused the Junkers staff of financial irregularities. Whatever the exact reasons for the split, it seems in retrospect an extraordinary decision. A staff of 30 Germans had operated eight aircraft from nine landing grounds, carrying a total of 20,000 passengers, the vast majority of them Iranians. Britain's ambassador in Baghdad, who might not be expected to praise German enterprise, said the Junkers team "are universally admitted to have given an admirably efficient service."[17] No service was introduced to replace that provided by Junkers, and 12 years passed before the country's own airline, Iran Air, was established.

Iran's decisions regarding the Imperial Airways licence and the Junkers accord had an impact that went beyond aviation itself. They put a brake on the internal development of the country which, with an air network shortening the vast distances between cities, was set to become by far the most advanced state in the region. They also left Iran increasingly isolated from its Arab neighbours and the wider world – a trend that has never been completely reversed.

By contrast, opportunities had now fallen into the lap of the Gulf's Arab states instead. In July 1932, the British government finally woke up to the reality that Imperial Airways had been perspicacious and that the short-term arrangements with Iran were no more than that. After the agreement with Sharjah had been signed, Britain formally announced that the Imperial Airways Empire Route, from 1 October, would follow the southern shore of the Gulf. An official statement said that a detailed examination of the whole question had shown that "the Arabian route possesses certain important practical advantages." This was a disingenuous statement from a government that, until the 11th hour, had banked on Iran changing its mind. But *Flight* magazine, for one, was quick to pinpoint, in jingoistic terms, the nature of those advantages: "The Arabian shore of the gulf is very much under British influence, whereas Persia is a foreign nation which is able to forbid or permit the use of aerodromes in its country by British aeroplanes as seems good to it. For the second time in the history of the India air mail service, this dependence on the will of a foreign Power has caused us inconvenience, and it is good time that we finished with that business." The blot on the landscape had been removed.

six

Lobster Mayonnaise for Lunch

By the early 1930s, Heliopolis airport outside Cairo had established itself as the region's aerial hub, synonymous with all the glamour and luxury attached to the early years of commercial aviation. Imperial Airways operated two empire services – one to India, the other to central and southern Africa. The latter transited Cairo, while passengers from Britain to India were taken as far as Palestine, where an aircraft from Cairo picked them up and flew them to their destination. The new India route involved various types of transport, passing across Europe, from Paris to Brindisi in southern Italy by train, and then by flying boat, via Corfu and Athens to Haifa on the Palestine coast. From here, passengers were driven to Tiberias, where they transferred onto the India flight that had set out from Cairo. For a few months in 1932, the seaplanes landed at Rhodes and Limassol in Cyprus instead of Corfu and Haifa. Then yet another change was made to the route: the Imperial Airways Kent-class flying boats flew from Castelrosso (Megisti – a small Greek island close to the southern shore of Turkey that in those days belonged to Italy) to Lake Tiberias in Palestine.

Among the aircraft based at Heliopolis were four of a new model, the HP42. Its manufacturers, Handley Page, called it "the first real airliner in the world". In some ways at least, this claim is valid. Never before had the world seen a four-engined transport plane;

and for seven years the HP42s were the only airliners providing a bar and a full catering service, with meals served by a steward. Only eight were built, but the HP42 remains an icon of the days of imperial flying. In appearance it looked anything but streamlined and the strength of its performance lay in reliability rather than speed, cruising at just 95-100 mph. An immensely stable aircraft, "it was said to be as steady as the Rock of Gibraltar – and about as fast. Up to forty passengers could be carried in ample space and comfort, and with excellent facilities for viewing from the fuselage slung below the lower wings."[1] Pilots christened this monolith of a biplane 'The Flying Banana'. As one historian has written, "it seemed a retrograde device, with its canvassed wings and many struts, compared with the giant Junkers four-engined G38 all-metal cantilever monoplane that flew into Croydon on the Berlin-London service of Deutsche LuftHansa."[2] Patrick Tweedie, who was a senior captain on the HP42s recalled that "flying the aircraft in severe turbulence was gruelling manual work. You wore gloves, took off your tunic and loosened your shirt and tie; when you'd come through it you felt as though you'd just rowed the Boat Race course. But despite that, and having wings that flexed a distance of eight feet at the tips in bad weather, it was a beautifully stable aircraft to fly, as strong and safe as houses."[3]

The one thing that the HP42 could guarantee was comfort – and luxury – on long flights. The *Imperial Gazette* described in some detail what passengers might expect when they boarded the plane: "In the liner are two cabins – fore and aft. Both are equally comfortable; large windows afford an unobstructed view, and beside each armchair seat are ventilating devices adjustable by the passenger, so that a constant supply of fresh air is ensured. The cabins are attractively panelled with wood painted in sea-like colours, the floor is thickly carpeted in beige, while the bright cretonne of the seats and the silken window curtains add tasteful touches of colour. Beside each seat is a light luggage rack, and a folding-table is provided for each person. Much could be written about the comfort, but it is sufficient to say that no train, nor car, nor ship has yet provided more thoughtful and comfortable accommodation for its passengers... So swiftly does the time pass after the steward has served chewing-gum, and little packets of cotton wool for the ears at the beginning of the flight, and so happily has the interval been filled in by an excellent lunch (served to each passenger at his own table) that it is with an apprehensive shock that one hears the engines stop and realises that the plane is heading earthwards."[4] This account failed to mention the silver cutlery and cruets, the bone china plates, the crystal glasses and the bunch of flowers on each table – perhaps such refinements were taken for granted in those days, as they would have been in the description of a first class railway dining carriage.

Before the aircraft entered service, a correspondent for *Aeroplane* magazine was taken up for a flight. He was less enamoured of the furnishings than the *Imperial Gazette* writer ("the cushions have too brilliant a pattern and the wall decorations remind one of the drop curtain in a provincial theatre") but was sufficiently impressed overall to conclude: "There were no bumps when airborne. We doubt whether there are more comfortable aeroplanes in the world than the HP42."[5]

Four of the HP42s (named Hannibal, Horsa, Hanno and Hadrian) had been stationed at Cairo for use on flights to African destinations. But when Imperial Airways was forced towards the end of 1932 to switch the India route from the Iranian coast of the Gulf to the Arabian side, it decided to assign the new aircraft to that service. The HP42s would fly from Cairo and land at Tiberias, Rutbah Wells, Baghdad, Basra, Kuwait (but at the start of the service not on a regular basis), Bahrain, Sharjah, Gwadar and Karachi. The RAF and a number of Imperial Airways officials involved in setting up facilities on the southern Gulf coast obviously knew what to expect and were confident that the new course was no more hazardous than any other long-distance air route of the day. But a common conception in Britain was that the little-known Gulf region was potentially hostile. *Flight* sought to allay fears. It acknowledged that the Trucial Coast was indeed that "tract with the ominous name of the Pirate Coast", adding that it was once a very dangerous part of the earth. Now, however, the publication assured its readers, "all the tribal chiefs have entered into treaties with the Indian government which forbid piracy and sea fighting, and which have earned for the sheikhs the title 'Trucial Chief' [sic]."[6] But when it came to previewing the journey down the Gulf as a whole, knowledge of the region was clearly patchy. After leaving Iraq, *Flight* continued, "the machine strikes the open Gulf at Kowait, after a flight of 75 miles. Kowait is the second largest city in all the Arab countries [sic] and the Sheikh of Kowait is a very friendly person to the British. There is a landing ground at Kowait, but the place is not a scheduled halt. To the south of this lies a stretch of territory more or less subject to the King of the Hedjaz[7]." The HP42 would then land for lunch at "the large island of Bahrein. This island is the centre of a group, which are under the protection of the Government of India... The capital is Manamah, and there is an aerodrome there. A second aerodrome has been constructed on the island of Muharraq." The *Flight* correspondent's grasp of the geography and topography of the Gulf grew increasingly vague as he commended Manama as "a pleasant place, possessed of many vineyards [sic] and natural wells which yield water of a temperature of 84 deg all the year round."[8]

The Ruler of Bahrain, Sheikh Isa bin Ali Al Khalifa, had given the RAF permission to establish an airfield near Manama a decade earlier, in 1920. An area was marked out by posts with a central white cloth circle and a 'T' to indicate the landing direction. But the site was far from ideal, causing Britain's political agent, Major Clive Daly, to comment in August 1923 that "the surface of this aerodrome is extremely bad. Although level, it is partly a hard surface, but in many places with heavy sand. It is, in fact, about as dangerous an aerodrome to land on as could well be found here. The aerodrome has never been used and it is doubtful whether it will ever be."[9] No doubt because of these problems, in 1930 another piece of land – at Gudaibiya, between Manama and Juffair – was leased to the RAF for use as an airfield. A second airfield was established on Muharraq Island, with dhows providing transport to Manama. It was on the Manama airstrip that the first eastbound HP42 of Imperial Airways landed in Bahrain on 6 October. The captain would not have had time to muse on imaginary "vineyards", or anything else for that matter, for as its wheels touched the sand, the plane (Hanno) became stuck in a silted water channel. A team of Bahrainis was assembled to pull it out using ropes. The HP42 then took off again without delay and landed a couple of minutes later at Muharraq, which became the Imperial Airways landing ground from then on and has remained the site of Bahrain airport ever since.[10] But landing on sand was often a problem for pilots of the lumbering HP42s. One, piloted by the athletic Captain Tweedie, became stuck before reaching Bahrain. The author Alexander Frater, retracing the old Imperial Airways route for a book published in 1986, interviewed Tweedie and recorded what the former captain had told him. On the flight southwards from Basra, the plane "ran into the worst weather ever recorded in the area and, his compasses malfunctioning, hopelessly lost, unable to raise anyone on the radio, was finally forced to put down on a salt flat. He ordered the bar to be opened and waited for the storm to blow itself out." But when he later went to start the engines he realised that the wheels of the aircraft had sunk deep into the sand. Dusk had fallen. A party of Arabs leading laden donkeys approached the plane, erected a tent nearby and "made it comfortable with carpets and cushions. A crackling fire was lit and a lamb roasted on a spit." A feast of lamb and rice was offered to crew and passengers. "To add to the gaiety of this extraordinary occasion Captain Tweedie turned on all the aircraft's lights. The meal over, his host, an official from a nearby village, packed everything back on the donkeys and vanished into the darkness, returning the next morning with ropes and a gang of able-bodied men" who pulled the HP42 out of the sand. Tweedie gave the official a box of 100 'Passing Cloud' cigarettes, and Imperial Airways later sent him a gold watch from London.[11] Adventures such as this one no doubt contributed to the exoticism and excitement that was attached to the early air routes.

Essential advice on etiquette when encountering Arabs after a forced landing was included in the RAF's *Air Route Book: Cairo to Karachi via North Arabia and the Persian Gulf* – an updated and expanded version of the *Pilots' Handbook* of the 1920s. "Remove footwear when entering their tents," the book said. "Completely ignore their women. If thirsty drink the water they offer, but DO NOT fill your water bottle from their personal supply... Do not expect breakfast if you sleep the night. Arabs will give you a mid-day or evening meal."[12]

More important than etiquette was the need, in the event of a sudden emergency, for the pilot to land his aircraft safely. To help, the *Air Route Book* described in detail all the landing grounds along the way between Cairo and Karachi and how to locate them. A pilot setting out on the southern Gulf coast route for the first time would find plenty of invaluable information. The new leg in the service began at Shaibah aerodrome outside Basra (situated on "undulating scrub-covered desert... an excellent landing ground, well drained and only unserviceable in very short periods to heavy aircraft during winter months"). Facilities at Kuwait were initially restricted to an emergency landing ground in the desert three quarters of a mile from the walled city ("wind indicator on city gate NW of airfield... Two W/T masts 100 feet high inside S end of city wall, near market"). The next emergency strip was at Ras Misha'ab, on the Saudi coast between al-Khafji and Jubail. The *Air Route Book* said the "nearest point of habitation is Ras Safaniya, 13 miles S along the coast. The island off the point is *not* a good landmark as mapped, as it alters shape." Further emergency landing grounds were available at Abu Hadriya (nearest water "from village 14 miles away"), Jubail ("surrounding country is composed of low sand dunes"), Ras Tanura ("Surface: Smooth, firm, rock, partially covered with saline crust") and Dhahran ("main camp of California Arabian Standard Oil Company"[13]) before reaching Bahrain. Muharraq airfield (no mention any more of Manama) offered "practically all-weather" serviceability, along with aircraft servicing and medical facilities provided by the RAF. There was even one hangar in the north-west corner of the field. By contrast, the facilities between Bahrain and Sharjah were minimal. Doha offered a strip for "use only in dire emergency", despite the fact that "the local Sheikh of Doha has extended hospitality to previous forced-landed crews", while Yas Island off Abu Dhabi was similarly to be avoided if at all possible. In Abu Dhabi itself, the "landing ground is not maintained and is to be used in extreme emergency only." Then came the welcome sight of Sharjah, located among "undulating sand and palm trees", one mile south-east of the town, with the aerodrome itself situated on "good hard sand". The last emergency landing grounds on Arab soil were at Kalba and Shinas on the eastern coast of the peninsula (where Imperial Airways had hoped to establish a permanent aerodrome for an overnight stopover) on the Gulf of Oman. Approaching Kalba, pilots were advised to look for the following landmarks: "Date gardens, soft sand and scrub with small trees. Landing ground shows up well as a dark rectangle patch immediately S of the town, and is an excellent navigation aid. Bounded by sea on eastern side and mountains rising up to 5,000 feet on western side."

In the absence of an airport on the east coast, Sharjah became the overnight stopover for the Imperial Airways Empire Service to India. A flavour of what it meant in that remote Gulf outpost whenever an HP42 passed through is found in a short public information film made in co-operation with Imperial Airways in the 1930s entitled *Air Outpost*. It is not a documentary that would have won prizes – the participants are clearly acting their parts in a self-conscious and stilted way, and the dialogue is far from natural – but it includes wonderful views of the desert airfield and the HP42. Sharjah, we are told in the commentary, is "a hot, desolate spot on the edge of the south Arabian Desert". The airport is built in the shape of "a square fort as a precaution against possible, but improbable, raids by wandering tribes of Bedouin." In charge is "a European station superintendent" – in the film, a stiff-looking, stern Scotsman in military uniform. After a brief look round the nearby town of Sharjah (home to "15,000 Arabs and a sprinkling of Indian and Persian merchants") we are shown an Arab in white robes and headdress leading a donkey towards the airstrip. Merchants like him bring "across the burning desert such fresh food as the markets can provide." Then, against the sound of Morse code messages, we see the station superintendent supervising preparations for the arrival late in the afternoon of the Imperial Airways flight from Basra and Bahrain. All through "the hot afternoon, cans of water are brought by donkeys to fill the tank in the courtyard – water to provide baths for the passengers and crew." Food is prepared and beds in the guest rooms are made up ready for inspection by the superintendent. Meanwhile outside, 10 men wheel a trolley bearing a "6,000-candle-power searchlight in case the aircraft should be delayed by headwinds and so fail to make Sharjah by sudden nightfall." The tone of the film becomes slightly tense, with everybody now waiting and listening for the approach of the HP42. Four boys sit, forming a square on the sand: "The Persian petrol boys pass the last few minutes with a game of cards." Finally, a silver bell with an Imperial Airways inscription is rung, and we see the giant biplane make a slow and shallow descent onto the sand runway, before taxying, a Civil Air Ensign[14] and an Air Mail Pennant[15] flying on small masts above the pilots' windows, towards the fort. Presumably keen to allay public concerns about the safety of the Gulf, the film-makers then focus on shots of Arabs carrying rifles and walking towards the airstrip. The commentary explains: "Arab guards provided by the Sheikh turn out to open the gates of the compound. If anything should happen to the airliner each man is liable to be punished in Arab fashion with the loss of an eye or a limb." Finally, the passengers disembark and are shown to their rooms and given a card telling them the schedule of departure times, meals and so on for the next leg of their journey.[16]

The comings and goings of HP42s following the transfer of Imperial Airways' Gulf route to the Arabian shore put the cities served by the airline on the map. A British minister visiting Bahrain in 1934 quoted the political agent there as saying "what a vast difference the coming of Imperial Airways had made to their lives. They were within a week of London instead of five weeks. They were in the world instead of out of it."[17] The new service also gave a big boost to commerce in Bahrain and Sharjah – as well as Dubai, traditionally the main trading station on the Trucial Coast. This helps to explain why the roots of commerce are so much deeper in Bahrain and Sharjah/Dubai than elsewhere in the Gulf. Both were relatively prosperous before the discovery of oil and remain well placed to maintain relative prosperity in the post-oil era. The impact that the arrival of the Imperial Airways airliners had on local traders was almost immediate. *Imperial Gazette* reported just a few months after the service began that it was "already proving of great use to merchants in the district. This district is the centre of the pearling trade in that part of the world, and the sheikhs find that they can now, by means of Imperial Airways' services, arrive at places in a few hours which it took them several days to reach by the older forms of surface transport. The fare is little more than by sea and the saving in times is so great that those who use the air services are almost sure to secure the cream of the business without much great initial outlay. The largest pearl-trading port is Dubai. The journey from Sharjah to Karachi takes nine hours by air and can only otherwise be made by a steamer which takes five days and only runs once a fortnight."[18]

Air travel meant not only that Gulf traders could do business with more ease, but also that far more foreigners than ever before were passing through the region. Very few European faces would have been seen in Sharjah, for example, before the advent of Imperial Airways in 1932. All of a sudden, European women, as well as men, were landing at the airport. Some were also taking the opportunity of visiting the town, where the inhabitants were largely conservative Sunni Muslims. The sight of European women, even in modest Western clothes, would have been shocking. On at least one occasion, it appears, clothes that were less than modest were worn. In March 1933, the British political resident in the Gulf received a report from his political agent in Bahrain, Lieutenant-Colonel P G Loch, that a "female Imperial Airways passenger had been seen going into the town [of Sharjah] wearing casual clothing, described as 'beach pyjamas'. Loch also wrote to the Imperial Airways Rest House superintendent at Sharjah asking him to discourage passengers from entering the town." The political resident wrote immediately to Imperial Airways, saying he had heard that "passengers at Shargah have begun going into the town, one lady passenger doing so clad in beach pyjamas. However suitable the latter garb may be in its right place, that place is obviously not Shargah." It must be remembered, he continued, "that the people of Shargah have not up to now been accustomed to having strangers, especially ladies, wandering about their bazaars, and it is of course most desirable from the point of view of the Company, as well as from my point of view, that any risk of passengers being molested should be avoided."[19]

Another stopover point where travellers were confined to their quarters was Rutbah Wells. Passengers' reactions to staying the night in this desert fort varied. Some complained of the extreme cold during winter nights. Others thought a night at Rutbah was a unique romantic experience – but with the trappings of civilisation conveniently on hand. One satisfied visitor called it "the most desolate and extraordinary hostelry in the world. It is practically 300 miles from any sign of civilization... Yet when you arrive out of the sky and taxi up to the gate, you pass in through the guards and enter a most pleasantly equipped restaurant in which you can have bacon and eggs, coffee, iced drinks, toast and marmalade and electric light."[20]

If there was little available to amuse transiting passengers at Sharjah or Rutbah, at other places they had more leeway. Indeed, Imperial Airways actively promoted the recreational facilities on offer. For example, passengers alighting at Gaza could entertain themselves with "duck shooting throughout the year and quail, grouse and plover during the winter, November to March." At Basra, too, it was possible to shoot "duck, geese, snipe, sand grouse, black partridge" and even wild boar. In Baghdad, fishing in the Euphrates could be arranged – "carp weighing up to 220 pounds have been caught and there is plenty of fishing in the upper reaches of the Tigris. The season is from November to June." On the other hand, if nightlife was what the traveller wanted then Imperial could recommend three clubs in Baghdad: the Alwiyah, the British Club and the Railway Club.[21] But not all passengers were enthralled by their overnight stopover in the Iraqi capital. Betty Trippe accompanied her husband Juan (who had founded Pan American World Airways in 1927) on a flight from San Francisco, across Asia and the Middle East to London. She wrote in her diary: "The hotel in Baghdad was dreadful. The fish at dinner, from the Tigris, was cold, and I found a dead fly in the tasteless cream sauce. The sheets were soiled, so we were even glad to know we would be called at 3.30am and could leave."[22]

By all accounts, Mr and Mrs Trippe were not enamoured of their brief Middle East experience and were happy when they reached Europe. There is also no evidence that Juan Trippe, during the couple's visit to Alexandria, was tempted – as many were – by the city's renowned fleshpots. Discreet and efficient Imperial Airways staff were, however, well prepared to cater for those who wanted to sample the vices on offer in the city. One manager recalled that it was "desirable that the traffic staff would know the going rate for a lady of pleasure and what time the nightclubs closed and what was the price for gin and tonic. If there were a sufficient number of passengers, as there frequently were, who found this the first fleshpot after two or three years' sojourn in the colonies or in extremely remote places, they would spend the night in a nightclub and we would offer to run the bus to the airport in the morning, say, at 4.15 from the nightclub."[23]

At Wadi Halfa, in northern Sudan (a stopover on the Southern Africa route), the pleasures on offer were much more innocent. Imperial Airways gave passengers the opportunity to play "golf and tennis. The golf, although confined to putting on a miniature green, is a source of much amusement and the newly opened tennis courts are being well patronised. The gardens with canna and oleander in full flower, and the green lawns surrounding the hotel show up in soothing contrast to the arid sands of the desert shimmering in the heat."[24]

Then, of course, there was the question – largely for female passengers – of what to wear in the evening during night stopovers. *Imperial Gazette* quoted one lady who, on a recent flight, had found the perfect solution: "I did not carry an evening gown with me. A change into an informal silk dress meets all the social demands of the night life on the air route, I consider, though for the gay travellers by air there is always dancing at Shepheard's in Cairo and a cabaret in Athens. Usually, however, a bath is, on landing, a greater luxury than all the jazz bands in the world!"

The same lady traveller went on to explain that "flying gave me a tremendous appetite. This seems a common 'complaint' among travellers, for the most wonderful meals were prepared... No lunch will taste as good again as that we took at a desert halt at the end of the Sudan, where we fared sumptuously in a marquee which might have been transported from the gay lawns of Ascot, it was so well appointed."[25] It was the food and service on board the slow and majestic HP42s that stuck in the memory of many people who wrote about their journeys along the Empire routes. Sir Montagu de Pomeroy Webb, Trade Commissioner in India, described lunch during a flight in the HP42, Hanno (the aircraft that had been pulled out of the sands of Manama), between Gwadar and Sharjah: "Hanno provides tables for his passengers. A steward now appeared; cloths were laid on the tables; also plates, knives and forks etc. And luncheon was served. And what a luncheon! – lobster mayonnaise, chicken, ham and salad, pears and cream, cheese and biscuits. Could any traveller by train or steamer expect more? Whisky and soda, or British beer completed this luxurious aerial repast." At Sharjah airport he saw the fort rest house ("surrounded by a barbed wire entanglement") for the first time, entering it with the other passengers "with pleasurable anticipations of a welcome bath and a good dinner. In both cases the expectations quickly became facts." The next morning at dawn they were off to Bahrain, "a long journey, 330 miles, mostly over the sea. Atmosphere calm; temperature cool; elevation 3,000 feet; visibility poor (owing to fine dust in the air)." But, as ever in the HP42, there was a fine meal to look forward to: "An excellent breakfast of cold tongue, scrambled eggs, fruit, bread, butter and marmalade was served about 7am." That evening, in Basra, the passengers enjoyed "a good dinner of fish, chicken, ice cream and fruit."

The next stage of de Pomeroy Webb's journey – to Cairo, via Rutbah Wells and Gaza – showed that, despite all the advances in technology and on-board comforts for passengers, the weather and technical snags could still have the last word on whether or not a journey would proceed smoothly. De Pomeroy Webb and his fellow passengers boarded Hanno at Baghdad ("after an excellent breakfast", of course). Between Baghdad and Rutbah Wells they encountered a headwind which, "while clearing away the haze and giving us a good view of the stony desert below, made the voyage a little 'bumpy'." On the next leg, to Gaza, the headwind was stronger, the 'bumps' more severe, so I slept (with one eye opened) whilst we passed over the 'hills' of Judea... And now the country becomes flatter, the headwind slackens, flying is smoother, and so, more comfortable. But what is this? Our engines are slowing down, and we are descending to earth. Landing so gently as to be almost unnoticeable our Engineer steps out and runs ahead to show the way to some unknown destination. Taxying after him, Hanno comes to rest over a small circular iron cover on what is clearly a large receptacle underground. In fact, it is an emergency petrol supply." The buried reserve, one of several installed by the RAF when they marked the track and ploughed the navigation furrow across the desert, was still proving useful a decade later. The captain – doubtless after consulting the 'Dr Balls' map in his copy of *Pilots' Handbook* – had decided "as a precautionary measure, to take in more petrol. So we all alight and watch the proceedings. But where are we? At Ziza [in Jordan], I am told." Fuel was duly pumped into the aircraft's tanks. Not all planes were so lucky. The dumps, Frater recounts, "were the subject of a long-running tactical battle between the airline and the desert nomads, who robbed and pillaged them like tombs. The nomads had no interest in the petrol, which they poured away into the sand, but they prized the tins, because they could be made into knives, cups, mirrors and water bottles. When Imperial put the dumps underground the nomads simply dug down, shot the locks off and carried on looting. Eventually London devised heavy-duty bullet-proof locks for which special keys were issued."[26]

Fuelling completed, de Pomeroy Webb and his fellow passengers boarded Hanno once more. But when the captain started the engines he noticed that something was wrong: the upper starboard engine was spluttering. After consulting his mechanic he decided to fly to the neighbouring military aerodrome at Amman instead of direct to Gaza which was nearly two hours away over the hilly lands of Palestine. So, de Pomeroy Webb wrote, "we fly north-west (instead of south-west), and, in about half-an-hour, we circle round and alight on the RAF ground at Amman much to the astonishment of a large number of military rank and file engaged in a cricket match."[27]

One of de Pomeroy Webb's main concerns during his travels was the standard of refreshments available, on the ground as much as in the air. For other writers, though, travelling during the 1930s to a new part of the world and seeing historical sites – sometimes from the air – was, in itself, a thrilling experience. The memoirs and travelogues of writers such as Robert Byron and Freya Stark contributed to a growing perception that, for the first time, long-distance international travel – for pleasure – was coming within the reach of the affluent middle classes, and not just heads of state, aristocrats and film stars. Without doubt, the creation of an air route across Egypt, the Holy Land and Iraq, all rich in antiquities, helped to draw people from across the world to see the treasures for themselves. The degree to which tourism contributes to the economies and social fabric of Egypt and the countries of the Holy Land owes much to the relative ease and speed with which travellers from Europe could reach them in the late-1920 and 1930s – and to the accounts they gave on their return.

In 1929, Sir Philip Sassoon, a British Air Minister, went on an extensive tour of the Middle East and India in a military flying boat. On the way he took many pictures of the sites he flew over. The material was collected subsequently and published as a book, which was reviewed in *The Times* under the headline, "Holidays by Air". The tone of the review indicates that the notion of commercial aircraft being used for sightseeing or for reaching far-off destinations for the purpose of pleasure alone was novel: "Sir Philip Sassoon disdains speed records in the air. They once were necessary to establish possibilities; we know now what can be done by daring flyers in fast machines. His book has another story to tell. Yet he cannot escape from the fact that speed is the essence of his narrative. That we can see the Pyramids, Palestine, the Nile, Jordan, Tigris and Euphrates, and walk the streets of Baghdad in one day is one of the wonders of our civilization that we shall not cease to marvel at for a year or two. And it is precisely because of what the more speedy ways of travel can offer to fading holiday appetites that Sir Philip Sassoon has written this charming description of the lands between here and the Himalayas... It is the deliberate intention of this enticing travel book to make flying popular. We are bidden to combine business with pleasure, or, on holiday, to scorn the familiar beauty of the Alps while we glide onward to the ruins of Babylon... But chiefly he is thinking of the time when long-distance air travel will stand on its own merits as the 'most enjoyable method of seeing the world.'"[28]

Other accounts by less distinguished passengers were also whetting the appetites of traditionally Europe-bound holidaymakers by describing the experience of flying over the Middle East. "After encircling the Holy City [of Jerusalem]," wrote a passenger on a flight to Baghdad, "the plane followed the Jericho Road winding like a ribbon throughout the Wilderness of Judea down to the Jordan and the Dead Sea. As I had expressed a wish to take some photographs, our pilot flew fairly low, enabling us to pick out quite plainly places of interest on this historic road – the little village of Bethany, the Apostles' Fountain, and the Good Samaritan's Inn; in the ordinary way all these spots can be detected. Seen from the air the whole region has an awe-inspiring appearance."[29] Another passenger – on a flight from Nairobi to Cairo – described what he saw at Aswan and beyond: "The machine was piloted across the famous Dam, and passengers were afforded an excellent opportunity of appreciating its features. As the water was very low, we also had a very good view of the Temple of Philae. The journey between Wadi Halfa and Assuan [Aswan] is very interesting. It includes also a view of the Temple of Abu Simbul, distinguished by three immense figures, and an opportunity for a very clear appreciation of the beneficial effects on the surrounding country of the construction of the Assuan Dam. Half-way between this point and Assiut the Nile describes enormous curves and on both sides there is evidence of intensive cultivation, supported by a wonderful irrigation system... the passengers evinced marked interest as we approached the land of the Pharaohs, and the pilot responded to a very pressing request to fly over the Pyramids. Having done so, he also circled round the Great Pyramid and the Sphinx. The machine landed at Heliopolis at 3.10, and the only regret was having to part again with a pilot who had been so helpful and instructive."[30]

Imperial Airways clearly realised that such descriptions were likely to entice armchair travellers (with sufficient disposable income) into attempting the real thing. So it began offering fortnight-long 'Aerial Tours' of the Middle East. For an all-in total of £80 each (a huge sum at the time), passengers would be flown to Paris, given first-class accommodation on the overnight sleeper train to Brindisi, before being flown to Athens, and then on to Castelrosso and Tiberias. Here, cars took them over the next three days on visits to Damascus, Jerusalem, Bethlehem and other places in the Holy Land. Back in Tiberias they would catch a plane to Cairo for sightseeing there. After that, a train journey to Alexandria would connect with a flying boat service to Crete, Athens and back across Europe to London. In those days, all the flights were at low altitudes, so "the aerial view of these ancient places was of dramatic interest".[31]

Thanks to the introduction of the British Empire air routes across the Middle East, then, the region was now well placed to capitalise on the emerging international tourism industry. Air services also opened opportunities for expatriates living in the Middle East to take vacations in fresh locations, without flying all the way back to northern Europe. During the brief spell in 1932 when Imperial seaplanes landed at Limassol in Cyprus, en route from Palestine to Europe, the island offered an escape from the severe heat of some of the countries to the east – just as it does today. *Flight* described what decades later would be dubbed a 'weekend break', in Cyprus – "a British possession which has such natural beauties, and so many historic monuments and associations." The magazine predicted that it would "prove a boon to those, say, in the desert countries of Iraq and Palestine, as it will be a swift and inexpensive flight to this beautiful island from either of these territories. Passengers, for example, who leave Basra or Baghdad on Friday will reach Cyprus before midday on Saturday, and, after spending a long weekend on the island, will be able to catch a return air service on Tuesday, alighting at either Baghdad or Basra on Wednesday afternoon."[32]

The 1930s was the decade when air transport began to make the world a smaller place, and the countries of the Middle East were part of this revolution from the start – far earlier than most other regions of the world. Planes, it was discovered furthermore, could carry a lot more than passengers and mail. Imperial Airways announced in 1930 that "a consignment of flowers, picked on Saturday morning in Egypt, were flown to London on the India airmail and exhibited in our window at Charles Street on the following Tuesday morning. Further experiments have been made in the transportation of flowers, and also of fruit and vegetables and a recent consignment contained, among other things, Egyptian cabbages, green tomatoes (which were subsequently ripened in London), bananas, and apricots which arrived in perfect condition."[33] Later that year, priceless artefacts were gathered together in Iran for a major exhibition planned in London in early 1931. These were taken by plane part of the way, a fact that was noted more than once with awe in the British press coverage of the event.[34]

Aircraft were becoming more functional than they had been in the immediate post-World War One years, and were now being designed and built specially to carry up to 20 passengers and cargo. But in the 1930s there was still an element of glamour and romance associated with flying – especially the extraordinarily daring long-distance solo flights made during the decade. The public's imagination was stirred still more by the performance of female aviators. In 1930, Briton Amy Johnson became the first woman to fly from England to Australia, while Amelia Earhart achieved international stardom two years later after her solo flight across the Atlantic. Some of the pioneering aviators were also gifted writers. One of these was New Zealander Jean Batten, who passed through the Middle East several times during her flying career – two decades after Baroness Raymonde de Laroche, at the Heliopolis flying week in 1910, had become the first woman to fly a plane in the region. In 1934, Batten flew solo from England to Australia, breaking Johnson's record. Her route took her from Athens to Nicosia in Cyprus. From there she headed for the Lebanese coast where her fragile de Havilland Moth biplane faced a challenge: "Away on the distant horizon I could see what looked like a great bank of cumulus cloud, but as I flew on I realized it was the great snow-covered range of the Lebanon Mountains. My altitude was 2,000 feet, and approaching Beirut I tried to gain more height. The down-draughts from the mountains were so violent, however, that any height that the Moth gained was lost in the succession of terrific bumps which shook the machine. Circling around Beirut for some time, I tried to gain sufficient height to cross the mountains, but it was not possible, so I flew along the coast, passing over ancient Sidon and Tyre where the great range gradually slopes away towards Nazareth. Eventually I came to a valley between hills festooned with terraces which looked so ancient that they might have been there even before Solomon took the cedars for his temple from the forests of Lebanon. On the hundreds of terraces I could see the most beautiful gardens and orderly-looking fruit trees and vineyards. Following the valley, I came to the Sea of Galilee. To the south I could see the River Jordan, and soon approached the edge of the Syrian Desert, which stretched before me like an endless sea of sand. In the distance Damascus, on the fringe of the desert, looked like a lovely city in the centre of a vast lake. Such was the illusion created by the River Barada, on the banks of which Damascus stands, and its many tributaries and irrigation canals, which reflect the intense blue of the sky."[35]

Of all the pilots who put pen to paper during the 1930s, one outshines the others. No one before or since has described flying with more sensitivity and such poetical – even spiritual – prose as the French writer, Antoine de St Exupéry. During the 1920s he was a pilot with the Latécoère Company, a predecessor of Air France, flying mail between France and Dakar in West Africa. In 1935, he set off with a mechanic named Prévot to try to set a new time record for a flight from Paris to Saigon. The pair reached the North African coast in Tunisia, and then headed for Benghazi in eastern Libya: "Off to Benghazi! We still have two hours of daylight. Before we crossed into Tripolitania I took off my glare glasses. The sands were golden under the slanting rays of the sun. How empty of life is this planet of ours! Once again it struck me that its rivers, its woods, its human habitations were the product of chance, of fortuitous conjunctions of circumstance. What a deal of the earth's surface is given over to rock and sand." They flew on into the night: "It was pitch dark when we came in sight of Benghazi. The town lay at the bottom of an obscurity so dense that it was without a halo.

I saw the place only when I was over it. As I was hunting for the aerodrome the red obstruction lights were switched on. They cut out a black rectangle in the earth." After taking on fuel, St Exupéry headed for Egypt, setting a course for a point midway between Cairo and Alexandria, reassured by the knowledge that even if he drifted slightly he would pick up the lights of one or other city. It was a moonless night: "I should not see a single gleam of light, I should not profit by the faintest landmark. Carrying no wireless, I should receive no message from the earth until I reached the Nile. It was useless to look at anything other than the compass and the artificial horizon... We had been flying for three hours. A brightness that seemed to me a glare spurted on the starboard side. I stared. A streamer of light which I had hitherto not noticed was fluttering from a lamp at the tip of the wing. It was an intermittent glow, not brilliant, not dim. It told me that I had flown into a cloud, and it was on the cloud that the lamp was reflected. I was nearing the landmarks on which I had counted; a clear sky would have helped a lot." After more than four hours in the air, St Exupéry knew that he ought to have reached the Nile, so began "a slow descent, intending to slip under the mass of clouds. Meanwhile I had had a look at my map. One thing was sure – the land below me lay at sea-level, and there was no risk of conking against a hill. Down I went, flying due north so that the lights of the cities would strike square into my windows. I must have overflown them, and should therefore see them on my left." Beneath the clouds, he spotted a light. "Oh!" he exclaimed. "I am quite sure that this is all I said. I am quite sure that what I felt was a terrific crash that rocked our world to its foundations. We had crashed against the earth at a hundred and seventy miles an hour." By some miracle St Exupéry and Prévot survived the crash, but stranded for several days in the desert they nearly died of dehydration. They were rescued in the end by Libyan Bedouin. The aircraft, it turned out, had encountered such strong headwinds that it had not even reached Egypt.[36]

While the heroic antics of lone pilots still made the headlines, the 1930s will be remembered for the rapid development of long-distance air travel, with several European operators inaugurating services through the Middle East. Aside from Imperial Airways, Germany's Lufthansa pioneered a route to the Far East via Cairo and Baghdad; KLM began flights to Jakarta, stopping at Istanbul and Baghdad; and Air Orient, one of the carriers that later merged to form Air France, flew from Marseilles to Beirut by seaplane, and by landplane to Saigon via (in the Middle East) Damascus, Baghdad, Basra, Bushehr and Jask. In other words, the inhabitants of the major cities in the region would have become familiar with the sight and sounds of aircraft, and the way that passengers, mail and other cargo could be transported safely by air from one region of the world to another. Many parts of the Middle East were indeed 'on the map'. "Today," a *Times* correspondent in the Gulf wrote, "the Arabs in Bahrein and Koweit regard the weekly air liners with as little interest as they regard the weekly mail boats of the British India Company, and divers out at the pearl banks hardly look up when an aeroplane circles over them. The people of Bahrein and Koweit are becoming air-minded; they enjoy travelling in aeroplanes and they use the airmail extensively for sending their pearls down to India and to Europe."[37] In 1929 (three years before the air route to India passed along the Arab shores of the Gulf), a pearl trader chartered an Imperial Airways plane for a flight to Bahrain, the arrival of which "caused great excitement among the local people. During the afternoon a total of 68 passengers took air flights and enjoyed bird's-eye views of their island home. Unfortunately, lack of petrol on the island did not permit the making of further flights, and over 200 of the inhabitants had to be disappointed."[38]

But opportunities for such air excursions were rare, and in the Middle East as a whole only a very tiny minority of Arabs would have set foot on a plane, let alone flown one. That state of affairs was beginning to change.

seven

The First Arab Professionals

In the Middle East, as in Europe, air travel in the 1920s and 30s was still very much an exclusive experience – within the grasp only of the rich and upper class. The overwhelming majority of passengers in Europe were male, chiefly government officials or businessmen in a hurry;[1] in the Middle East, by contrast, business travellers were outnumbered by British civilian and military officials. An Imperial Airways manager in Cairo recalled several decades later that he had identified clear categories of air travellers: "There were what would today be called the jet-set, the very rich who are constantly perambulating about the world. Africa was, of course, a Mecca for the safari business. There was big business in transporting very rich people down to Africa, Kenya and Uganda particularly. That was perhaps two per cent of the passengers. The balance was made up almost exclusively of colonial civil servants going to and from leave and member of His Majesty's Services going to and from postings or leave, with or without wives, according to seniority."[2] But air travel was by no means the norm for middle-ranking professionals. My father, a relatively senior employee of the Imperial Bank of Persia, was posted to the Middle East in the 1930s. It was not until the end of World War Two that he and his family were allowed to travel to and from Britain by air. His first diary mention of air travel – characteristically staccato, without colour or emotion – was in

August 1945: "Left Tehran by air for Cairo 1.30pm. Arrived Cairo 10pm. Stayed Metropolitan Hotel."

Throughout the Middle East the ruling elites, too, were increasingly keen to sample the experience of flying. Some took to it more readily than others. In 1924, an RAF seaplane from Basra landed for the first time off the coast of Bahrain. The following morning, the Deputy Ruler, Sheikh Hamad bin Isa Al Khalifa, was taken for a flight of nearly two hours. He expressed, an RAF officer reported later, "the liveliest interest". On landing he "repaired to his great tent where all his friends and admiring relations were assembled and, if the volume of the ensuing converse be any indication, the story of the flight lost nothing in the telling." Three years later, Sheikh Hamad was taken up in an RAF aircraft again – this time with a clear mission: to fly to Doha for a meeting with the ruler of Qatar.[3]

Far away from the Gulf – in Sudan – Imperial Airways was also doing its bit to introduce local rulers to the advantages of air travel. During the early 1930s, it organised pleasure flights at Khartoum airport to celebrate the birthday of King George V. The chiefs of the 15 provinces were given rides and word travelled fast around the country. Imperial Airways staff were told that the "Sheiks and notables of Wadi Halfa are now expressing themselves anxious to be given a similar flight in order that they may have an opportunity of seeing their own town from the air."[4]

Some Arab rulers even sought to acquire aircraft of their own. In 1932, a British member of parliament with contacts in the Anglo-Persian Oil Company (in which the British government held a 50 per cent share) relayed a message from an employee in Kuwait to a minister in the Department of Overseas Trade in London. The MP said the ruler of Kuwait, "that Island or Country [sic], whichever it is, would like particulars of small cabin aircraft of British make with a view to purchase." Neither the Overseas Trade Department nor the Air Ministry voiced an objection to the request. But the prime minister's office was more cautious, fearing that the issue might be linked to ongoing oil concession negotiations. A Downing Street official explained that "there are two sets of people negotiating with the Sheikh for oil concessions: The Eastern and General Syndicate who represent United States oil interests and the Anglo-Persian. The Syndicate gave the Sheikh a large car some time ago and this may be the retort courteous on the other side. There is also the risk of trouble if the Sheikh goes flying into Saudi Arabia and crashes there. (He is no stranger to flying and lately was taken to Baghdad by a Royal Air Force machine and back by a 'Puss Moth'). So we shall have to consult the Foreign Office and India Office before we can reply even on a silly point like this."[5] British government archives do not specify whether Kuwait's ruler ever received the plane he apparently wanted.

Of all Arab dignitaries of the 1920s and 30s, the man who appeared to be most attracted to air travel was King Feisal of Iraq. Perhaps this is not surprising. Feisal, a son of the Sharif of Mecca, had fought alongside T E Lawrence during the Arab Revolt in the First World War. While there is no evidence that he went up in an aeroplane himself during that campaign, he would have been brought face-to-face with aviation's potential. At the level of individual convenience he saw how Lawrence often flew to meetings with his superiors in Cairo and elsewhere. From a broader strategic perspective he was all too aware of the role that air power had played in securing the Allied/Arab victory over the Ottoman forces. In 1927, Imperial Airways announced that it had had "the distinction of carrying on the Cairo-Basra service HM King Feisal and the Emir Ghazi of Iraq. Earlier in the month, the heir to the throne of Iraq, who was returning from Harrow accompanied by his tutor, travelled in the 'City of Baghdad' between Cairo and the Iraqi capital. HM King Feisal, attended by Tashine Bey Khadri and other members of his suite, later flew from Baghdad to Gaza. During the flight the King sent out by wireless a message of brotherly greeting for the Emir Abdulla of Transjordania [later King Abdullah of Jordan]."[6] In May 1933, the king was airborne again, chartering an Imperial Airways plane to fly to Amman and Cairo, and later that year – on his way to England for a state visit – he flew to Cairo, with a stop for breakfast at Gaza.[7]

King Feisal also bought his own aircraft – a de Havilland Puss Moth, a three-seater high-wing monoplane with a closed cabin. Its delivery to Baghdad coincided with the creation of the first military air wing in an Arab country and what was almost certainly the first professional training scheme for pilots from the region. Six Iraqi army officers, who had passed through the Military College in Baghdad with honours, had been sent to Britain in 1928 for instruction. After completing a course at the RAF Cadet College at Cranwell they were attached to various RAF squadrons for further practical training. Once the officers had achieved competence, the next step was to organise a flying unit for Iraq. It was decided, according to an account written at the time, "to make a humble beginning with a flight of light aeroplanes, and the Gypsy Moth [single-engined two-seater biplane] was chosen as the standard type. It has the advantage that when the unit is re-equipped with more powerful aeroplanes, the Moths can still be used for training work and other general flying." Five aircraft were ordered from de Havilland (four of them equipped to carry bombs), "complete with wireless installation and cameras, as well as extra petrol tanks, drinking water tanks, and other special desert equipment." With a range of 600 miles, they would be "very suitable for light reconnaissance and offensive duties".

Five of the original six Iraqis officers were selected to fly the Gypsy Moths to Iraq. A photograph taken on the day of departure shows Lieutenant Jawad, who was in charge of the squadron, along with Lieutenants Mushtaq, Ali, Aziz and Tae, standing in front of one of their aircraft on a grass airfield, looking serious and self-conscious in front of the camera. They are wearing RAF-style uniforms and shiny black shoes. On 8 April 1931, they and a seconded RAF officer (piloting King Feisal's plane) set off in formation for Paris, the first leg in a long and historic flight by Arab pilots across Europe and the Middle East. When they landed in Baghdad two weeks later King Feisal was at the aerodrome to greet them and to take delivery of his Puss Moth.[8] Iraq's air force had reached its embryonic stage.

A year later, Egypt took a similar step towards creating its own military air wing. But the development was not without difficulties, becoming the subject of public controversy and official embarrassment. As was the case with the Iraqis, Egyptian army officers were trained as pilots by the RAF in Britain, and by the end of 1931 they, too, were ready to fly five Gypsy Moths from England to their home country. Bad weather across Europe caused their departure to be postponed many times. It was a bad omen. The creation of the Egyptian Army Air Force, as it was called, was intended as a goodwill gesture on Britain's part to placate rising nationalism and anti-British feelings. But it did not have the desired effect. While the Egyptian government had approved the formation of the air wing and had allocated a sum in the national budget for the upkeep of buildings and hangars at Almaza aerodrome outside Cairo (close to Heliopolis), the Egyptian press was critical of the authorities' total reliance on Britain in this respect. The daily *al-Balagh* quoted a statement from the Egyptian Ministry of War saying the latter was seeking "the service of British pilots, engineers and other experts for the new air force since it is difficult to find them among Egyptians." *Al-Balagh* was furious, accusing the Ministry of organising "the air force in a manner which is absolutely inconsistent with Egypt's interest and which leads to placing the air above Egypt in the hands of the English... [which is] a crime against the country and its future... We agree with the said ministry that Egyptians were not born trained in the art of aviation and that airplanes are not sown like cotton in the land of Egypt. But such was the case with all the other countries in the East and West which possessed independent civil and military air forces from the very beginning." The paper added that Iraq had Iraqi pilots, with "a few English pilots who can be counted on the fingers of one hand and whose services were considered by the Iraqi government as indispensible."[9]

More problems followed. Continuing bad weather in the spring of 1932 delayed the departure of the men and machines still further, prompting the Director of Aviation in Egypt, former RAF Air Commodore A G Board, to take a unilateral decision: the five aircraft would be packed up in crates and transported to Egypt by sea. The airmen would follow later, also by sea. The ship carrying the consignment of aircraft was approaching Gibraltar when the Egyptian press heard what was happening. It expressed outrage. The government, caught in an embarrassing position, had no choice but to respond to public criticism. So, against the background of disquiet at Britain's role in the whole affair and mindful that the Iraqi pilots had flown themselves back home to an ecstatic and patriotic welcome, the Egyptian authorities put their foot down: the five Gypsy Moths would arrive by air, piloted by Egyptians, come what may. The crated planes were consequently unloaded at Gibraltar and put on the next ship back to Britain. The Egyptian pilots, who were still in England and about to embark for Alexandria, were told to stay put. The Egyptian government accused the British authorities of disobeying orders by refusing to allow the planes to be delivered by air. Board had no choice but to resign. Crucially, he had failed to understand that the delivery of the planes was, first and foremost, a matter of national pride. Short-term practical and strategic considerations were of secondary importance. The *Egyptian Gazette* spoke of "an unfortunate incident" marring the formation of the country's air force and explained that it had been considered "contrary to Egypt's dignity that the planes should not be flown as machines ordered to the Iraqian [sic] Air Force were flown out by Iraqian officers trained in England."[10] Following government orders a formation of five aircraft left England on 24 May, three piloted by Egyptians (Second Lieutenant A Abdel-Razik and Lieutenants Abdel-Moneim Mikati and Fuad Haggag – Lieutenant Nagi, who had been ill, went by sea).

Nine days later ("after a great deal of slightly unpleasant publicity – due to no fault of the pilots") the five aircraft touched down at Almaza aerodrome, having circled Cairo twice, accompanied by a larger plane (with a British pilot), one of two that had been acquired by the Egyptian air wing a short time before. The aircraft taxied to the Royal Stand where King Fuad, Prince Farouk and other dignitaries were waiting. The king "warmly congratulated" the Egyptian pilots. On the completion of this ceremony, "the crowd, which had been very orderly, broke through the cordons and rushed towards the planes, mobbing the airmen."

The arrival of the formation marked the inauguration not just of the country's air force but also of the Almaza aerodrome – an occasion for pomp and ceremony of a kind witnessed at Heliopolis in 1910 at the start of the aviation week. Stands decked with flags had been erected along one side of the aerodrome and "contingents of the Egyptian Army were drawn up opposite, cavalry on the right, infantry in the centre and light gun sections on the left. The massed bands of the Egyptian Army were in the middle of the aerodrome." The march past – for reasons best known to the organisers – was accompanied by the strains of the Welsh song, *Men of Harlech*.[11]

As the music chosen for the occasion demonstrates, there was a firm British hand involved in the founding of Egypt's air wing, as there had been in Iraq. Nevertheless, the establishment of the two forces in the early 1930s gave both countries a strong regional lead in the development of aviation. By the 1950s Iraqi and Egyptian pilots were acknowledged as the best and most experienced in the Arab world. The air forces subsequently became important and politically powerful institutions in both states. Much of the status they enjoyed was due to their perceived role as agents of change and reform. They were seen as ushering their respective countries into the 20th century, whilst simultaneously sending a message to the rest of the world that Egypt and Iraq should now been taken seriously – equal with the most technologically advanced nations of the West. In practice, this was far from being the case. For a start, both countries were under British domination. But the reputation at home of the Egyptian and Iraqi air forces would in time provide those associated with them with considerable political leverage. For example, three of the nine men in Egypt's Free Officers' Movement that overthrew the monarchy in 1952 were from the air force, and former president Hosni Mubarak rose through the ranks to become air chief marshal. So it would be no exaggeration to say that the presence of the RAF in the Middle East after the First World War and the development of the commercial air corridor to India and Australia through Egypt and Iraq helped to shape the destiny of these two states in later decades.

But even as the Iraqi and Egyptian air wings developed, the RAF retained overall control of the skies of the Middle East. The RAF had remained deployed in Egypt, Palestine, Transjordan and Iraq after the First World War, and at the Cairo Conference of 1921 it was assigned the task of peacekeeping in the latter two countries

– a role that it began in October the following year. In Iraq, this was a particularly difficult, but ultimately crucial, task. It was at that Cairo Conference, too, that Feisal was appointed king of Iraq – as compensation for being ousted by the French after a very brief spell as king of an independent Syria. To justify the imposition of an Arab leader from the western edge of the Arabian Peninsula as ruler of the people of Iraq the British government gave instructions that "every effort would be made to make it appear that the offer came from the indigenous population rather than Britain."[12] In reality, the Iraqis were looking to one of their own notables to rule them, and the announcement in August 1921 of overwhelming support for the new king in a referendum could have fooled few people. In that same month Feisal was crowned King of Iraq, with the name of the country changed from Mesopotamia. But Britain's single-minded policy ignored the existence of strong pan-sectarian resentment in many areas of the country at the British military occupation. This culminated in a full-scale uprising involving Sunni and Shi'i Muslims, as well as Kurds. The British military responded with tough measures, and within a few months the revolt had run out of steam. But the large and rebellious Kurdish minority in the north continued to cause difficulties to the British in Iraq for several years because it "felt it had been deprived of its hopes of self-determination by the post-war settlement" – having had demands for an independent state in the post-Ottoman world ignored by the big powers.[13] In 1919, British forces had already quelled one attempt by the Kurds to assert their independence, and over the following decade RAF planes were frequently in action helping to put down further Kurdish revolts, resulting in the deaths of many innocent people. British air strikes on the Kurds are regarded infamously as the first in which air power was used specifically to terrorise civilians as part of a military campaign against their leaders. It was a tactic employed many times since then by a number of leaders, not least against the Kurds themselves by a later ruler of Iraq, Saddam Hussein. In one particular British campaign in the early 1930s "RAF bombing had destroyed 1,365 out of 2,382 buildings in 79 villages. In addition, the use of delayed action bombs, in violation of the 1907 Hague convention and of the British *Manual of Military Law* (1914), caused widespread civilian casualties. The Kurds were among the first to learn that aerial war was both devastating and indiscriminate in its victims, something which fuelled Kurdish indignation with Baghdad. As Arthur ('Bomber') Harris[14] wrote in 1924: 'They [Arabs and Kurds] now know what real bombing means, in casualties and damage; they now know that within 45 minutes a full-sized village can be practically wiped out and a third of its inhabitants killed or injured.'"[15]

Shameful and unacceptable as the use of air power was in these circumstances, as a tactical instrument of war it ensured nothing less than the survival of Iraq as a national entity in the form that it has kept ever since. Not only were ethnic groups pulling the new nation state in different directions, but Turkey, recovering after its defeat in World War One, still contested Britain's control of Mosul, at the centre of the oil-rich area of northern Iraq. One military historian is unequivocal in concluding that the RAF's brutal and effective action in subduing uprisings helped to cement the cohesion of the country: "Had the air control scheme not offered a cheap but effective alternative to military occupation, it is likely the British presence would have been curbed or ended, the Arab Kingdom would have been stillborn and the reviving power of Turkey would have engulfed the Mosul and possibly the Baghdad and Basra vilayets."[16]

Another irritant facing the British-backed authorities in the Kingdom of Iraq came from border raids conducted by Wahhabi tribesmen on the Arabian Peninsula, where Abdulaziz Al Saud (Ibn Saud) had taken control of the central region, the Nejd. There were also boundary disputes between King Feisal and Ibn Saud, "exacerbated by Hashemite-Saudi rivalry" – but a measure of reconciliation was achieved through British mediation.[17] Since the First World War, an agreement between Ibn Saud and Britain meant that the lands captured by the former were given British protection. In return, Ibn Saud had agreed during the First World War to launch a military assault on the followers of one of his main rivals, Ibn Rashid – an ally of the Turks. Ibn Saud did not succeed in overpowering Ibn Rashid until 1922, long after the Turks had been defeated. But the huge territorial gains he had made whilst doing so were recognised by Britain in another treaty between the two. Ibn Saud, as his part of the deal, agreed not to infringe British-controlled territory, including Iraq.

Britain maintained good relations with Ibn Saud, despite having made an alliance during the First World War with another of his biggest rivals, Sharif Hussein of Mecca, who controlled the Hejaz, the western region of the Arabian Peninsula. But by the mid-1920s, Britain's support for Hussein (who, after the war, called himself King of the Hejaz) had evaporated. With two of his sons, Abdullah and Feisal, installed safely as the leaders of Transjordan and Iraq respectively, and with the Ottomans defeated, Britain chose not to stop Ibn Saud's advance westward and the noose that was closing around the remaining Hashemites on the peninsula. There is no doubt that, had it chosen to do so, through the use of air power Britain could have slowed, if not halted, Ibn Saud's advance and propped up Hussein's fiefdom – a move that, once again, would have had immense implications for the political shaping of the Arabian Peninsula and required the rewriting of the modern history of the Middle East. As it was, Hussein was left helpless, with just his eldest son, Ali, by his side. Ibn Saud's forces captured the sacred Islamic city of Mecca in December 1924; Hussein realised that he was faced with overwhelming odds and could not expect help from outside. He sailed away, with British help, to temporary exile in Cyprus. But his eldest son, Ali, remained, proclaiming himself king as he prepared for a last stand in the Red Sea port city of Jeddah.

A dynasty once courted by the world's chief imperial power to help defeat the Ottoman army had been left at the mercy of its enemies. One intriguing and little-known aspect of the final days of Hashemite rule in the Hejaz is the way that Ali made one last, despairing and ultimately futile effort to repel the attackers with air power – using foreign pilots in what must be the first time that mercenaries were employed as aviators in a Middle East conflict.

The pilots in question were Russians, formerly members of the Imperial Army who fled after the 1917 revolution. One of them,

Colonel Ivanoff, subsequently absconded from Ali's meagre air wing in March 1924 and made his way to Baghdad en route to Iran where he hoped to find another job as a pilot. During his stay in the Iraqi capital he told his story to a correspondent for *The Times*. It makes for depressing reading. Colonel Ivanoff was "one of several Russian airmen who found their way to the Hejaz, some before and others after the fighting with the Wahhabis [ibn Saud's supporters]." Ivanoff explained to the correspondent that the war had entered a new phase with the siege of Jeddah. All was quiet for a time while the Ibn Saud forces awaited the arrival of reinforcements and guns. For their part, Ali's troops, "being inferior in numbers, decided that it was politic to remain behind the barbed wire defences of the city."

Practically every day, Ivanoff said, "the Russian airmen were sent out from Jeddah to make reconnaissances of the road leading to the town. Sometimes they bombed the Wahhabi camps. For the two months succeeding the evacuation of Mecca King Ali busied himself turning Jeddah into an armed camp." The king had sent trusted officials to Europe to purchase arms and ammunition. Their return must have been a bitter disappointment to him. Most of the equipment unloaded at Jeddah was "absolutely useless to the Army. Absurd prices were paid for ancient munitions, which in some cases had been lying rusting for years in ordnance dumps in different parts of Europe. They purchased 'tanks', the arrival of which was awaited with great impatience; but when they were received they turned out to be merely old American motor lorries which had been lying idle in Germany, without cover of any kind, since the war."

Of the aeroplanes they had purchased, "only two were more or less capable of flying. One was a DH9 with an open body, while the other was a DH9 with a closed 'limousine', which made it practically useless for war purposes. The latter machine very seldom left the aerodrome, and when it did go up it remained in the air for only a few minutes." There were, however, some aircraft in the Hejaz before the Wahhabi offensive began. One was destroyed at Taif and the Russian pilot and his Arab observer were killed – directly as a result of the Hejaz authorities' incompetence, in Ivanoff's view. The pilot had been ordered to fly to Taif – only to find that the Hejazi troops had withdrawn from the town. When the plane landed it was "soon shot to pieces and the wounded pilot and his observer were brutally murdered... Colonel Ivanoff went on to say that, in his opinion, the high command of the Hejaz Army had no idea of the proper role of aeroplanes in war, and frequently the pilots were given ridiculous orders. It was not uncommon for them to be asked to fly to some remote spot in the desert to kill a group of five or six Bedouin said to be implicated in the theft of a few sheep." On one occasion they were told to drop hand grenades on Ibn Saud's camp – an order that led to the death of another Russian pilot and two Arab observers. One of the grenades exploded in the plane which then crashed from a height of 4,000 feet. The Russian colonel also told how, despite Ali's instruction that Mecca was not to be attacked from the air, he received a written order from the Minister of War for the Hejaz, Tahsin Pasha, which read: "To M le pilot Ivanoff: I hereby order you at 7 o'clock tomorrow morning to fly over Mecca, and to throw bombs and leaflets on the city. Before starting you must call at the office of Tahsin Pasha to obtain your flying orders."

Ivanoff added that the climate of Jeddah was "very trying for the pilots and the five Russian mechanics who assisted them. The supplies of food and water were bad, and the airmen were asked to undertake long flights when they were suffering from fever, with high temperatures." As for the civilian population of Jeddah, "many of them expressed their wish that Ibn Saud would be victorious. In official quarters a hostile spirit was displayed towards Great Britain which was considered to be a friend of the Sultan of Nejd [Ibn Saud]. This spirit was so strong that if any of the pilots was seen talking to the British Consul in Jeddah suspicions were immediately aroused, and at times they were openly accused of treachery."[18] In December the same year, Ali abdicated, like his father before him, realised that his cause was lost and fled into exile in Iraq. The Wahhabi forces captured Jeddah and Ibn Saud became King of Nejd and the Hejaz.

But not all the tribes were loyal to Ibn Saud and sporadic outbreaks of unrest continued on the Arabian Peninsula. Despite agreements with Britain that forbade Wahhabi border incursions into Jordan and Iraq, these continued on a sporadic basis – usually involving only small groups of nomads. The RAF dealt "very severely with such unauthorised incursions. From time to time rebel groups would flee for safety into Kuwait or Iraq where the RAF would be charged with suppressing them." For example, towards the end of 1929 Britain's Under Secretary of State for Air, Frederick Montague, told members of parliament that the RAF had "rendered signal service in dealing with two rebellious tribes subject to Ibn Saud, the King of Nejd, whose leaders, accompanied by their followers, after an unsuccessful rebellion against that monarch, took refuge in Kuwait and Iraq. We had given an undertaking to Ibn Saud that we would not afford refuge to those rebels... In order to implement that undertaking, the political officer ordered the refugees to withdraw across the frontier." The rebels refused either to leave or surrender to the British authorities. Eventually the high commissioner authorised air action on a limited scale, the immediate result of which was the unconditional surrender of both tribes: "I may say that in this case the dropping of bombs as a warning proved sufficient, and there were no casualties to the rebels or on our own side."[19] Targeting Bedouin from the air was most difficult in winter when tribes pitched their tents singly or in twos and threes, over a large area of country, "each group of tents being separated from its neighbour by a distance of anything from a quarter to half a mile. This is done for support purposes in case of Arab attack, and to ensure that camels are well scattered and get full benefit from grazing." The opposite is the case in summer.[20]

So, British air power helped Ibn Saud tighten his grip on the peninsula, which would later be recognised as the Kingdom of Saudi Arabia. Ibn Saud himself was no stranger to aviation. In 1923 he had encouraged the formation of a small air arm intended primarily for coordination with ground forces and the subjugation of dissident tribesmen. A few surplus DH9 bombers were supplied by the British government, and a base was established at Dhahran, with workshops – after 1925 – at Jeddah.[21] Efforts to set up a more effective air wing began in 1930 when four ex-RAF Westland Wapiti bombers (single-engined biplanes), with British pilots, flew from Baghdad to the Hejaz "to form the nucleus of an air force...

and should enable Ibn Saud to exercise better control over the frontier tribes and check their raiding tendencies."[22] British pilots and ground personnel were contracted to operate and service the aircraft. But the arrangement was not a happy one. Ibn Saud complained that he was being overcharged and that the pilots' conduct on the ground (not least their consumption of alcohol) was unacceptable. In June 1931, he dismissed the three pilots and demanded replacements at lower salaries. He also insisted that six Hejazi personnel be taught to fly in England. The Air Ministry in London was in no rush to comply, recommending to the Foreign Office that more should be gleaned from Ibn Saud about what he had "in mind in regard to his Air Force... For example, to undertake the training of six Hejazi pilots now, without making any provision for the training of a suitable number of mechanics would be a most impractical and short-sighted policy." Then there was the question of where they should be trained: in the view of the Air Ministry it was "more suitable for them to be trained at the RAF School in Egypt. Also the language difficulty should be made very clear, especially in regard to the training of pilots, as the services of an interpreter would not overcome the difficulty during training in the air. As a first step it might be desirable to have selected personnel taught English." A further spanner in the works was inserted by the British high commissioner in Egypt who said that while "Egypt would be a more suitable place than England for the training of Arabic speaking officers, the fact that there is more talk than ever today of 'Pan-Islamic Movements' and the 'Arab Union' makes it incontestable that from the political point of view England would be a healthier training ground."

The issue on which the contract between Britain and Ibn Saud eventually foundered was that of who would have ultimate control of the pilots. The British government said the airmen were not to be used in war – and sent a note to this effect to the Ministry of Foreign Affairs in Mecca. The reply from the Ministry said the king wanted to remind Britain "that we did not buy the aeroplanes with the intention of warring against anyone... we bought them for operations against those of our own subjects who disobeyed us and secondly to repulse any move that anyone might make against us. But we have not been able to profit from the aeroplanes in the time of need... Let the British government choose one of two courses, either to send us airmen and mechanics or engineers sufficient for four aeroplanes and let them be under our authority for every purpose, or else send us engineers and instructors and we will ourselves look for airmen other than English, and the English will be for training and the others for war." The British government rejected the proposal and in 1933 the agreement was terminated.

No matter how one judges the positions adopted by the two sides, the outcome was beyond dispute: the Kingdom of Saudi Arabia (formed in 1932) missed an opportunity to develop both its air force and the aviation sector in general – in the way that Egypt and Iraq had done. After the last British personnel left (the pilots sacked two years earlier were never replaced), other foreign advisers were hired, but without great success. A British consular official reported at the end of 1933 that one of the Wapitis had crashed after a German pilot was forced from his sick bed to fly it. He added that the expected arrival of a passenger aircraft from Egypt "will be the first machine of any kind to fly in or near the Hejaz since the ill-fated Wapiti crash... Its arrival may serve to focus local attention on the parlous condition of the Saudi Air Force. The latter still consists of the four Wapitis and five old DH9's bought from His Majesty's government; but the former, which alone might be made to fly, still remain, as they have remained since the time of the crash referred to above, in their ramshackle hangar, with absolutely no attention except an occasional greasing by an inexpert hand; while Ibn Saud remains without a single pilot capable of flying the machines and without a single competent air-mechanic. No attempt has been made to develop any ground organisation, and projects, which have been reported on various occasions from this post, of engaging Turkish pilots and/or training Saudi subjects in Turkey, have remained unrealised." Three years later there was no sign of improvement: "There has been no material change in the equipment or personnel of the force. The aircraft taken over from the Hashemite regime can be dismissed as completely valueless.

Two certainly, and possibly one other, of the Wapitis bought under the auspices of HMG in 1929-30, are in working condition. I have heard lately of some idea of attempting to recondition the fourth, which crashed in the lagoon just north of Jeddah in September 1931, but I doubt the feasibility of this." The only pilots available to Ibn Saud at this stage were Russians, who, like those who flew for King Ali of the Hejaz, had been part of the Imperial Army.

In the mid-1930s, in an attempt to break the deadlock, Saudi officers were sent to Italy to train as pilots. The British consul in Jeddah said the press had published from time to time "optimistic accounts of the progress of the Saudi student-aviators, whose departure for Italy was reported... Private information is less glowing." On their return the Saudi "eagles" – as they were called in the press – appeared, according to the consul, more keen to enjoy the kudos of their status as foreign-trained airmen than to keep up their flying skills: "The belief that the Saudi 'eagles' trained in Italy would be less likely to cleave the empyrean with bright wing than to make a mess in the eyrie is confirmed from no less an important person than Said Bey-al-Kurdi, Commandant of Jeddah. During a courtesy visit which was paid to him by Commander Bowen of HMS Weston, the conversation turned to aviation, which Said Bey said would be of the greatest use to Saudi Arabia, both for ordinary administration purposes and as a means of controlling the tribes. He then broke out into a violent tirade, which, although nominally against all young Arabs educated abroad, was obviously aimed at the newly-returned 'eagles'. Such people, he said, were good for nothing but to live a life of luxury and try to teach their grandmothers to suck eggs... They expected pay, food, clothes and servants on European scales, but to work as men work in Europe was the last thing they would do."[23] Not until the early 1950s – when Saudi Arabia was becoming a major oil exporter – did its air force develop in a modern and systematic way.

Flying in Egypt, by contrast, progressed steadily during the 1930s. Aside from the formation of the Egyptian Army Air Force, a handful of private individuals qualified for pilots' licences, some of them acquiring their own aircraft. In 1930, the Royal Aero Club of Egypt was founded under the presidency of Prince Abbas Halim, the second cousin of King Fuad.[24] One issue of the *Egyptian Gazette* in 1932 mentioned how "the young Egyptian Aviator Ahmed Salem is planning to return to England, in the near future, in a Puss Moth that he has recently acquired... R Moursi Effendi, a young Egyptian student in England, is shortly contemplating flying out to Egypt via France, Italy and the usual North Africa route... The director of Almaza aerodrome is Kamel Bey Eloui, a well known Egyptian pilot [and later one of the first Arab airline executives]..."[25] *Al-Mokottam* newspaper, in an editorial, praised the developments of flying in Egypt, pointing out that "quite a good number of Egyptians and naturalised Egyptians will form the nucleus of civil and military aviation." It also suggested that an internal air service might be launched, as well as one linking Egypt with its neighbours.[26] In fact, initial steps towards achieving these goals had already been taken.

The first commercial aviation company in Egypt was a joint Egyptian-British venture. The Egyptian partner (with a 60 per cent share) was one of the leading financial institutions, Banque Misr, while the remaining 40 per cent was in the hands of Airwork, a British aviation company that, among other things, operated Heston airport near London. The first contacts were made in early 1931 between Alan Muntz of Airwork and Talaat Bey Harb of Banque Misr. The British high commissioner supported the move, telling Talaat Bey that "the Residency would look favourably on the conclusion of an arrangement with Airwork Ltd for the formation of an Egyptian Aviation Company and would do what it could to facilitate matters." As discussions progressed, it was decided that the new venture would: offer flying instruction; provide hangarage, servicing and sales of civilian aircraft; and carry out charter and air taxi services.[27] To publicise and seek support for the proposed firm, Muntz organised a flying display in his Puss Moth at Almaza aerodrome before a number of "notables and Egyptian aviators". The Minister of Communications, Tewfik Pasha Doss, and Talaat Bey were among many present who were taken up for 10-minute joy rides. The *Egyptian Gazette* correspondent was also given a flight, reporting that "there is little vibration or noise. The machine is extremely light and easily handled, which Mr Muntz demonstrated to a reporter of the *Egyptian Gazette* who was foolish enough to ask during the flight if it were possible to do any stunting." Among the spectators was "Sir Ahmed Hassanein Bey who was taught flying at Heston aerodrome" and another pilot, Rushdy Bey.[28] Formal authorisation for the establishment of Société Anonyme Misr Airwork was given at the start of 1932, and a Royal Decree issued five months later.

Despite being forced to loop the loop, the *Egyptian Gazette*'s aviation reporter was enthusiastic about the prospects for Misr Airwork, describing its establishment as a move that would take the country into a different sphere of aviation: "At Almaza now, we shall be able to learn to fly; for a few shillings we can enjoy all the thrills of a bird's-eye view of Cairo; and if by chance we wish to visit friends at one of the Lost Oases we have only to telephone Zeitoun and a white-winged taxi will be at our disposal. We have little doubt that public interest will be stimulated, and that the British and Egyptian pilots at Almaza will be kept busy."[29] Within days, 12 students had enrolled for lessons and Almaza was busy: "Planes were flying round, landing, taking off again, taxying rapidly across the aerodrome, being tested, with motors roaring and propellers making miniature sandstorms; some were totally, others partially, dismantled; mechanics were preparing two planes that were leaving the next day for England; budding pilots were receiving their first lessons; and passengers were arriving for flights round Cairo." But Misr Airwork was soon offering more than joy rides or air taxi flights. A year after its formation – with airfield lighting now installed at Almaza enabling night flights to begin – the new company was running regular services, twice daily, to Cairo and Alexandria – with Mersa Matruh added to the route at weekends. Luxor and Aswan became the next destinations, and services linking Cairo with Port Said, Jerusalem, Lydda, Jaffa, Tel Aviv, Haifa and Nicosia were inaugurated in 1935. During that year alone, Misr Airwork carried nearly 7,000 passengers – and this figure was trebled in 1936, with Beirut and Baghdad also becoming regular ports of call. A Misr Airwork advertisement offered charter services "To Anywhere at Any Time – The Romance of the East with the Speed of the West".

Misr Airwork was the first domestic and regional airline based in an Arab country – yet another aviation distinction for Egypt. The country seemed set to dominate the development of flying in the region for the foreseeable future and be the model that others would seek to emulate. But circumstances over subsequent decades conspired to prevent Egypt realising its full potential in the aviation sector. One factor was the failure of Egyptian pilots to receive professional training and acquire commercial ratings – whether by choice, insufficient education or because they were prevented or discouraged by their European colleagues is not clear. In 1933, an Egyptian (Muhammad Fawzi Effendi) obtained the highest ground engineer's rating – but there is no evidence of an Egyptian pilot taking controls of an airliner before the Second World War. So, for example, when a Misr Airwork aircraft crashed at al-Arish en route to Palestine, killing two Swiss passengers, it was no surprise to learn that the pilot, who died later in hospital, was an Englishman, Captain Spooner.[30]

Despite this setback, Misr Airwork continued to thrive – expanding its presence at Almaza aerodrome. A measure of its success was Imperial Airways' reaction to its formation: it regarded some of the new services as a direct threat to its own ones. In particular, it fought hard to secure the right to fly passengers between Cairo and Alexandria (instead of transporting them by rail), and sought – unsuccessfully – to have exclusive rights on services linking Cairo with Lydda and Baghdad.

The discovery of oil in the Gulf led to a significant increase in demand for flights – passenger and cargo – linking Cairo with the Arabian Peninsula and the Gulf. The first oil wells went on-stream in Iran in 1908 and were subsequently operated by the Anglo-Persian Oil Company. Discoveries were then made in Iraq (1927), Bahrain (1931), Kuwait and Saudi Arabia (1938) and Qatar (1940). The rising global demand for oil prompted frenetic activity in all these countries as foreign firms sought to expand production and accrue greater revenues. From the very earliest days, the use of aircraft to reach remote and distant oilfields and installations

boosted the efforts of all those involved in the exploitation of oil
– as, of course, it has continued to do. In 2004, I boarded a Boeing
737 airliner belonging to Saudi Aramco that flew dignitaries and
journalists from Dhahran to Haradh, a small town at the northern
fringe of the Rub' al-Khali (the Empty Quarter, a desert larger than
the area of France). The occasion was the inauguration of a gas
treatment plant, a vast and intricate cat's-cradle of chrome – pipes,
towers and tanks – glinting in the sunlight. Four gas-flaring towers
marked the plant out at night. The facility included fully-equipped
accommodation for the 1,000 workers there, alongside an airstrip
capable of receiving medium-size jet airliners. Building the plant,
there in the middle of the desert, and keeping it operating smoothly
would have been unthinkable without air support.

Aviation's association with the oil industry goes back almost to
the earliest days. In 1910, an aircraft was sold in London for laying
oil pipes in Iran – the first recorded sale of its kind. But it was not
until the 1930s that aviation started to play a significant part in
oil exploitation. As Misr Airwork was being established in Cairo,
for example, Shell already had a base there, with a plane used "for
covering the wide territory supplied by the Company in Africa and
the Near East."[31] The Anglo-Persian Oil Company, at about the same
time, stated in an annual report that "in the search for new fields
our geologists are applying the most modern physical methods, and
they are much assisted by the air service which we have introduced
for the greater mobility of the management."[32]

Of all the areas for potential oil exploration in the 1930s the
most challenging was undoubtedly that presented by the vast deserts
of Saudi Arabia. Standard Oil of California negotiated a concession
with Ibn Saud in 1933 – one of the most important conditions of
which was the company's right to use aircraft in its exploration
work. Two pilots were recruited in the United States and a single-
engined Fairchild 71 ordered by the newly-formed Californian-
Arabian Standard Oil Company. The aircraft would have "a hole in
the bottom for taking vertical photographs, a removable window
on each side for taking obliques, and in deference to the expected
sand it would have the biggest tires they could find." An extra fuel

tank restricted the seating capacity to four but gave the plane a cruising radius of 350 miles. The Fairchild was shipped to Egypt and eventually, after bureaucratic problems were resolved, was flown (using a borrowed RAF pilots' guide and map) to Iraq and on to Saudi Arabia, where the pilots were promptly arrested for landing without authorisation. The reason for Ibn Saud's sensitivity, it turned out, was that "he was having trouble with the Imam of Yemen (trouble that was to break out into war the following May); and he was afraid if they [the pilots] flew too low or too far in toward the Nejd, the Bedouins might be tempted to try out their shooting eyes... For these reasons the King insisted they use no radio, fly high and stay out of the interior. The prohibitions reduced the usefulness of the plane, but it was still better and faster than the car-and-camel reconnaissance."

The pilots worked out a plan of "flying straight parallel courses six miles apart, over any areas to be studied, while geologists with drafting boards mounted by the window sketched everything in the three-mile strip on each side... and if they saw anything that looked particularly interesting they photographed it. The most interesting thing they had so far found, the Dammam Dome, they photographed very thoroughly from the highest altitude they could get the Fairchild to reach."[33] Drilling of the Dammam Dome began in the summer of 1934. Finally, after a series of disappointments, oil was discovered there in March 1938. Ibn Saud and Saudi Arabia "were on the road to fortune."[34] Aviation had given the country a strong push along that road.

Saudi Arabia used its Gulf and Red Sea ports to export its oil to markets in Europe and elsewhere. But for Iraq, with access to the sea limited to the Shatt al-Arab waterway at the northern end of the Gulf, the options were more limited. The biggest oilfields were around Mosul in the north and a way needed to be found to pump that oil to the Mediterranean in order to secure quick and easy access to customers in Europe. The Iraq Petroleum Company (IPC) was a consortium of British (through the Anglo-Persian Oil Company), French, Dutch and US companies. As early as 1930, Anglo-Persian Oil was telling shareholders that transporting oil to the Mediterranean coast would involve the laying of "what is likely to prove one of the most costly pipelines yet constructed since the area where the most important discovery of oil has been made lies some hundreds of miles from the coast, from which alone it can find its natural outlet to the world's markets."[35] All in the IPC consortium agreed that the starting point for the pipeline should be Kirkuk. But the British and the French had different views about its outlet to the sea. Britain wanted the pipeline to run to an export terminal at Haifa in British Mandate Palestine, while France favoured Tripoli in French Mandate Syria – now Lebanon – as its destination. In the end, a compromise was reached by laying a double pipeline from Kirkuk to Haditha on the Euphrates, from where one headed for Haifa and the other for Tripoli.

The pipeline network was completed in 1934, and the following year an official opening was planned – involving a form of aviation that differed markedly from that used in rough and ready oil exploration and development in remote desert regions. IPC hired an Imperial Airways HP45 airliner named Syrinx that normally operated on European routes. The HP45 was a modified version of the HP42, that gentle giant of an airliner used to open up the southern Gulf route to India. Standards of service on both were comparable. Each of the dignitaries on board was handed a brochure entitled: "Imperial Airways: Special Flight of the Air Liner Syrinx to Iraq on charter to the Iraq Petroleum Company on the occasion of the opening of the Iraq-Mediterranean Pipe Line." Passengers were told that "a fully equipped buffet will be carried throughout the journey. Lunch and tea will be served in the air on each day between London and Cairo. Dinner will be served at the following hotels where overnight accommodation has been arranged: Lyon – Hotel Carlton; Naples – Hotel Excelsior; Benghazi – Hotel Italia; Cairo – Shepheard's Hotel. The company's special representative will be at your disposal throughout the journey and will advise you each evening of the hour of departure on the following day." From Egypt, the HP45 flew its first luxurious leg to Iraq. Opening ceremonies were subsequently held at Kirkuk, Tripoli and Haifa. "The days when journeys were made through the wilderness on pemmican and water, or, failing these, locusts and wild honey, are over," *Flight* commented in its curmudgeonly report of the VIP charter flight, "and the lonely cache of today contains caviar and Veuve Clicquot."[36]

But this opulent and ostentatious display did not mark the end of aviation's involvement in the pipeline project. Even as the HP45 lumbered its way back across Europe, IPC were acquiring four de Havilland Rapides (twin-engined biplanes) for much more prosaic duties: to operate services the length of the two pipelines, carrying personnel, equipment and mail. A firm link between flying and the oil industry of the Middle East was all set to be established. But the outbreak of World War Two put this on hold – and stunted the growth of Arabs' involvement in civilian and military flying as a whole.

eight

Arab Planes in Action

The fate of the first Arab air force was not a happy one: it suffered a crushing defeat within a decade of its formation at the hands of the RAF, the institution that had created it and which, at the time of its annihilation, was continuing to train its personnel. The story of how the Royal Iraqi Air Force (RIAF) was put out of action has its roots bedded deeply in both the turmoil of Middle Eastern politics and in the struggle for military dominance of the region in the Second World War.

There is a tendency to assume that the war paralysed the Middle East, causing Arab political action to be frozen. This was far from the case, either in Iraq – or in British Mandate Palestine. Serious rioting by Palestinians in 1929 in protest against rising Jewish immigration and Britain's failure to halt it left hundreds of people dead. Violence worsened in the 1930s as Jewish immigration rose sharply, and 1936 marked the start of what became known as the 'Arab Revolt' – not to be confused with the Arab Revolt against Ottoman domination during World War One. The 1930s revolt took the form of strikes, the withholding of taxes and acts of violence against both Jewish and British targets. The uprising, lasting three years, was directed by a newly formed Arab Higher Committee led by a staunchly anti-British, anti-Jewish and pro-Nazi nationalist, the Grand Mufti of Jerusalem, Hajj Amin al-Husseini. Some Arab volunteers from around the region also took part in the revolt. Late in 1937, the British cracked down on the Arab Higher Committee, arresting and deporting some of its members. Hajj Amin al-Husseini fled to Beirut, and at the outbreak of World War Two in 1939 moved to Baghdad where he continued to be vocal in support of Arab nationalist and anti-British politics.

An important aspect of the revolt was its effect on Arab nationalist feelings throughout the region. The Palestinian issue became – as it remains today – the key Arab grievance against Britain and the West. In particular, it stoked already strong nationalist and anti-British sentiments among the majority of Iraqis. While Iraq had been nominally independent since 1932, the Anglo-Iraqi Treaty of 1930 gave Britain considerable freedom to operate as it wished in the country – including the right to maintain two military airbases and to recruit Iraqi levies to defend them. The bases were at Lake Habbaniya on the Euphrates River, 55 miles west of Baghdad (replacing the previous RAF cantonment at Hinaidi) and at Shaibah, south-west of Basra.[1]

By the time the Second World War began, in September 1939, resentment towards the British had created deep political divisions within Iraq. Earlier that year, King Ghazi (who had succeeded King Feisal when the latter died in 1933) was killed in a car accident. His son, Feisal II, was only three years old, so a regent was appointed: Prince Abd al-Ilah, the son of Ali, who had briefly been King of the Hejaz in the late 1920s after his father, Sharif Hussein, had gone into exile. The regent was openly pro-British, as was the Prime Minister, Nuri al-Said – a fact that put them directly at odds with a prominent group of four nationalist officers in the Iraqi army, who were collectively known as the 'Golden Square'. Nationalists in the army were strongly influenced by the example of Hitler's National Socialist Germany, the image of which had been "assiduously promoted by the German ambassador to Iraq during these years, Fritz Grobba." Even though Grobba had been forced to leave Iraq at the outbreak of war in 1939, his influence lingered on, and Iraqi nationalists remained convinced that the Axis powers would win the war.[2] France had fallen to the Nazis; the Italians had penetrated

Egypt; and Greece was about to fall to the Germans. It was a bleak moment for the Allies.

At the outbreak of war, the Iraqi government had complied with a British request to break off diplomatic relations with Germany and intern all Germans in the country. But the move was controversial and revealed the split between supporters and opponents of British policy – inside the cabinet as well as the army. In an attempt to sideline the nationalist officers, the regent announced the formation of a national coalition government led by a nationalist, Rashid Ali al-Kailani, with Said as foreign minister. Rashid Ali tried to steer a middle course, aware that the British "were still a power to be reckoned with in Iraq, whatever setbacks they were experiencing elsewhere." With the Allies apparently facing certain defeat at the hands of the Axis powers, the prime minister decided that the government need not risk doing anything more in the short term than remain neutral. But in justifying neutrality "he became increasingly associated with the more openly pro-Axis sentiments of the Golden Square… [and] became ever more closely identified as the figurehead or symbol of the anti-British (and in the context of the war pro-Axis) movement in Iraq."[3] A subsequent decision by the regent to dismiss Rashid Ali led to a sharp increase in tension in Baghdad. This rose still further when the regent tried to break up the Golden Square. On 1 April 1941, the four colonels launched a coup, installing Rashid Ali once again as prime minister. The regent was smuggled out of Baghdad, taking refuge for a time at RAF Habbaniya before being transported under British protection to Jerusalem.

Britain was alarmed. Iraq was a significant oil producer. Not only did the British war machine need that oil, but it also had to stop the Germans having access to it. Equally importantly, Iraq was a key stepping stone on the civil and military air route to India and Australia, with BOAC (as Imperial Airways had become in November 1939) seaplanes landing on Lake Habbaniya. Britain informed the new Iraqi government that, in compliance with the terms of the Anglo-Iraqi Treaty, it intended to land troops in Basra. On the same day, Rashid Ali received a letter from Berlin assuring him of German support if Iraq found itself at war with Britain. Perhaps emboldened by this, the Iraqi government protested strongly at the planned British troop landings. The protests were ignored and in mid-April, the RAF transported 364 British troops to Basra by air from India – stopping at Sharjah and Bahrain to refuel – in what was the first ever strategic airlift by British forces in war.[4] Towards the end of the month, still more British troops arrived, prompting Rashid Ali to send urgent appeals to Germany for military support.

The military coup and the ousting of the regent, along with the outpouring of anti-British sentiment in Iraq, took the RAF totally by surprise. Shortly thereafter, the officer commanding British forces in the country had appealed to the British military headquarters for the Middle East in Cairo for support. But the Commander-in-Chief, Middle East, General Sir Archibald Wavell, rejected the request: military intervention, he argued, might inflame anti-British feelings across the region; and he could not spare forces for Iraq as he feared this would further endanger Egypt and Palestine. But with the war in the Mediterranean going badly for the Allies and the prospect that German forces might reach Iraq via Vichy Syria[5], other senior British officers, backed by Prime Minister Winston Churchill, overruled Wavell, and Indian troops were dispatched to Basra.

Until this point, Rashid Ali had remained convinced that, given Britain's precarious position in the war at large, it would not provoke a military confrontation within Iraq. Nevertheless, because the British were defiantly landing troops and equipment at Basra against the wishes of the Iraqi government, the prime minister heeded the calls of his military commanders who wanted to increase pressure on them. On 29 and 30 April, Iraqi troops seized the Kirkuk oilfields, shutting the pipeline that ran to Haifa (to stop the flow of oil to the British), but reopening the supply to Tripoli (in Vichy Syria) that had previously been cut. At the same time, a large force of Iraqi troops was ordered out of Baghdad to deploy around RAF Habbaniya, while the River Euphrates' embankments were cut, flooding the low-lying areas around the airbase and effectively cutting it off from the east. Rashid Ali's intention was to place RAF

Habbaniya under siege, with the aim of forcing Britain out of Iraq without a fight, "the fear of a bloodbath at the cantonment being sufficient, he believed, to frighten the British into withdrawal."[6]

One of the main reasons why British officers in Iraq were so alarmed by the 1 April coup was the fact that RAF Habbaniya was a training base, rather than one designed for combat, and consequently ill-equipped to respond to the latest crisis. A variety of aircraft ("a mixed assortment of obsolete and obsolescent bombers, fighters and trainers") were deployed there, although not all could be used for offensive operations. Only 39 pilots were available to fly the aircraft. The RIAF, for its part, constituted "formidable" opposition, with "a substantial and modern air force with many British-trained pilots".[7] The RIAF was equipped with 116 aircraft, although only about 57 were reported to be in a serviceable condition in early 1941, most of which were based at Rashid airfield (previously known as RAF Hinaidi before it was handed over to the RIAF) in Baghdad.[8]

With RAF Habbaniya under siege and so poorly equipped to defend itself, Rashid Ali assumed he could "create a political crisis and drag out the resulting impasse through negotiations."[9] The last thing that the Iraqi government expected was an aerial attack on its forces. But that was what happened. On 1 May, 12 RAF Wellington bombers arrived at Shaibah to back up the force at Habbaniya. Senior RAF commanders had received a message from Churchill saying: "If you have to strike, strike hard. Use all necessary force."[10] The commanders decided that, indeed, attack would be the best form of defence, with the added key element of surprise. Officers at the base gathered together as many pilots as they could find (including Greeks who were on a training course) and ordered the aircraft into action, with the Wellingtons from Shaibah bombing Iraqi positions around Habbaniya. While several RAF planes were shot down, the surprise factor was decisive – dealing a severe blow to the morale of the Iraqi armed forces and the government alike.

Late on the first day of hostilities, the RIAF launched a number of attacks on Habbaniya, but failed to inflict significant damage. Over the next two days, RAF planes ventured further, attacking Rashid airbase and Baghdad airport. An RAF statement on 4

May said bomber aircraft had carried out another heavy raid on the Iraqi aerodrome at Rashid airbase, causing severe damage to buildings and workshops, and "at least 22 Iraqi aircraft were put out of action. A number of air combats occurred resulting in several hostile aircraft being disabled."[11] A further 13 RIAF planes were destroyed at Baaquba. On the following day, the RAF reported that "the greater part of the Iraqi Air Force has been destroyed by our air action, either while attempting to attack British camps or as a result of attack by our air forces on Iraqi airbases."[12] These successes for the RAF came at a price: four days after the hostilities started, only a handful of planes were still airworthy. But the RAF's tactics achieved their aim: the Iraqi army withdrew from Habbaniya.

Rashid Ali's failure to use his air force against Habbaniya before the RAF planes could get in the air proved to be a fatal mistake. He had not believed for one moment that "in its straitened circumstances Great Britain would defend its interests in Iraq by force." Instead, he had assumed that the protracted period of negotiations that would follow his blockade of the airbase would give Germany time to bring arms and aircraft into the country. There was one unmistakeable outcome of the Habbaniya crisis: "Iraq's air force was largely destroyed".[13] One cannot underestimate the damaging effect that the RIAF's defeat, so soon after its creation, must have had on its personnel and on Arab prestige as a whole. The rebuilding of the force did not begin until 1946 – again under British supervision. But if the RIAF had been given different orders and directed to strike sooner, then it would almost certainly have acquitted itself well against the motley opposition. Such action would have significantly boosted Arab and Muslim pride – just as the successful arrival of the two Turkish airmen despatched by the Ottoman authorities from Constantinople to Alexandria in 1914 would have done. These two aviation setbacks contributed to sense of failure and despair that were to permeate the Arabs towards the end of the century.

While the siege of Habbaniya was lifted on 6 May 1941, Britain's battle to oust the new government in Iraq continued. By mid-May, a ground force was on its way to the country from

Palestine. Also en route to Iraq, via Vichy-controlled Syria, were 33 German and Italian warplanes (14 twin-engined Messerschmitt 110 fighter-bombers, seven Heinkel 111 bombers and 12 Italian-made CR42 biplane fighters), the majority of which had taken off from Greece. Rashid Ali's pleas for help were finally being heeded. The first the British knew about this was when ground forces heading for Iraq were shocked to find themselves being attacked from the sky. The German planes were refuelled in Syria, using airfields at Rayak (in modern-day Lebanon), Mezze outside Damascus, Aleppo and Palmyra, before being based at Mosul in northern Iraq. Germany had reached an arrangement with the (Vichy) French High Commissioner in Syria, General Henri Dentz, that overrode the professed neutrality of the Vichy administration and enabled both German and Italian planes (painted in French or Iraqi colours) to use airbases there and in Lebanon. On 15 May, the British government announced that German aircraft, including Messerschmitt 110s, had landed in Iraq and that, as Foreign Secretary Anthony Eden told parliament, "the French authorities in Syria are allowing German aircraft to use Syrian aerodromes as staging posts for flights to Iraq. His Majesty's Government have in consequence given full authority for action to be taken against these German aircraft on Syrian aerodromes. The French Government cannot escape responsibility for this situation."[14] Two days later, *The Times* commented that "French Syria is now to all intents and purposes in the occupation of the German Luftwaffe, which designs to use it as a base of operations against Iraq and eventually, no doubt, other countries of the Middle East."[15] Some members of the Vichy forces defected and joined a detachment of Free French in Palestine – including a significant number of air force personnel, following a stirring appeal from General Valin, head of the Free French air wing: "You in Aleppo and Damascus... who rage in your hearts to see German planes landing on your aerodromes on their way to Iraq, know full well that by receiving and refuelling the planes full of troops you are committing a hostile act against Free Frenchmen... In all conscience you must not do it; you will not do it. You cannot go down to history under the weight of such an infamy."[16]

But before British planes could start attacking German aircraft in Syria, the 'Fliegerführer Irak', as the German force was called, went into action against RAF Habbaniya, with three Heinkels supported by Me110s catching the base off guard. Two RAF planes were destroyed on the ground and an engineer was killed. Reinforcements were flown immediately to Habbaniya from Basra, and during the subsequent two days the RAF took the fight to the Germans in the north of the country, destroying about one third of their aircraft – a rate of attrition "that did not augur well for the continuance of a strong Luftwaffe presence in Iraq." By the end of May, only five per cent of German aircraft in Iraq were fit to fly. The German intervention, too small and too late, had been a failure.

There was another important reason for the Germans' failure that is linked directly with the way that aviation had developed in the region. Britain, through experience gained during the First World War, from the solo pioneering flights and from the establishment thereafter of commercial air routes, was firmly entrenched in the Middle East, not only with airbases, but also with dependable lines of supply. An article in *Flight* in December 1941 highlighted this advantage: "Britain's airbases in the Middle East are not only supported by locally available fuel, labour and material resources: sea and air routes stretching outside the immediate combat area link them with important production centres of the Empire and the USA. The position of the Axis is entirely different. The favourable geographical distribution of the Axis bases in the Middle East is heavily outweighed by their inferior supply position. These bases have not the advantages of a hinterland of substantial supply potentialities nor of secure supply lines. To a great extent they are dependent on either the existing stocks or the maintenance of communications with the Italian and Greek mainland."[17]

So, after suffering losses so soon after arriving in northern Iraq, the remains of the German air force had no choice but to withdraw to bases in Syria. Inadequate supply lines meant it could not easily bring in spares or reinforcements into Iraq – a factor that greatly inhibited its performance and effectiveness. Allied land and air forces, meanwhile, pushed northwards, cutting the road from

Baghdad to Mosul. On 30 May, Rashid Ali and around 40 supporters fled across the border to Iran. Grobba, who had requested and subsequently coordinated the military intervention, crossed into Syria. The following day, the coup leaders in Baghdad surrendered to the British, paving the way for the return of the regent.

British control of the skies was once again the deciding factor in securing Iraq in 1941, just as it had been during the First World War. Britain had learned then the dangers of losing aerial supremacy at the time of the siege of Kut. It was to learn an even more painful lesson elsewhere in the region during the Second World War. Even as the RAF and British and empire troops were regaining control of Iraq, a massive German aerial assault was under way on the island of Crete. This was the "first exclusively airborne invasion in history". Around 5,000 paratroopers were dropped on the island, occupied by almost 30,000 British and Commonwealth troops. They seized and held the airfield at Maleme, where Luftwaffe transport aircraft were then able to land with large-scale reinforcements and heavy equipment. Success in Crete depended on aircraft also providing "effective close air support and flying in fresh men and supplies to reinforce the initial attack".[18] The Allies did not have a sufficient number of fighter aircraft to stop the assault, and by the end of May they had retreated ignominiously from Crete, leaving the island in German hands. The expectation then was that the Germans would seize the island of Cyprus, to the east, before moving into Syria and the oilfields of northern Iraq, using Vichy French bases and, where necessary, French aircraft. The Allies' priority now became to deny the Germans the use of Syrian soil and maintain mastery of the air by destroying French facilities there.

The RAF had already been in action against Vichy airbases in Syria, including Palmyra, Damascus and Rayak. These attacks were sufficient only to keep the German and Vichy air forces at bay. The Allies decided that nothing short of the toppling of the Vichy administration would prevent the Axis powers obtaining a foothold in the Eastern Mediterranean. On 8 June, British, Australian, Indian and Free French forces launched an invasion of Syria and Lebanon along three fronts: northwards from Palestine towards Beirut;

and westwards from Iraq towards Damascus; and to the Rayak airbase. The Vichy French air force (Armée de l' Air de Vichy) in Syria and Lebanon had 112 aircraft at its disposal, with a similar number having been sent from North Africa as the crisis in Iraq developed. RAF and Royal Australian Air Force (RAAF) aircraft – including Hawker Hurricanes – went into action in support of the ground units, strafing and bombing targets in Beirut, Sidon and Tripoli, along with the oil installations at Dora and many targets in the mountains and the Beqa'a Valley.[19] The Allied pilots were told to target as many airfields as possible, and dozens of Vichy French planes were hit before they could take off. In one raid alone, the RAF and RAAF reported destroying eight aircraft on the ground at Rayak and Baalbek and damaging "a very large number of others... At Quseir, near Homs, one Vichy Glenn-Martin aircraft was destroyed on the ground. A number of [French-built] Dewoitine fighters were intercepted over the aerodrome, and two of them were shot down, while a number of others were damaged."[20]

But the Allies did not have a free hand: several of their planes were lost in aerial combat, and Vichy aircraft, operating out of Aleppo, carried out at least one sustained raid on Haifa, inflicting considerable damage. In general, the Allied advances into Syria and Lebanon were slower than had been expected: far from there being mass desertions, the French (particularly a regiment of the French Foreign Legion) put up fierce resistance. Damascus finally fell to the Allies on 22 June, and Beirut on 9 July (after major battles at the Litani River and later at Damour, just to the south of Beirut). General Dentz surrendered and an armistice was signed. The Allies could now concentrate their efforts in the Middle East on defeating the combined German and Italian armies in Libya. Once again, air power had played a decisive role – when Allied planes had "speedily established a superiority over the Vichy aircraft, which greatly assisted the troops on the ground."[21]

One sad and highly unusual feature of the Syria campaign was the spectacle of Frenchmen (Vichy and Free French) pitted against each other in war. Another equally rare occurrence, which created particular problems for the airmen involved, was the sight of the same model of aircraft in service on both sides. When Vichy French and Allied fighter pilots encountered American-built Martin Maryland light bombers in the skies over Syria they had to swiftly assess whether they were friendly or hostile before engaging them. A number of Marylands had been delivered to France before its surrender to the Germans, and the RAF had taken over the residue of the contract – those aircraft finished after France had fallen – complete with instruments and cockpit instructions written in French.

In terms of the impact of the campaign on Syria and Lebanon themselves, leaving aside the deaths and destruction caused by warfare, both could be said to have benefited from the Allied victory: the withdrawal of the defeated Vichy French forces in 1941 enabled Syria to declare independence; and in the same year, during a visit to the region, Free French leader General Charles de Gaulle, announced that Lebanon, too, would become independent. But neither country began building an air force until well after the Second World War was over.

With the Iraqi air force wiped out by the RAF, Egypt was now the sole Arab country with its own air wing, the Egyptian Army Air Wing (EAAW), which had expanded since its formation in 1932. Four years after that, an Anglo-Egyptian Treaty was signed that required Britain to withdraw all its forces from Egypt, aside from 10,000 troops deployed in the Suez Canal Zone. Britain also agreed to provide training for the Egyptian armed forces. Under the treaty, the EAAW and the RAF took joint responsibility for the air defence of Egypt, the Canal Zone and Sudan, while Britain agreed to hand the supervision and control of the air wing to an Egyptian, Brigadier Ali Islam. Without delay, the EAAW ordered six Avro 674 (Audax) biplanes (unarmed, they were intended for liaison and personnel transport), followed over the next two years by a further 30 aircraft, including a four-seater biplane for the Royal Flight. A measure of how relatively advanced aviation had become in Egypt was the fact that the EAAW, during 1937, took over its own flying training, with a flight school established at Almaza staffed by EAAF instructors who had qualified at the Central Flying School in the UK. Seconded

RAF personnel now acted in an advisory rather than an executive capacity, while the air wing became increasingly detached from the army, with its name changing in 1939 to the Royal Egyptian Air Force (REAF). That year the force acquired 78 new training and combat planes from Britain and the REAF was restructured to form five squadrons, two of them fighter wings.[22]

Given the nationalist feelings in Egypt at the time, it is remarkable that during the first year of World War Two the REAF operated in partnership with the RAF, the former's main task being to patrol the country's western frontier with Libya against possible Italian incursions and to provide an aerial defence of Alexandria in order to protect the seaplane base there. But when Italy entered the war on the German side and invaded Egypt in 1940 the Egyptian government declared the country neutral. As a result, the REAF withdrew from active service, and its bases and some of its aircraft were taken over for RAF use, causing morale to sink to a low ebb. However, young Egyptian airmen keen to see some action were not entirely disappointed: under the pretext of training, "the REAF fighter squadrons were 'scrambled' whenever enemy aircraft approached", without engaging in aerial combat.[23] The decisive Allied victory in the 'Battle of Egypt' in November 1942 finally drove the Axis forces out of the country; but the REAF took no active part in the fighting. Nevertheless, it acquired more aircraft, including Spitfires and Hurricanes, and by 1944 it had expanded to six squadrons. Two of these were deployed alongside RAF units at airfields in the Nile Delta region. By this time, REAF personnel consisted of 200 commissioned officers and 2,000 non-commissioned officers. Egypt, the cradle of aviation in the Middle East in the pre-World War One years, could now boast the largest and most advanced air force in the region.

There is a curious diplomatic footnote to the REAF's development: the aircraft received by the REAF during the war were never paid for, and when hostilities ended the British government sent a bill to the Egyptian authorities. A "somewhat bemused" Egyptian government countered this with a bill for RAF wartime use of bases and facilities in Egypt and "the services rendered to the UK by the REAF at a time when Egypt was not officially a belligerent. The entire matter was quietly dropped by mutual consent."[24]

After the war was over, Britain retained its air force in the Suez Canal Zone under the terms of the 1936 treaty, and a British advisory mission remained attached to the REAF. Egyptian pilots continued to be trained by the British – in Egypt and at RAF establishments in the United Kingdom. The REAF also acquired a small number of four-engined heavy bombers, including Avro Lancasters, from war surplus stocks. But while they may have looked impressive, the bombers were of little practical use, their presence being "largely in the nature of a token force because of manning and maintenance difficulties."[25] The "difficulties" were soon to become glaringly evident when the REAF went into action for the first time – in 1948 against the newly created state of Israel (described in Chapter 10).

Control of the Suez Canal – and therefore of Egypt as a whole – had been a strategically vital objective for Britain during both World Wars. But there was another factor that strengthened Britain's determination to keep a foothold in Egypt. In the years after World War One, Cairo had become a crucial hub for air routes to and from British colonial possessions. That importance increased between 1939 and 1945. As France fell to Nazi German forces and Italy entered the war, Britain's access to Africa, the Middle East, the Far East and Australia became significantly more difficult. These problems were overcome by the establishment of a BOAC seaplane route from Poole Harbour on the coast of southern England to Lisbon in Portugal (which was neutral). From there, planes refuelled at Rabat, Port Etienne, Bathurst in French Equatorial Africa (today's Banjul in Gambia), Freetown, Takoradi (Ghana) and Accra before ending their journey at Lagos. Here a DC-3 Dakota took passengers eastwards across Africa to Khartoum where the flight connected with a weekly Short C-Class Empire flying boat service that began in Durban and headed northwards to Khartoum, Wadi Halfa, Luxor and Cairo. From the Egyptian capital the planes followed a route through Tiberias, Habbaniya, Basra, Bahrain and Dubai, before crossing into India and onwards to Australia and New Zealand. It was known as the 'Horseshoe route' because of the way it passed northwards across Africa before curving eastwards around the Middle East.

The 1941 pro-Axis coup in Iraq meant that the Horseshoe route could no longer pass through Iraq, so, according to a breathless *Flight* report written close to the end of the war, "under strict secrecy, land and sea aircraft of the RAF and the BOAC surveyed an alternative route for an emergency. Instead of going north from Egypt via Palestine and Iraq, the route would strike south from Cairo to Port Sudan and Asmara, and thence east across to Aden, via the southern fringe of the Arabian Peninsula to Karachi. One's imagination does not have to be very flamboyant to realise what was involved in breaking this virgin route. Even from schoolboys' maps one can gather a picture of this region, deprived of water, cultivation, etc. Because of heavy surf during the monsoon period it was decided to use land aircraft, and bases had to be established at Salalah and Masirah [in today's Oman] from scratch. Runways, buildings, hangars, dormitories, distilling plants for water and wireless equipment had to be set up. Even food had to be supplied by air when the work was in progress."[26] The route was later used regularly by RAF and US Air Force aircraft transporting supplies to China. But once again Egypt occupied a pivotal position in the new air link between West and East. That same 1945 article highlighted Egypt's wider role, pointing out that Middle East routes "radiate from Cairo in a spoke-like fashion to Ankara; to Tehran via Damascus and Baghdad; to Jeddah via Port Sudan; to Aden via Asmara; and once weekly to Addis Ababa." Egypt at this time was so important that it was immediately associated in the minds of aviation officials when they spoke of the route between Europe and the Far East. For example, when the BOAC Chairman in 1944, Viscount Knollys, looked ahead to commercial aviation in the post-war period he asked his audience to imagine "leaving England on a cold January night and looking down ten hours later on the Pyramids."[27]

During the 1910 Heliopolis aviation week, none of the entrants had felt capable to take up the challenge to fly the relatively short distance to the Pyramids. Huge advances had been made in the three decades since then, and Egypt was now immersed in the new world of commercial and military flight. As the leading aviation player in the Middle East and North Africa and it must have seemed impossible in the years following the end of the Second World War that it could ever lose this commanding position.

nine

Aerial Crossroad

One morning in the Jordanian capital, Amman, in the 1980s I sat in a taxi heading up one of the hills over which the city sprawls towards Marka, the city's military airport. Marka was built on the site of the original RAF landing ground, and is now used to receive VIP flights to the kingdom. At that moment, a skeleton of memory started to form in my mind: I was about four years old, in a car with my parents and driving towards the same airport to watch my father play cricket. This he did most Fridays. My journey there more than three decades later was to report on the arrival of a senior British dignitary. King Hussein was standing at the end of a red carpet, and a band and a guard of honour were on parade. As the plane from London arrived, I remembered those Friday games of cricket, this English peculiarity closely associated with lush grass pastures and the shade of broadleaved trees being played, in this instance, on a concrete wicket covered by matting, with incongruous figures dressed in white dotted about the desert outfield. It was a scene similar to that witnessed in a previous era – in the 1930s, when the HP42 carrying Sir Montagu de Pomeroy Webb, Trade Commissioner in India, made an unscheduled stop at Amman airport.

Often as we had our picnic tea by the boundary rope we would watch King Hussein practice landings and take-offs in a de

Havilland Vampire jet, one of nine donated to Jordan by the British government. His instructor was Wing Commander Jock Dalgleish, a wartime RAF pilot, who commanded the Royal Jordanian Air Force. The enthusiasm for flying that the late King Feisal of Iraq had displayed clearly ran in the family (King Hussein's grandfather, King Abdullah, was Feisal's brother). Decades later, Dalgleish recalled that the king's journeys by air could sometimes be hair-raising affairs. A few years after qualifying as a pilot, Hussein took off in a de Havilland Dove of the Royal Flight and headed north on a route that would take him eventually to Switzerland, where he had planned a holiday with his mother. Dalgleish was co-pilot. Passing through Syrian airspace the king was ordered by air traffic control to land at Damascus because, he was told, the aircraft did not have clearance to fly over the country. The king feared that the order might be part of a plot to capture him – at a time of strained relations between Jordan and Syria – so refused to comply. Two Syrian Mig-17 jet fighters were then scrambled and ordered to intercept the royal plane. The two fighters made aggressive passes close to the Dove, with the intention of forcing it to land. Dalgleish took over the controls, "plunged the royal plane earthward, hedge-hopped for 20 minutes as it fled back to the Jordanian border while the Syrian Migs, flown somewhat amateurishly, made five more 'quarter attacks' at the plane, but without firing." The king and his co-pilot landed the Dove safely back at Marka airport.[1]

The twin-engined Dove was a small (it carried only up to 11 passengers) post-war airliner that was in production during the 1950s and 60s, therefore a modern plane at the time. By contrast, when I arrived in Amman with my parents in April 1952 – my father had been appointed manager of BBME there – we travelled in a de Havilland Rapide of Arab Airways, an eight-seater biplane dating back to the 1930s – the last decade when, in the view of historian Professor Robert A Wohl, commercial flying was considered an adventure: "What happened right around the beginning of the war was that the circumstances in which people flew began to change. The essence of flight had always been the risk and danger associated with it – the unpredictable aspects of flight. As flight became more predictable and as it became safer it was hard for people to feel the same sense of adventure."[2] But there was adventure enough in the Rapide, tossed mercilessly by air currents over the mountains and valleys between Lebanon and Jordan.

By the 1950s, aircraft were becoming significantly safer and more sophisticated. The Second World War had acted as a catalyst for the development of aviation in an even more spectacular way than the 1914-18 conflict had done. Reliable navigation methods using radio and radar were introduced, and engines and airframes became more dependable. Aviation had taken yet another enormous leap forward, and once again – just as in the previous war – it became clear how commercial peacetime aviation had the potential to shrink the globe. "There are no distant places any longer," said American politician Wendell Willkie. "The world is small and the world is one."[3]

While the Second World War had seen the emergence of large, powerful aircraft that could fly, by the standards of the day, vast distances without refuelling, these were not immediately suitable for passenger use. But until new airliners fit for the purpose could be designed, built and tested, former bombers and wartime aircraft of various kinds were adapted and kitted out with seats and other amenities to enable them to carry passengers. One example was the Avro York, a snub-nosed derivative of the four-engined Lancaster bomber. Travelling in such aircraft might not have been quite the adventure that flying was in the 1930s, but unpressurised cabins meant that cruising above bad weather was not always an option, so a journey could still be something of an endurance test. My father's diary of 1948 outlines a journey from Tehran to London on a BOAC airliner: "June 30: Completed packing then went to BOAC office to weigh in.... July 1: Up at 4am, airport 5.30am, took off 6.50am. 2hrs 40 mins flight to Baghdad. Highest altitude 14,000 ft. Oxygen masks worn over 10,000 ft. John [my eldest brother] sick once. Stayed 1 hr Baghdad, then left for Nicosia (4 and a half hours). Very hot at first, then OK. Flew at 8,000 ft. J sick once, then all right after pills. Motored to hotel, where we stayed the night. All paddled in the Mediterranean...." Then in 1949, my parents, my second brother and my sister flew on a BOAC York from London to Tehran. The journey to Rome was "rather bumpy through much cloud. Flying 9,500 ft. Children both sick frequently." After a night in a Rome hotel the plane flew at 6,000 feet to Nicosia ("Cloudy at times but conditions mainly good. Light refreshments and lunch on board. Children all right."). The following morning the weather in Nicosia was fine, but "as Tehran is snowbound the pilot has decided to wait for further information before leaving. Expect to take off early tomorrow."

By the end of the 1940s, BOAC was able to fly once more over most of the routes in the Middle East that had been disrupted by the war. But the British carrier was by no means the only airline offering services across the region, for several newly independent countries were forming their own carriers. In general, these began from a standing start: the war years had stifled what little existed of Middle Eastern commercial aviation. As one historian wrote in 1945, local airlines "were at a low ebb". There were only two substantial regional airlines that could trace their history back to pre-war days: Turkish state airline Devlet Hava Yollari (DHY); and Misrair of Egypt (formerly Misr Airwork). In February 1946, Misrair suspended operations for two years because of the inadequacy of its equipment. There were no other significant Arab airlines in operation.[4]

Even as the newly independent Arab countries planned the start-up of national carriers, their governments were inundated with requests for landing rights – not least from United States-based airlines. *Flight* reported in August 1945 that "plans of United States airlines to fly to Europe and the Middle East on the routes recently approved by the Civil Aeronautics Board[5] will require landing rights in 33 countries, including the nations of the Middle East... Interest in the establishment of air routes that eventually will circle the world centres on the Middle East region, which has been called the aerial crossroad of the world." The American carriers also hoped to attract passengers by promoting tourism in the region, but were initially prevented from doing so because "advertising portraying the historic and cultural regions of the Middle East, particularly Cairo, which was designated as a key stop on the TWA [Trans

World Airlines] through-route to India", could not be circulated until landing rights in Egypt had been approved by the Egyptian government.[6]

While TWA was eventually assigned a route through the Middle East that included Cairo, its big rival, Pan American World Airways (PAA – more often referred to as Pan Am) received permission to make a comparable stopover on its Europe-Far East services at Beirut. It would be Beirut, rather than Cairo, that emerged later as the region's commercial aviation hub in the 1950s and 60s.

Beirut's fortunes rose as a result of the post-war development of the oil industry in Saudi Arabia and the Gulf states. The oil boom created a demand for small aircraft and helicopters to service the needs of the exploration and development companies, and more significantly for larger airliners to ferry the many thousands of foreign technicians in and out of the region. With increasing oil production came greater wealth and consumer spending power, with corresponding demands for fresh produce from those working in remote desert locations. Fruit and vegetables, meat and other foodstuff were transported by air from Lebanon. At the same time, wealthy Gulf Arabs and foreign workers with bulging pay packets adopted the habit of escaping the extreme summer heat by flying to Lebanon for vacations, by the Mediterranean or in the cool air of the mountains. Because of all these factors "an air traffic pattern quickly became established after the war, centred on the Persian Gulf in the eastern side and along the Levantine coast to the west, with the city of Beirut suddenly assuming the status of a major traffic junction, assisted by the decline of Lydda because of political troubles in Palestine."[7]

Palestine's 'political troubles' were the result of worsening violence there, as thousands of European Jews, survivors of the Nazi purges, tried to join those who had already reached what Jewish leaders were determined would become the state of Israel. British troops and police attempting to administer the territory, found themselves targets of both Jewish and Arab violence. Amid this mayhem, in February 1947, Britain admitted defeat in its attempts to find an equitable solution to the Palestine problem and handed the issue over to the United Nations. On 14 May 1948, the Union Flag was lowered for the last time on Government House in Jerusalem. Spitfire fighters and Lancaster bombers patrolled the skies as the car carrying Sir Alan Cunningham, the last British high commissioner, drove to Kalundia airfield north of the city. From there he flew to Haifa and sailed back to Britain.

On the same day, the Jewish People's Council, representing Jews in Palestine and in diaspora, approved the declaration of the establishment of the State of Israel. The Zionist movement had achieved its goal. The Palestinians felt demoralised – first betrayed by Britain through the 1917 Balfour Declaration and then finally abandoned by it three decades later. Unlike the Jews, the Palestinians had no military organisation, and looked to neighbouring Arab states to come to their support. Egypt, Jordan, Syria and Iraq were the main participants on the Arab side, with Saudi Arabia and Yemen sending volunteers. In the ensuing war the Jewish state was able to expand the area of territory under its control, despite its population being numerically far outnumbered by those of the surrounding Arab states. The Arabs' humiliating failure to inflict defeat on Israel prompted much soul-searching and questions about what had gone wrong. A group of young Egyptian officers quickly came to the conclusion that the poor performance of their army resulted from it being ill-prepared and ill-equipped, and from high-level corruption. The Egyptian soldiers had found they were using "defective arms which had been purchased by the king's [King Farouk's] cronies, a collection of petty crooks who profited from the war by realizing huge commissions from arms deals."[8] The anger felt by officers (who later formed the Free Officers Movement) led eventually to the coup of 1952 that toppled the monarchy and later installed Gamal Abdel-Nasser as president. Initially, Nasser sought good relations with the West, but his socialist reform policies, which prompted an exodus of foreigners and foreign capital, his increasingly strident denunciations of Western imperialism and his tirades against Israel damaged Egypt's standing abroad as a destination for both business travellers and tourists from Europe and America. Relations between Egypt and the West cooled dramatically and Cairo airport suffered correspondingly from a drop in the volume of arrivals and departures. Beirut, by contrast, with its free market economy, its mountain scenery and attractive beaches, and its relaxed lifestyle appeared a far more attractive proposition. In 1952, the number of flights in and out of the Lebanese capital increased by 223 per cent on the previous year, rising again over the next two years by 10 per cent and 18 per cent respectively. A new airport was opened at Khaldeh, on the coast to the south of Beirut (the site of the capital's airport ever since), replacing the one at Bir Hassan, close to the Hippodrome. A survey of Lebanon and Syria by the Royal Institute of International Affairs in London, published in 1954, noted that the "new airport of Beirut (Khaldeh) receives the Comet [made by de Havilland in Britain, it was the world's first jet airliner], and is beginning to rival Cairo as a gateway to the East."[9]

The 1950s and 60s were golden decades for Lebanon, when it acquired the sobriquet that became a cliché: 'The Switzerland of the Middle East – a cosmopolitan playground attracting businessmen and pleasure seekers from around the world. A July 1957 edition of *Lebanon This Week/Le Liban Cette Semaine* gave details of performances of *The Merchant of Venice* and *Antony and Cleopatra* staged by the Old Vic Theatre Company at the Baalbek International Festival. Aside from a choice of bars and restaurants, the publication listed nightclubs ("Opening at 21hrs. Floor at Midnight"), including 'Kit-Kat', offering "Les Night and Day Follies et un programme d'attractions de 90 minutes", and 'Eve', hosting "Rafael de Cordova et sa Troupe; Les Conty Girls".

My father was briefly posted to the Beirut branch of BBME in the late 1950s. My mother and I joined him there, travelling from London in a DC-6B airliner of Pan American Airways, one of the last of the great piston-engined airliners that dominated civil aviation in the decade after World War Two. The plane stopped at Munich, Rome and Istanbul on the way. We arrived in Beirut late in the evening and I still remember what was for me the romantic and exciting sight of lights glowing on the other giant airliners on the tarmac as we came down the steps of the DC-6B and boarded a bus for the terminal.

During this time in Beirut, my parents had social events to attend most evenings. From the balcony of our house near the end of rue Bliss, next to the old lighthouse, I would await their return, watching the lights of aircraft descending over the sea from right to left towards Beirut airport. Many of the planes would have belonged to Beirut-based Middle East Airlines (MEA) – for that airline was closely associated with Lebanon's golden era and remains central to many of my own memories of childhood in the Middle East.

The Lebanese carrier had been the first to be established in the post-war wave of airline start-ups in the Middle East (it began operating in November 1945). The launch of MEA was followed shortly by that of Iraqi Airways and Arab Airways of Jordan. These and other carriers that came after were all supported either financially or technically by foreign companies or individuals, and ownership patterns changed frequently as the airlines became more self-sufficient. Most Arab airlines have had their ups and downs as they have weathered political unrest and even war. But nothing matches the experience of MEA, or rivals the way it became a victim of countless local and regional conflicts, forcing it to close for long periods and rebase temporarily abroad. Yet, against the odds, MEA has survived.

MEA was formed and registered in Beirut on 31 May 1945. Its president/general manager was Saeb Salam (a Sunni Muslim who later became prime minister of Lebanon) and its technical manager was another Sunni, Fawzi el-Hoss. An agreement was reached with BOAC under which the latter provided technical advice and staff training. The new airline then leased from Britain three de Havilland Rapides which carried the cedar tree emblem on their tails, as MEA aircraft still do today. (Incidentally, MEA is one of the few airlines in the world with a radio call-sign that relates to its emblem, rather than the more prosaic airline name alone. MEA pilots calling up air traffic controllers on the radio identify their aircraft with the prefix 'Cedarjet' followed by the flight number.) Shortly after the creation of MEA, another competitor airline was formed in Beirut: Compagnie Général de Transport (CGT – later called Air Liban). Najib Alamuddin, who later became chairman of

MEA, recalled in his memoirs that "in line with the true political tradition of Lebanon, where MEA was founded by Moslems, CGT was founded by Christians. MEA was associated with the British (BOAC); CGT was associated with the French (Air France)."[10]

The arrival of a competitor on the scene did not, however, disrupt MEA's expansion. The success of its inaugural Rapide services prompted the airline to seek bigger aircraft, in particular the ubiquitous American-built Douglas DC-3 Dakota. This led to a rupture in relations with BOAC and the signing of an agreement in 1949 with PAA, in which the latter acquired a 36 per cent share in MEA. But excitement at the arrival of the Dakotas was dampened by a suspicious incident at the airport. For no explicable reason, an aircraft operated by CGT swung off the runway and crashed into two of the Dakotas, causing one to be written off. Alamuddin wrote later: "Perhaps it *was* an accident, but such was the atmosphere of suspicion that many people in MEA were convinced their splendid new aircraft had been deliberately sabotaged by their competitors."[11]

As MEA's fleet grew and its route network expanded, Beirut's commercial success continued. By the mid-to-late 1950s, the capital's airport had secured its position as "one of the most important centres of air communications in the Middle East", the focal point of an "extensive network of air services operated by the airlines of the Arab states", and with an increasing number of long-haul international carriers serving it.[12] Beirut itself was applauded as a capital "as cosmopolitan as any in the world", with a "fine airport serving the needs of 34 airlines."[13]

In the 1950s, Arab aviation still had the potential to become a powerful and influential player in the worldwide industry – but only if governments coordinated both the purchase of equipment and the provision of services. Commercial aviation in the Arab world could have been a shining example of regional co-operation. In the end, it remained as fractured as the Arab region itself. Co-operation among airlines or between individual Arab states remained impossible as long as regimes were motivated more by narcissism and hollow expressions of national pride than by a desire to see benefits accrue to the region as a whole. The result, throughout the second half of the 20th century until today, has been a region wracked by political instability that has periodically spilled over into war.

Initially, efforts were made to persuade governments to work together in the best interests of regional aviation: as early as 1955 *Flight* was reporting on a proposal that might give "the Middle East a single Arab airline in place of 11 of the present operators." The idea was to merge Aden Airways[14], Air Jordan, Air Liban, Arab Airways, Gulf Aviation, Iraqi Airways, Kuwait Airways, Middle East Airlines, Misrair, Saudi Arabian Airlines and Syrian Airways. Such a combination, it was argued with good logic, "would cut out much wasteful competition and improve aircraft utilizatio". Alamuddin was a strong proponent of a pan-Arab airline, and he hoped that MEA's merger with Air Liban in 1963 might be a first step towards achieving one. This merger, incidentally, made Air France a shareholder in MEA, and with its arrival on the scene the Lebanese airline added French-built Sud Aviation Caravelle jets to its fleet.

In the event, the merger with Air Liban was a one-off. The quest for a joint regional Arab airline came to nothing. By the late 1950s and early 60s, many airlines – Arab and others – were serving the Middle East and, as Alamuddin recalled, "we needed to face the uncomfortable fact that too many aircraft seats were chasing a limited number of passengers. MEA was facing alarming competition from two sides. Government-owned European airlines were busy squandering their taxpayers' money by offering more and more flights in the region, while the airlines of the oil-rich Arab states ran their companies with prodigal disregard for cost." A body to regulate the global airline business had been formed in 1945, the International Air Transport Association (IATA); but Arab airlines did not join until a decade later – and even then they still failed to act cohesively. In the opening years of the 1960s, a number of Arab airline executives sought IATA's help to set up a regional body that could work closely with the international one. The formation of the Arab Air Carriers Organization (AACO) in 1964 was intended to "control the chaos of Arab airlines". A senior MEA manager, Salim Salam, was appointed AACO's secretary-general for the initial three-year formation period. But, as things turned out, Salam remained in his 'temporary' post for 22 years because the Arab airlines could not agree on which country should next host the organisation: "Many wanted that honour. Unable to agree, they settled on leaving it with Lebanon. Finally, in November 1986, Salim was relieved of his 'temporary' appointment and replaced by someone acceptable to all the Arab airlines – a stateless Palestinian ['Adli al-Dajani]."[15] Since then, top AACO jobs have been distributed among a number of countries.

While the formation of AACO admittedly represented a small step towards greater regional co-operation on aviation, MEA faced the far greater challenge of maintaining regular operations in the face of growing political instability in the Middle East. This was a time when the Cold War was at its height. In an effort to create a political barrier against the spread of communism in the region, Britain and the United States in 1955 organised an alliance of countries across the northern tier of the Middle East. Signatories to the Baghdad Pact, as it was called, were Britain, Turkey, Iraq, Iran and Pakistan. Britain also wanted Jordan to join. But President Nasser of Egypt, the popular champion of anti-Western sentiments among the Arabs, regarded the pact as a tool of British imperialism and put pressure on King Hussein to refrain. There was also strong popular opposition to the pact among Jordanians. Angry crowds, chanting anti-Western slogans, swarmed through the streets of Amman, smashing property associated with Britain, including the BBME. As the riots worsened I remember crowds tramping through the garden of our house and the sounds of explosions and gunfire. We remained trapped inside, terrified. In early January 1956, during a curfew, my mother and I were driven by a Jordanian military unit through the deserted streets strewn with stones and broken glass to the airport. A BOAC Argonaut flew us to safety.

These protests were followed less than a year later by the Suez crisis. President Nasser's nationalisation of the Anglo-French Suez Canal Company had created alarm and indignation in London and Paris, where it was seen as a direct threat to European interests. In response, the British and French governments hatched a secret plot with Israel under which the latter's forces would invade Egypt and advance towards the canal. Without informing the United States, Britain and France issued an ultimatum to both Israelis and Egyptians to withdraw from the canal zone. President Nasser obliged by rejecting the ultimatum, thus giving the two European powers the pretext they had been seeking to launch a joint attack. British and French troops were parachuted into Port Said, while the RAF attacked Egyptian Air Force bases, destroying large numbers of newly acquired Soviet fighter jets before they could take off. For the second time, the RAF had defeated an Arab air force that it had developed and trained.

The Suez campaign did not last long. Under pressure from Washington and Moscow, the foreign forces withdrew. Britain and France, the two countries that had plotted successfully to carve up the Middle East during the First World War, had on this occasion been humiliated.

As the Suez crisis was developing, my father was managing the BBME in Aleppo in northern Syria. I, along with the rest of my family, flew out from London to join him for the summer holidays. Our BOAC Argonaut stopped at Düsseldorf and Rome en route to Damascus. From there we drove through the night past numerous military checkpoints to Aleppo. But within a matter of days the anti-British feelings aroused by the political crisis in Egypt led to angry and violent demonstrations. My mother, my two brothers, my sister and I were whisked very early one morning to Aleppo airport where we boarded an MEA DC-3 Dakota and headed to Beirut. There a BOAC Lockheed Constellation, one of the most graceful airliners of the piston-engine age, flew us back to London. My father stayed for a while, eventually being forced to lock up the bank and flee Aleppo.

My family's untimely and hasty escapes from Amman and Aleppo within the space of a year were indicative of the changes taking place in the region. Britain's influence in the Middle East was in terminal decline. President Nasser's standing as champion of pan-Arab nationalism, by contrast, was stronger than ever, and his relations with the Soviet Union and with countries of the newly formed Non-Aligned Movement were growing warmer. Western governments considered that Egypt represented a grave danger to their interests in the region, both through Nasser's support for pan-Arab, anti-Western nationalism and his flirtation with the Soviet Union – either one of which might eventually threaten to disrupt oil supplies from the Gulf.

The controversy over the Baghdad Pact and the war over Suez had pushed Egypt onto the centre of the Middle East's political stage. But in commercial aviation terms these developments were a disaster: the volume of air traffic at Cairo airport dropped still further. Once again, Beirut benefited briefly from Cairo's woes. But Lebanon, too, was about to face a series of political and military challenges. The country played host to thousands of Palestinian refugees who had fled across the southern border after the creation of Israel in 1948. Their presence, when combined with the country's numerous sectarian divisions, made Lebanon politically volatile and unpredictable. Periods of prosperity were frequently disrupted by violent interludes. In May 1958, civil war broke out, with Muslim factions (backed by Syria) seeking to bring the country within the United Arab Republic (UAR) – the brief (1958-61) and unhappy union of Egypt and Syria. Lebanese President, Camille Chamoun, a staunchly pro-Western Christian leader, resisted the rebel demands for Lebanon to join the UAR. Then, two months later, the monarchy in Iraq was overthrown in a brutal coup – believed by the West to have been inspired by Egypt. Chamoun grew increasingly alarmed and appealed for American help, prompting the landing of US Marines close to Beirut airport. British troops, meanwhile, were flown into Jordan to be on hand to protect the monarchy there if the need arose. These various crises all ended quickly, but while they lasted they caused immense disruption to daily life and the running of normal air services. Alamuddin wrote in his memoirs that the turbulence in the Middle East between 1958 and 1960 "played the very devil with the running of MEA. Airports were frequently closed to traffic, services rerouted, aircraft grounded in troubled airports, passengers unable or afraid to go to airports, and employees prevented from going to work. Inevitably, it led to losses of revenue and increases in expenditure."[16]

Worse was to come for MEA. But for most of the 1960s Beirut continued to party, and MEA flourished. In those heady and carefree days everything seemed possible. In an interview in 1964, Alamuddin spoke confidently of his airline's plan to buy two Concorde supersonic airliners.[17] Of course the order never materialised, and in the light of Lebanon's subsequent fate, the unbridled optimism of the time seems tragic. The next crisis to confront MEA was not political but financial. Two years after he gave that interview, Alamuddin was struggling to save the airline from financial ruin. The Intra Bank, a major shareholder in MEA, collapsed and for two weeks the company was without cash or credit. Then, the Arab-Israeli war in June 1967 (described in Chapter 10) forced MEA temporarily to suspend operations for a further two weeks.

The Arabs' defeat in that war gave birth to the Palestinians' armed resistance movement under the umbrella of the Palestine Liberation Organisation (PLO). From this point on, Lebanon, with its large population of Palestinian refugees, became entangled inextricably in the Arab-Israeli crisis, and in particular in the growing tension between various Palestinian groups and the Israeli armed forces. The consequences for MEA were disastrous. A Palestinian attack on an airliner of the Israeli carrier, El Al, at Athens airport in December 1968 prompted a retaliatory raid on Beirut airport by helicopter-borne Israeli commandos. No fewer than 13 aircraft belonging to Lebanese airlines were destroyed on the ground. Eight were owned by MEA and included a brand new Boeing 707-320C – as a *Flight* report from Beirut a few days later described it: "the most expensive item in a most expensive inventory of destruction." The article said the Israeli raid had taken place when MEA had been looking forward to "a period of consolidation after the hard knocks it has taken lately, particularly the Intra Bank affair of 1966, a storm which few people expected MEA to survive."[18] That raid in 1968 established a pattern that has been followed ever since: Beirut airport and MEA aircraft are automatic targets for Israeli retaliatory raids.

Six months before the attack on the El Al plane in Athens, in the summer of 1968, a Boeing 707 was hijacked on a flight from Rome to Tel Aviv and diverted to Algiers. The hijackers, members of the Popular Front for the Liberation of Palestine (PFLP – a left-wing faction within the PLO) demanded the release of Arab prisoners in Israel. After 40 days of negotiations, the passengers and crew were released. The hijacking demonstrated that airliners constituted a "vulnerable point at which otherwise well-defended states – and world capitalism – could be attacked, with maximum impact on the media. As the world entered the era of international terrorism, airliners and airports found themselves in the front line."[19]

From 1968 onwards, civil aviation became a pawn in the violent politics of the Middle East, a grim association that reached its nadir in the terrorist attacks on New York and Washington in September 2001. The association began with hijackings, acts of terror that seem almost innocent in retrospect, when measured against the ruthless suicide bombings of later years. In 1969, a group of hijackers belonging to the PFLP took over a TWA flight from Rome to Athens and forced the pilots to land in Damascus. Everyone was allowed to leave unharmed and the aircraft was blown up. The hijacking received particularly wide coverage around the globe because a woman, Leila Khaled, was among the group that carried it out.

The PFLP continued its policy of hijacking airliners to draw attention to the Palestinian cause. The most dramatic event of this kind occurred in September 1970 when a TWA Boeing 707 with 155 people on board en route from New York to Frankfurt was hijacked over Belgium and forced to land at a disused desert airstrip in Jordan, about 50 miles from Amman. Dawson's Field, as it was called, had been built by the RAF in the 1940s and was named after Air Chief Marshal Sir Walter Dawson. A short time later, a Swissair DC-8, seized on a flight from Zurich to New York, was also on the ground at Dawson's Field. An attempt to hijack an El Al airliner over England on its way from Amsterdam to New York failed. A male hijacker was shot dead and his female companion overpowered. She turned out to be Leila Khaled, who was taken into custody in London. Meanwhile, a Pan Am Boeing 747 Jumbo, also on its way from Amsterdam to New York, was forced to fly to Cairo where, for reasons that were never explained, it was blown up after the passengers and crew had been freed, rather than flown to join the other hijacked planes in Jordan. At Dawson's Field, meanwhile, passengers remained at gunpoint on board the two airliners. Three days into the siege a BOAC Vickers VC-10 flying over the Gulf en route from Bombay to London was also made to land at Dawson's Field – in an attempt to force the release of Leila Khaled. After five days of frantic diplomatic contacts, all the 402 hostages were freed and the three aircraft destroyed – the picture of black smoke and debris at the moment when the VC-10 was blown up, after being marooned incongruously in the desert with the other two aircraft, remains an iconic image of that era.

The PFLP's choice of Jordanian soil for an exploit that shocked the world and blackened Jordan's name had infuriated King Hussein. The majority of the population in the kingdom were Palestinians, and the use of Jordan by PLO groups as a base for cross-border attacks on Israel and the planning of hijackings and other acts of violence was not only provoking Israeli retaliation, but was also starting to undermine the authority of the monarchy. The Dawson's Field affair, for King Hussein, was the last straw. He ordered the Jordanian army to launch an offensive against the Palestinian fighters – an intense, urban confrontation that began in September and continued over several months, despite frequent Arab efforts to mediate a truce. The PLO forces were eventually defeated and forced out of Jordan. The defeated Palestinian fighters regrouped with their light and medium weapons in Lebanon, which consequently became more enmeshed than ever in the regional turbulence.

From then on, tension between the Lebanese authorities and the Palestinians increased as the latter gradually expanded their influence in a country where both the government and the army were weak. Clashes between the Lebanese army and Palestinian fighters broke out in 1973, with Beirut airport coming under fire. MEA moved its operations base temporarily to Nicosia in Cyprus. That year, an MEA Caravelle, chartered to Iraqi Airways, was intercepted in Lebanese airspace by Israeli fighter jets and forced to land at an airbase in Israel. The Israelis justified their action by saying they had been informed that PFLP leader Dr George Habash had been on board, brushing aside – as they have always done on occasions such as this – the chorus of international condemnation. Also in 1973, Israeli fighters had shot at and damaged a Libyan airliner (with a French captain at the controls) that had strayed into Israel's airspace while lost during a sandstorm. During an emergency landing in Egypt all but five of the 113 people on board were killed. Once again, Israel shrugged off international criticism of its actions.

MEA's troubles began in earnest when hostilities erupted between armed Palestinian factions and right-wing Maronite Christian militias during 1975 – the opening year of the long, complex and destructive period of war that ended in 1990. The conflict is called for convenience the Lebanese Civil War. But several outside groups (Iran, Israel, Syria – and their international backers) had parts to play, directly or indirectly, at different stages. Except for during a few relatively brief periods of calm, Beirut airport and MEA were frequently in the firing line. The effect, Alamuddin said, was "crippling": throughout 1975 the airline "maintained its operations under virtually impossible conditions" as the country tore itself apart. Remarkably, despite staff being kidnapped and killed, the company continued to offer regular services. One employee fortunate enough to survive a kidnapping was Assad Khorchid, an MEA executive at the time. He was abducted from his car at a roundabout on his way to the airport by a group of Palestinian gunmen armed with Kalashnikovs. They took him to their base and questioned him before eventually letting him go. But despite the dangers, employees remained loyal – with up to 1,500 camping at the airport during the worst periods of violence. Beirut was divided in two by a confrontation line (Green Line), and the airport lay to the west of the divide, in territory controlled by Muslims. "During the war," Khorchid said, "it was very difficult and dangerous for Christians to get to the airport. So when they got there they used to remain for long periods." Yet, he added, "when we were at work the atmosphere was just perfect. Nobody asked what religion you were."[20] Throughout the years of conflict in Lebanon

MEA has been the sole institution to remain free of sectarian tension. As Alamuddin wrote later, Sunni and Shi'a Muslim, Druze and Christian employees, from various backgrounds and levels of society, were often cooped up together for months at a time in confined premises and living under constant stress. Under these difficult circumstances "the political phobia then so contagious in Lebanon" could have developed. But it did not happen. The employees decided to respect each other's opinions and "to keep Middle East Airlines outside politics. They lived together as a true Lebanese family."[21] It is difficult to pinpoint the reasons why this might have been the case. Perhaps the staff and crew of MEA felt the same sense of national pride – and responsibility – as the tragic Ottoman aviators who had crashed in Palestine in 1914. Or perhaps the sense of camaraderie and professionalism that binds so many pilots and aviation enthusiasts enabled them to transcend sectarian tensions and escape – for a while at least – to a simpler environment.

In any event, the MEA 'family' remained an anomaly. The fighting in Lebanon became more intense during 1976, leading to the closure of the airport in June. MEA had already shifted spares, including aircraft engines, to Orly airport in Paris. The shut-down of Beirut airport meant that the airline's base of operations would also have to move. MEA's preference was London, home and business/vacation destination for many thousands of Arabs and a good place from which to lease out aircraft. But when the company's management team arrived in the United Kingdom it was disappointed by the absence of help or encouragement from the British government or British Airways (as BOAC had become after merging with British European Airways – BEA – in 1974). So MEA decided to set up its base-in-exile at Orly. In an interview at the time, Alamuddin expressed bitterness not just at Britain and British Airways, but also at other airlines (not least Arab ones) that had failed to come forward at MEA's hour of need. "After 24 years in the airline business," he said, "I am saddened by the lack of understanding and co-operation in the airline fraternity." He also took issue with IATA's claim to be the airlines' club: "You can't have a club without the club spirit, which means that members should co-operate and help each other.

MEA has had no so such help. With the notable exception of Air France and Saudia, not one international airline has come forward with offers of assistance." Approaches for even moderate assistance had been "vigorously rejected", he complained, while the airlines concerned were doing good business by picking up MEA traffic.[22]

By now, any lingering dreams of a united Arab airline had faded once and for all. Arab airlines, as much as the governments that supported them, were in the game for what they could get for themselves. The trend reflected the mood in the region as a whole: the pan-Arab movement espoused by President Nasser had collapsed in dramatic fashion after the calamitous defeat by Israel in the 1967 war. The Lebanese civil war demonstrated how much further the region had fragmented into groups allied with the United States, with the Soviet Union, with Saudi Arabia, with Syria, with Israel, and so on. A pan-Arab force (the Arab Deterrent Force) sent by the Arab League to intervene in the fighting quickly disintegrated, providing a convenient cover for the Syrian army to entrench itself in Lebanon. Against the background of inter-Arab fighting and fluctuating allegiances to regional and international powers, there was no hope of Arab airlines bucking the trend by moving towards greater integration. If Lebanon had not been the region's battleground, then it is possible that Middle East Airlines, with its dedicated professional staff, might have managed to become just that: the airline of the Middle East. Instead, it needed all of its resources merely to survive the many challenges that it faced.

For long periods during the 1980s and 90s Beirut airport remained closed. Foreign news teams and others trying to reach Lebanon in those days travelled by boat from Larnaca in Cyprus to Jounieh, north of Beirut, with the vessel frequently stopped on the way by the Israeli navy, which would check the identities of all those on board. Once ashore, I remember seeing vast columns of smoke rising out of Beirut and, as often as not, the sound of Israeli jets bombing it. From Jounieh, it was a dangerous car journey into the city with the hope of finding a safe place to drive at full speed – to avoid sniper fire – across the confrontation line to reach the BBC office in West Beirut where I was based at the time.

The status of the airport during these times took on considerable importance. Its opening or closure tended to reflect the level of hostilities and had a noticeable effect on morale. When, after a prolonged closure, the first aircraft descended low over the roof-tops on its approach to the airport people would take to the streets and cheer.

The first plane to land would inevitably be one of MEA's – it was the flight crew who would find out before anyone else if conditions were really safe. MEA pilots operated under very difficult conditions, not just because they were flying in and out of a war zone, but also because they had to cope with Lebanon's collapsed infrastructure. For most of the 15 years of warfare, the main navigation aids at Beirut airport were unserviceable. But one aid, an old-technology non-directional radio beacon with the code 'BOD', worked miraculously throughout the conflict. It consisted of a single radio mast rising from the rocks off the Corniche opposite the campus of the American University of Beirut, almost due north of the main runway. BOD enabled pilots not only to track their course to the Lebanese shore but it also helped them to align their planes with the runway at times of poor visibility.

During the Israeli invasion of Lebanon in 1982, Beirut airport became once again the invaders' front line as the Western half of the city, where the Palestinian fighters were situated, came under siege. The airport was subject to further heavy destruction and looting during this period. The eventual departure of PLO fighters from Beirut, under international supervision, changed the balance of power yet again in Lebanon. The majority Shi'i community, traditionally sidelined when it came to the division of power in the country, saw a chance to assert the claims that their numerical strength entitled them to. Through the Amal movement and later through Iranian-backed Hizbollah, Shi'i political and military influence increased. I remember in June 1985 watching a Royal Jordanian airliner flying over Beirut in its descent towards the airport, a seat-belt flapping from the closed back door, indicating the hurried and chaotic circumstances surrounding its departure an hour or so earlier from the same airport. The aircraft had been seized by a group of five Lebanese Shi'i gunmen and forced to fly first to Larnaca and then to Palermo in Sicily. It returned to Beirut, but after negotiations to secure the release of the passengers failed it took off again – only to return once more. The passengers were eventually freed and the airliner was blown up. Thereafter, Royal Jordanian assigned two armed and plain-clothed security guards on all its flights. A few days later, a TWA airliner was hijacked by a group of Lebanese Shi'a, members of the Hizbollah organisation, en route from Cairo to London. It landed at Beirut where 19 passengers were freed before continuing to Algiers where a further 20 passengers were allowed to leave the aircraft. The hijackers then forced the plane to fly again to Beirut. While on the ground there, one of the passengers, a US Navy diver, was murdered. The aircraft subsequently made another flight to Algiers before returning finally to Beirut. After protracted negotiations, the remaining passengers and crew were at last released. During the course of the hijacking, a photograph was taken of the captain of the TWA plane, with a pistol to his head, being interviewed by a reporter on the tarmac below. As with the image of the Dawson's Field explosions, it remains an icon of its time – one when Beirut was a byword for anarchy and danger.

Visiting Beirut these days, looking at the apartment block that has replaced the house where my parents and I lived on rue Bliss, and looking from the outside at the flat where my own family lived off the Corniche before they had to flee Lebanon in 1983, I feel no strong feelings of nostalgia, sadness or regret. But Beirut airport, while almost unrecognisable from the way it was in the 1950s, still excites me, stirring memories of when it was a magnet for many of the great airlines of the world. I have no memory of my first departure from Beirut airport – as a child – in 1957. I travelled with my parents in a Vickers Viscount to Bahrain where my father had been posted. The journey itself was remarkable, however, because of the extreme turbulence that the plane encountered in the long flight eastwards over the Saudi desert. The thermals rising from the scorching summer sand made the plane shudder and sway, causing me accidently to pour a bottle of Coca Cola over the man sitting behind me who – it turned out – was one of the best customers of my father's bank, a senior member of the Kanoo family of Bahrain. The arrival was memorable, too – stepping out of the doorway of the aircraft at Muharraq and being hit by a wall of August heat and humidity, with the smell of oil from the Sitra refinery in the air. The civil airport doubled as an RAF base, RAF Muharraq, where I attended school, distracted frequently by the arrival of veteran York and Hermes aircraft, and later by the turboprop Bristol Britannia and the Comet 4 jet, both of BOAC. Amid the comings and goings of these larger planes I would look out for the smaller DC-3 Dakotas and de Havilland Herons and Doves of Gulf Aviation – the precursor of Gulf Air.

The Gulf had lain on the earliest pioneering air routes linking Europe with India, the Far East and Australia. But until the 1950s, there was no commercial company linking the small airfields of the region with Bahrain and Sharjah. A former RAF officer, an Irishman named Freddie Bosworth, took steps to fill that gap. He arrived in Bahrain in 1950 with a seven-seater twin-engined Anson, a slow, workmanlike aircraft. He had ambitions to start a charter operation to serve the oil companies operating in the Gulf. The writer Nevil Shute based a character in his 1951 novel *Round the Bend* on Bosworth. In the novel, the fictional Bosworth describes the circumstances that attracted men like him to the region: "The Persian Gulf is full of industry – new oilfields being laid out, wells being sunk, pipelines being laid, new docks and harbours being built all over the place. There are no roads outside the towns and no railways, and no coasting steamers and few motor boats. The country is full of engineers to whom time is money, and there are always people wanting to get about in a hurry. The country is mostly desert, good for landing a small aeroplane when you have learned the different look of hard and soft sand from the air, and I was right up to the neck in work from the day I got there. Most of the oil companies had their own aircraft, but there was plenty of work left over for me."[23] A leading Bahraini businessman, Hussein Yateem, put up the money for Bosworth to set up his operation, which was initially licensed by the Bahraini government merely to offer joyrides. The success of these convinced Yateem and Bosworth that the potential was even bigger. Yateem put together a business group (including members of the Kanoo family) that established Gulf Aviation, providing scheduled services to Dhahran and Sharjah, as well as charter flights. To meet the expanding demand, Bosworth travelled to Britain to buy an eight-seater de Havilland Dove. But he was killed in a crash while getting his accreditation to fly the plane.[24] After Bosworth's death, BOAC bought a controlling stake in Gulf Aviation, which initially operated several Ansons, a Dove and a de Havilland DH86 twin-engined biplane, linking Bahrain with Dhahran, Doha and Sharjah. The biplane and the Ansons were gradually replaced by three more Doves. In May 1952, BOAC advertised for Dove pilots, offering them a tax-free salary of £1,335, plus "generous allowances for local cost of living and separation from family. Quarters equipped with heavy furniture, free for single and separated men, but subject to nominal charge to married men with families. (Due to accommodation shortage married men must be prepared to accept an initial period of separation.) Home leave with free passages at the rate of eight weeks for each year's service in Bahrain."[25] But despite Bosworth and Yateem's initial optimism, making the new airline a paying concern was not easy. BOAC, in its annual report of September 1952 said that in its first six months of owning Gulf Aviation the latter lost £11,138; the sum of £14,737 was written off as goodwill and accumulated losses prior to the corporation's purchase of shares.[26]

As the 1950s progressed, Gulf Aviation acquired DC-3 Dakotas and four-engined de Havilland Herons (an expanded version of the Dove), broadening its network to include Kuwait, Dubai and Abu Dhabi. In 1959, the airline appointed Alan Bodger chief executive with a mandate to modernise operations and make the company profitable. The new appointee faced many difficult challenges. When Bodger joined Gulf Aviation its fleet of small piston-engined airliners served only local routes in the Gulf. Bodger's obituary in *The Times* in 1995 recalled how, at that time, "in-flight drinks on Gulf Aviation flights consisted of a flask of iced water which, in the blistering heat of the Gulf, was generally at blood heat before the aircraft even took off. Once airborne, passengers were able to savour this uninviting fluid from paper cups... No cabin staff were employed at that stage, neither were aircraft equipped with a toilet until a senior director of Gulf Aviation was caught short between Sharjah and Bahrain. The next board meeting cured this problem, instructing management to install toilets in the Herons regardless of the fact that one fifteenth of income would be lost (a matter of serious concern in those days)."[27]

My father at the time, as BBME manager in Bahrain, also had responsibility for branches in Qatar and the Trucial States. So my parents were frequently required to endure the hardships of travel on Gulf Aviation's Dakotas and Herons that took them initially to Doha, Dubai and Sharjah. Dubai airport consisted of a single small arrivals and departure building in the desert. From Dubai, my parents would travel overland by a four-wheel-drive vehicle along a desert track to Abu Dhabi that consisted only of the ruler's fort and a few outlying buildings. As my father negotiated the opening of the first bank in the emirate, the Abu Dhabi emergency landing ground was still in the state it had been during World War Two, described by the RAF as being "not maintained" and to be used "in extreme emergency only". Gradually the sand was flattened sufficiently for Dakotas and Herons to land there, with passengers stepping down onto the desert, in much the same way as those arriving on the HP42s had done at Sharjah in the 1930s and 40s.

Bodger oversaw the conversion of Gulf Aviation from a small regional airline operating out of desert airstrips into one serving the wider Middle East and Europe. Viscounts were chartered from MEA and Kuwait Airways, turboprop Fokker F-27 Friendships replaced the Dakotas, and BAC-111s were bought from Britain for longer routes. Eventually, in 1970, Gulf Aviation inaugurated its service to London with a Vickers VC-10 jet chartered from BOAC.

Two years before this inaugural flight, the British government had announced that it would withdraw its remaining political and military presence from the Gulf by the end of 1971. This prompted the seven emirates of the Trucial States (Abu Dhabi, Dubai, Sharjah, Ras al-Khaimah, Ajman, Umm al-Quwain and Fujairah) to form the United Arab Emirates (UAE). At around the same time, Bahrain and Qatar became fully independent of Britain. The first steps towards the creation of a regional airline were taken in 1973 when Abu Dhabi, Bahrain, Oman and Qatar bought BOAC's shares in Gulf Aviation. (Significantly, Dubai declined to do the same.) The following year, Gulf Aviation changed its name to Gulf Air. At last, it seemed, the template had been created for an Arab regional airline. Gulf Air expanded rapidly, with the purchase of new long- and short-haul aircraft and the inauguration of services as far afield as Australia and South Africa. The creation of the Gulf Cooperation Council (GCC – Bahrain, Kuwait, Oman, Qatar, Saudi Arabia and the UAE) in the early 1980s seemed to open the possibility of Kuwait Airways and Saudi Arabian Airlines coming under the Gulf Air umbrella. With Beirut incapacitated by the civil war, Bahrain was set to become the new aviation hub for the Middle East. But the political and economic integration that the GCC appeared to offer failed to materialise: while the Gulf did become the undisputed centre for commercial aviation in the Middle East it happened in a way that could not have been predicted when the GCC was created, with individual rather than joint projects. Dubai, which continued to remain aloof from Gulf Air, in 1985 created Emirates Airline. This move was gradually to change the face of aviation in the Gulf, and the subsequent upheaval saw the demise of Gulf Air as a regional carrier and the emergence of Dubai as the new regional civil aviation hub for the Middle East, taking over the role that had earlier been played by Cairo and Beirut.

ten

Aerial Defeat

Buildings in Lebanon during the periods of war and upheaval since the 1970s have frequently been shaken by exploding bombs or the firing of mortar shells and artillery rounds. But even at times of peace, windows are often rattled by what sound like loud explosions close by. In fact they are sonic booms many thousands of feet above the earth, caused by Israeli jets breaking the sound barrier high in the sky over Lebanon. The motive for these flights might be, in part, the need to maintain aerial reconnaissance. But more important is the psychological factor: Israel wants to demonstrate that it has absolute air superiority. While Israeli military commanders are less likely to risk such brazen infringements of national sovereignty in the airspace of Arab states like Egypt and Syria, which have effective air defences, it is keen to impress upon the region as a whole that it has mastery of the skies. For despite the Arabs' exposure to aviation from the earliest pioneering days and the region's close association with the development and modernisation of flight, Israel's aerial superiority has rarely been challenged.

The Arabs' best chance was their first one. Before Israel came into existence on 14 May 1948 the Jewish community in Palestine had no air force to speak of. The underground Zionist paramilitary organisation, Haganah, had an air wing, but its fleet of aircraft consisted only of single-engined Taylorcraft and Auster light aircraft that were on the Palestine civil register, intended for initial pilot training or recreational use. Before the British mandate expired, these two- and three-seater planes were used clandestinely for supply dropping, reconnaissance and, eventually, ground-attack sorties, with the pilots operating hand-held machine-guns and dropping small bombs.[1]

Egypt, by contrast, had more than 30 ex-RAF Hurricanes and Spitfires, and 20 C-47 Dakotas that had been converted into makeshift bombers. On 15 May 1948, as Egyptian ground forces invaded Israel from the south, the Royal Egyptian Air Force mounted the first offensive action of the war when two Spitfires attacked Tel Aviv and the nearby Sde Dov airfield. One of the aircraft was shot down and the pilot taken prisoner. Ex-RAF Westland Lysander liaison aircraft based at al-Arish flew support missions for the Egyptian army and C-47s carried out bombing attacks deep inside Israel. With Jordanian, Iraqi, and Syrian troops also joining the war against Israel, it was within Egypt's power to make its air superiority felt. But it did not. Why, for example, were only two Spitfires despatched to attack Tel Aviv? Why did the air force not mount round-the-clock attacks on Israeli military positions? These have to remain rhetorical questions. Yet two elements that contributed to Egypt's failure are beyond question. The first was poor planning. For example, on 22 May, Egyptian Spitfires attacked Ramat David airfield, apparently unaware that it was still occupied by the RAF. Two RAF Spitfires and a Dakota were set on fire. In a subsequent attack on the same airbase by five Egyptian Spitfires, three were shot down during aerial combat with RAF aircraft – a complete waste of Egypt's resources. The second element was Egypt's gross underestimation of Israel's resourcefulness at a time of crisis. Three weeks before the declaration of independence, Jewish leaders had signed a contract with Czechoslovakia for the purchase of 10 Avia S-199 fighters – a derivative of the World War Two German Messerschmitt. In agreeing to the order, Czechoslovakia was ignoring a UN embargo on military sales to the Middle East. Jewish pilots who had flown with the Allies during World War Two (Ezer Weizman, later a president of Israel, was among them) underwent a conversion course in Czechoslovakia, and transport aircraft bought in the United States flew the dismantled S-199 fighters to Israel between 20 and 26 May. The initial plan was to use the fighters to attack al-Arish airbase. But with only 20 miles separating the advancing Egyptian army and Tel Aviv, the mission target was changed. Four S-199s attacked an Egyptian army column near Ashdod on 29 May. An Israeli air warfare historian believes that while the attack caused little damage (and resulted in the loss of one aircraft) "the element of surprise should not be dismissed – up until that time, the Egyptians had been completely unaware that Israel had acquired fighter aircraft. The IDF [Israeli Defence Forces] counteroffensive against the Egyptian column ultimately failed, but its cumulative effect deterred the Egyptians from any additional advance northwards towards Tel Aviv."[2]

Israel sought aircraft of any type, wherever it could find them – sometimes by "extreme methods of cannibalisation". For example, several Spitfires and de Havilland Mosquito fighter-bombers were built up from components salvaged from the aircraft dumps that remained at the former RAF bases. A military flying school, staffed primarily by American instructors, was set up at an airfield in Italy, close to Rome. As the weeks passed, Israel acquired many more aircraft, including 300 Mosquitoes – from France, Britain and elsewhere – "mostly as scrap, many being cannibalised to provide spares for those that could be made airworthy."[3]

Another factor in Israel's favour was the aerial combat experience that those pilots who had flown with the Allies in World War Two could draw on. While Egypt could muster good and experienced pilots, some of whom had flown support missions for the Allies until Egypt declared itself neutral, none had flown in combat before. Israelis, through wartime connections with Europe, were also able to recruit many non-Jewish personnel. In addition to the fighters, Israel acquired a few Boeing B-17G Flying Fortress bombers (four-engined aircraft of the type that had been based in Britain and attacked German targets during the war) and various American transport aircraft. Several of the latter were converted into rudimentary bombers by the addition of external bomb racks, and joined the Flying Fortresses "in making nuisance raids at night on some of the Arab capitals, principally Cairo. Although the damage created by these night raids was limited, they played a major part in reducing the morale of the enemy."[4] In the meantime, aircraft began to shuttle arms and equipment acquired in the United States and Europe, via Czechoslovakia, to airfields in Israel.

Egypt did not succeed in circumventing the UN embargo on military sales and its air force began to suffer from a shortage of spare parts. Within months, the clear advantage that it enjoyed in the air at the beginning of the war with Israel had evaporated. Just as Iraq's leadership in 1941 had missed the opportunity to launch pre-emptive air strikes on RAF Habbaniya, so Egyptian commanders failed to exploit their country's air superiority quickly and decisively enough. By the end of the hostilities, Israel had complete ascendency in the air over all its Arab neighbours.

One reason for Egypt's apparently half-hearted use of its air force at the start of the conflict could have been King Farouk's reluctance to order his forces to become involved. In the event, he sent the Egyptian military into Israel only because his main political opponents, the Muslim Brotherhood, had joined the fight, and if the Egyptian government had not committed itself to the Palestinian cause then the Brotherhood would have consolidated their popular appeal. There was also an element of inter-Arab rivalry. Farouk was conscious that "his old adversaries, the Hashemite kings of Transjordan and Iraq, could strengthen their position in the Arab world if they intervened and he did not."[5]

Rivalry of this kind and poor coordination account in large measure for the failure of four Arab armies to defeat the forces of the small Jewish state. Their apparently determined action "masked their fatal disunity. It was a unanimous decision of the Arab League to intervene in Palestine, but the unity was no more than a façade. There was no effective liaison between the Arab armies and they did not act in concert. Their military capacity did not reflect the overwhelming Arab superiority in numbers, with 40 million Arabs confronting some 600,000 Zionist Jews."[6] Mutual Egyptian-Iraqi hostility meant also that the region's most powerful and experienced air forces (both created in the 1930s) acted independently and ineffectively, a failure their common enemy was quick to exploit – with disastrous results for the Arabs.

The Arabs' unsuccessful war with Israel (which left the new state with more territory than it had been allocated under a UN partition plan) ended in January 1949. Arabs in general and Egyptians in particular felt humiliated, betrayed by their political and military leaders. Aside from the loss of self-esteem, the majority of Egyptians were also facing increasing economic difficulties, while they watched corrupt officials become richer. Given the prevailing mood of simmering hostility towards the creation of Israel on Arab land and resentment at the role that Britain had played in the process, the continued presence of British forces, including the RAF, in the Suez Canal Zone suddenly became totally unacceptable. As a way of seeking popular support, the government in October 1951 abrogated the 1936 Treaty with Britain – a move that the British immediately rejected. The Egyptian authorities next ordered a state of emergency, and the cutting of fresh food supplies to the British garrison in the Canal Zone. After Egyptians working in British garrisons had been withdrawn, the bases themselves became the targets of violence perpetrated by government-supported squads. In January 1951, anti-British riots broke out at Ismailiya. The British army, its 80,000 troops pinned down in the Canal Zone by guerrilla and sabotage attacks, decided to pursue a group of suspects who had taken refuge in the town's police station. The police refused to hand them over. The British set an ultimatum for the suspects to surrender. It was rejected, and the British responded with force. In the ensuing battle, around 50 Egyptian policemen were killed and many were injured. The following day, serious rioting broke out in Cairo, with the crowds attacking British targets and those associated with Western affluence. During Black Saturday, as it became known, the offices of BOAC and Shepheard's Hotel, where so many of the airline's passengers had spent the night en route to the Far East or Africa, were among the many buildings destroyed by fire.

Given the anti-British mood at this period, it is surprising that the Cairo government still turned to Britain as it sought to rebuild its air force – acquiring jet fighters (Gloster Meteors and de Havilland Vampires) for the first time. But in the aftermath of Black Saturday it seemed inevitable that Egypt's course would have to change. In the face of such widespread and powerful street anger the government and the king appeared weak and helpless. Farouk had become, in the one historian's assessment, "a cartoon satire of middle-aged debauchery... Although intelligent and quick-witted, he lacked *gravitas*; his character was as light as his body was heavy."[7]

The 1952 military coup, which forced the king to abdicate and later saw the monarchy abolished, presaged a change in the composition and character of Egypt's air force. After lengthy negotiations with the regime of President Gamal Abdel-Nasser, Britain agreed in October 1954 to the progressive withdrawal of the RAF from the 14 bases in the Canal Zone. Early the following year the Egyptian Air Force (with 'Royal' removed) took over the defence of the canal with its newly acquired Vampires. But the balance of power in the Middle East was about to change still further. In 1955, a three-year trade agreement was signed between Egypt and Czechoslovakia involving the supply of Soviet military equipment. At this time, Egypt's air force consisted of around 120 (mostly British-built) aircraft of various kinds. Through the Czech deal the Cairo government ordered no fewer than 86 Russian Mig-15 fighters and conversion trainers, 39 Ilyushin Il-28 light attack bombers, 20 Il-14 transports and 25 Yak-11 trainers. The first Mig-15s arrived by sea at the end of 1955, along with Russian and Czech technicians, who were to assemble and organise maintenance and flight training programmes for the Egyptians.[8]

Egypt, yet again, appeared to have an opportunity to capitalise on its long experience in aviation to develop a powerful and highly professional air force with the latest equipment from the Soviet bloc. But even as the Migs were being unloaded at Alexandria port, the Suez crisis was developing. After Nasser failed to secure Western financing for a project to build a new dam on the Nile at Aswan he decided to nationalise the Anglo-French Suez Canal Company. The revenue from the canal, he told a cheering crowd in Alexandria in July 1956, would finance the dam project. The British Prime

Minister, Sir Anthony Eden, was enraged by what he regarded as this impudent action and began what became an obsessive personal campaign to bring down Nasser at any cost. His obsession led to the secret Anglo-French-Israeli plot to lure Egypt into war and justify British and French military intervention in the Canal Zone. By the time of Israel's attack on the Sinai in October 1956 the Egyptian Air Force had received its full complement of Mig-15s and a small number of Mig-17s. However, few Egyptian pilots were yet trained to fly the Russian fighters and the air force did not respond to the initial Israeli attack. On 31 October, British and French planes attacked Egyptian airbases with the aim of knocking out the whole force within 48 hours. They were largely successful, for "despite camouflage and dispersal, the bulk of Egypt's newly acquired combat aircraft was destroyed without taking to the air. Under cover of darkness, 20 of the Il-28 bombers were flown to Riyadh in Saudi Arabia, a few Mig-15UTIs escaped to Hama in Syria, and the 10 Il-14 transports that had already been delivered were also flown out. All were piloted by Czech and other East European personnel, and had it not been for these aircrews, the machines would undoubtedly have shared the fate of some 250 assorted aircraft which fell victims to the Allied attacks."[9]

This disastrous outcome for Egypt suited all three parties to the Suez plot – but Israel in particular. The most populous, powerful and influential Arab country (and therefore the biggest threat to the Jewish state) had, in terms of air power, been emasculated. But the sense of jubilation in Arab countries that Britain and France had been humiliated shifted the focus away from military setbacks and on to what it was hoped would be a new era of regional coordination, free from outside colonial interference. The Egyptian aircraft that had survived the Anglo-French onslaught returned to their bases, and another large consignment of Russian jets arrived at Alexandria port. By April 1957, 50 Mig-17s had been supplied, and the arrival of 50 more, plus a batch of Il-28s, prompted the Commander-in-Chief of the Egyptian Air Force, Air Marshal Muhammad Sidqi Mahmoud to boast on 23 July 1957, the fifth anniversary of the coup, that in the nine months since Suez the air force had doubled in size.[10] New Russian training aircraft were also delivered to replace those destroyed during the Suez fighting, while Egyptian pilots were sent to Eastern Bloc states for training. Soviet, Czech and East German instructors were engaged at Egypt's air academy at Bilbeis on the edge of the southern Nile Delta.

Just as the 1952 bloodless coup in Egypt had opened the door to Soviet and Eastern European military equipment, so the distinctly bloody 1958 coup that overthrew the monarchy in Iraq swung that country away from its dependence on Britain and British aircraft. Although it still operated 50 Hawker Hunter jets from Britain, the mainstay of the Iraqi offensive arm consisted of various models of Mig fighters. Migs had also become the mainstay of the Syrian Air Force, although its first batch was destroyed in 1956 during the Israeli attacks on Egypt, where they and their Syrian pilots had been sent for a conversion and training course. The courses were then continued, with Russian instructors, at Syrian airbases. Soviet-made planes were operated by a number of other air forces in the Middle East, including those of North and South Yemen. Jordan, Iran and Israel were the main three states to stick exclusively to Western-built aircraft.

As the Arab countries built up their air forces, Nasser continued to raise popular hopes that the defeat of Israel and pan-Arab unity were achievable goals – even after the collapse of the United Arab Republic. As the 1960s progressed, Nasser's rhetoric became more bellicose, and popular expectations rose accordingly. The subsequent humiliation of the June 1967 Arab-Israeli war was all the greater because the Arab people had been led by Nasser to believe that the conflict would end unquestionably in triumph. The outbreak of war came against the background of rising tension between Israel on one side and Egypt and Syria (bound by a defence pact) on the other. On 13 May 1967, the Soviet Union confirmed Egyptian and Syrian intelligence reports that Israel was preparing for an imminent attack on Syria. Three days later, Nasser requested the withdrawal of a United Nations deterrent force which had been stationed along the Egyptian-Israeli border in Sinai since 1956. Once the UN had left, a large force of Egyptian troops entered Sinai. The danger of all-out war was growing fast; and the Arab people, hanging on every word spoken by Nasser, were still confident of victory. In a speech to senior air force officers on 25 May, the Egyptian leader announced a move that made armed confrontation inevitable: he declared the Strait of Tiran (the entrance to the Gulf of Aqaba), closed to Israeli shipping. He spoke of Egypt's rights and sovereignty over the Gulf "which constitutes Egyptian territorial waters. Under no circumstances will we allow the Israeli flag to pass through the Gulf of Aqaba." With rhetorical flourish he continued: "The Jews threaten war. We tell them you are welcome, we are ready for war."

On 30 May, Jordan signed a defence pact with Egypt. War broke out on 5 June. It was effectively all over in just a few hours. Vice-President Anwar Sadat, who subsequently succeeded Nasser, said he first heard that the conflict had started when he switched on his radio in the morning. The official Cairo news report said that 27 Israeli jets had been shot down by Egyptian fighters. Sadat went at once to army headquarters. There he found the commander of the armed force, Field Marshal Abel-Hakim Amer, standing behind his desk in tears. He remained silent for a full minute after Sadat's request to know what was happening. So Sadat asked others in the room. With one voice they said: "The Israelis have destroyed our entire air force."

Sadat said the shock of what had happened was all the more devastating because just a few days earlier Nasser had been assured by his senior commanders that they expected the Israelis' first strike to be against the air force and had made plans accordingly. In the event, the first wave of Israeli jets arrived over Egypt when Amer was flying back to Cairo from a meeting with his commanders in Sinai. Instructions had been given to anti-aircraft batteries not to open fire while the commander-in-chief's plane was still in the air. The Israelis had struck at 8.30am, the time when pilots had breakfast after the daily inspection shift. Even though the country was on the brink of war their routine had not been changed. Amer's plane turned back when those on board realised what was happening and the field marshal witnessed for himself the destruction of the country's airbases. The element of surprise was total. Within the first hour, the bases at Abu Sueir, al-Arish, Kabrit, Cairo West, Beni Sueif, Fayid, Bir Tamada, Bir Jifjafah, Inshas, Gebel Libni and Ras Umsid were paralysed because their runways had been cratered. A further five airfields (including those at Luxor and Hurghada) were later put out of action. The Israeli Air Force then targeted the aircraft as they sat trapped on the ground, destroying 309 of the 340-plane fleet. Later in the day, Israeli jets struck airbases in Syria, Iraq and Jordan – which lost 21 Hawker Hunters. By the end of the second day, 427 Arab aircraft had been destroyed, 333 of them on the ground.

The destruction of Egypt's air force was, in large part, a product of leadership incompetence. According to the memoirs of an aide to President Nasser, Sami Sharaf, the government had received numerous tip-offs about a planned Israeli attack, from embassies abroad and other sources, three days before it happened. Yet somehow this information was never passed on to senior military commanders. When Amer flew to the Sinai front to review his forces on the day when the devastating air strikes occurred, his senior officers seemed unaware that anything unusual was about to happen. According to Sharaf, when Amer reached his destination in Sinai, officers and troops left their positions and operation rooms to accord him an official welcome. Just a few hours later, the Egyptian armed forces had lost all hope of air cover, and the war was, to all intents, over.[11]

Not surprisingly, the morale of Egyptian Air Force pilots and other personnel was shattered by the humiliating destruction of so many of their aircraft on the ground. Air Force Commander Muhammad Sidqi Mahmoud, and the commander of the Eastern Air Zone, Air Vice-Marshal Ismail Labib were both given long prison sentences, having been found guilty of "dereliction of duty which obstructs victory".[12]

Not only did the 1967 war wipe out the Egyptian air force for the second time in just over a decade, but it also changed the face of the Middle East, with Israel occupying the West Bank (including East Jerusalem), the Gaza Strip, the Sinai Peninsula and the Golan Heights. Arab governments have shown little more in the way of planning and coordination than they had during the 1948 war. The

Arabs' catastrophic defeat also deflated the bubble of optimism that had surrounded the dream of regional unity. At a practical level, Arab air forces had been pushed and pulled in different directions by the whims of their political leaders. Governments fostered alliances with outside powers, then switched them, each change signalling a new source of military equipment, including planes, and new training courses. The continuity needed to develop effective air forces by senior personnel drawing on experience and passing on skills was missing.

Egypt's defeat took a heavy toll on Nasser's physical and mental health. On the day the war ended, the president had announced to his people in a speech on state television that he was resigning. But within minutes, millions of people took to the streets, in Egypt and other Arab countries, urging him to change his mind. In the face of this overwhelming public pressure, he remained in office. In April 1969 Nasser launched a 'War of Attrition' against Israel. This took the form of land and air attacks against the Bar Lev Line, the line of Israeli defensive positions on the eastern bank of the Suez Canal, and further into the Sinai Desert. Nasser hoped that the War of Attrition would eventually force Israel to make territorial concessions. Israeli planes and helicopters retaliated against Egypt, hitting military and civilian infrastructure targets, including bridges over the Nile and electricity generating plants in Upper Egypt. Soviet advisers told Egyptian commanders how and when to respond – a source of growing resentment within the military. From time to time, Israeli and Egyptian aircraft engaged in aerial combat, with the result that by the time a ceasefire had been signed in August 1970, Egypt's air force "had acquired valuable experience: it had carefully analysed Israeli operational methods and tactics that had been demonstrated and was evolving countermeasures, and it had gained some of the confidence that would be necessary if it was to avenge the humiliating defeat that had been inflicted on it three years earlier."[13]

Within weeks of the War of Attrition ending, Nasser died of a heart attack. Under Sadat, air force training was modified and intensified, and the Russian advisers were increasingly ignored.

While vast quantities of Soviet equipment were imported into Egypt, relations between Cairo and Moscow began to come under strain. The differences came to a head in July 1972. Without warning, the Egyptian president ordered the estimated 15,000-20,000 Russian military advisers out of the country within a week and decreed that the equipment they left behind would become Egyptian property. From that moment on, Egypt looked to European countries and the United States for military aircraft.

Israel, too, was looking to America as it sought to expand and modernise its air force. During the first two decades of its existence, Israel had depended largely on French-built fighter jets and other aircraft. President Lyndon Johnson had promised in 1968 to supply Israel with McDonnell Douglas F-4 Phantoms, and the first batch arrived the following year, in time to take part in the War of Attrition. The arrival of American military equipment, Sadat's break in relations with the Soviet Union and Israel's mood of self-confidence after the 1967 victory led Israeli leaders to the conclusion in 1973 that their country was invulnerable to Arab attack.

It was not; and for once, it was Israel that was caught napping. Sadat knew that Egypt had no hope of reaching military parity with Israel in the near future. Nor was Israel likely to make territorial concessions in the absence of pressure from the Soviet Union or the United States. So he calculated that a carefully prepared war would attract the international attention needed to achieve Middle East peace. Sadat realised that Egypt had to contend with "Israeli air, technological and tactical superiority. This had to be matched by exploiting Israeli weakness in manpower, and fighting a two-front war with Syrian assistance... Surprise was to be the essential element. On 31 January 1973 the armed forces of Syria and Egypt were put under a unified command." King Feisal of Saudi Arabia and President Houari Boumediene of Algeria were informed of the developing war plans.[14] During August that year, senior Egyptian and Syrian officers met to work out the details of the military campaign.

When Egypt and Syria went to war with Israel, on 6 October 1973, they enjoyed spectacular early successes. It was Yom Kippur, the most sacred day in the Jewish calendar when Israelis *en masse* stay at home. It was also the Islamic month of Ramadan when Muslims fast during the day. War was the last thing on the minds of the Israelis. The Egyptians achieved that day what most people (including the Israelis) thought would be impossible. They crossed the Suez Canal and penetrated the Bar Lev Line. The Egyptian Air Force (commanded since 1972 by Hosni Mubarak) targeted those Israeli installations in the Sinai Desert which could have provided support and reinforcements for the Bar Lev Line, including a string of former Egyptian airfields, missile batteries, artillery emplacements and command posts. The Egyptians claimed to have destroyed 90 per cent of the assigned targets within 20 minutes of launching the strike. A force of 220 Egyptian aircraft, including assault helicopters carrying commandos, took part in the assault. Within 24 hours, Egypt had despatched 90,000 men and 850 tanks across the Suez Canal. At the same time, the Syrian Air Force had taken to the skies in support of three divisions and an armoured brigade that broke through Israel's defences on the Golan Heights.

After its stunning offensive in the early hours of the war the Egyptian Air Force was called on to defend its own airbases from Israeli counter-attacks from the air – which the Egyptians did with considerable success. Not one airbase was put out of action nor was a single plane destroyed on the ground. After sustaining considerable losses in attacks on airfields the Israelis switched their attention to targets around the Suez Canal.

Israel had been dealt a severe blow; but its recovery was swift, helped by a massive airlift of sophisticated arms from the United States. In the days that followed, the Syrian advance was reversed, and the Israeli army inflicted heavy losses on the Egyptian army during fierce battles in Sinai. Eventually, an Israeli force established a bridgehead on the western bank of the Suez Canal and "Egypt's Third Army was surrounded and cut off in Sinai... Israel had snatched a stunning military victory from initial defeat."[15] But without such substantial air-lifted American support for Israel the course of the war and perhaps even its outcome would have been very different.

When a UN-sponsored ceasefire came into effect on 24 October, both sides had suffered heavily. While the outcome of the war was another defeat, Arabs have always described it as a victory. The initial successes enjoyed by Egypt and Syria are still celebrated in Arab countries, while the later setbacks are largely overlooked. The euphoria generated in particular by the crossing of the Suez Canal and the delivery of a body blow to Israel was massive because the two actions served to bury some of the humiliation suffered in 1967. In the words of Sadat: "The wounded nation restored its honour."[16]

The important part played by Egyptian Air Force pilots tends to be overlooked when the 1973 war is discussed. For once they had an opportunity to show their prowess. In contrast to previous clashes with Israel, military commanders had made meticulous plans in advance, and there was close collaboration between the two Arab states involved ahead of the conflict. As one aviation historian wrote nearly a decade later, "the Egyptian Air Force had every reason to be proud of its showing during the October 1973 war. It fully regained its pride and confidence, and completely refuted the widespread belief that, with the departure of its Soviet mentors, the Egyptian Air Force would collapse as an effective force."[17]

As the 1970s continued, Soviet involvement in Egypt's air force became a distant memory, with the United States and France taking over as the major suppliers of equipment. In 1979, Egypt had 61 French Mirage 5 supersonic attack aircraft in service and was awaiting delivery of 34 American-built F-4 Phantoms.[18] Eleven years later, the number of Mirage jets had risen to around 100, and F-16s were operating alongside the F-4s. But none of these and subsequent generations of aircraft has been in action against Israeli jets, for in November 1977 Sadat became the first Arab leader to visit Israel, setting in motion a process that led two years later to the Camp David Accords. While the peace agreement between Egypt and Israel has not resulted in anything like a warm relationship between the two countries it has, at least, put an end to years of conflict.

Arab critics of Camp David – and there are millions of them – argue that the withdrawal of the most powerful and influential Arab state from the front line against Israel has given the Jewish state a freer hand to take action elsewhere. In particular, they say, Israel would not have dared launch its 1982 invasion of Lebanon, designed to crush the PLO, unless it had been certain that its southern flank would not be attacked. Once again, Israeli control of the air was a determining factor. In the opening days of that war I drove from Damascus to Syria's border with Lebanon. Halted at a military checkpoint, I watched a brief aerial encounter between Israeli and Syrian jets in the sky over Lebanon. The outcome was unclear – aircraft from both sides eventually dispersed. I later learned that this had been Syria's final engagement in the air war: after losing 29 of its aircraft, Damascus decided to withdraw from the conflict, leaving Israel's air force challenged only by ineffectual anti-aircraft fire from the ground. Israel made the most of its aerial mastery, carrying out extensive bombing sorties throughout southern Lebanon in support of its army, eventually forcing PLO fighters to take refuge in the western half of Beirut, where the BBC office was located. There, under siege by land, sea and air we heard aircraft screaming overhead, targeting buildings where Israel believed that senior PLO commanders were hiding or where arms and ammunition were stored. The Palestinian leaders kept on the move, never spending two nights in the same building. So while the Fakhani district in the south of the city where PLO offices were to be found bore the brunt of the bombing, we never knew what other buildings elsewhere might be hit. Within seconds, high-rise blocks of flats in residential districts were flattened. Those terrifying bombardments, by night and day, were precursors of later attacks on Lebanon and on the Gaza Strip. Some years later I met an Israeli Air Force pilot who talked about the raids on Beirut in 1982 and said he could not believed that anyone had survived. He was flustered to hear that I had been one of the civilians sheltering from the air attacks. For a brief moment the comfort that wartime pilots enjoy of remaining both anonymous to and distant from possible victims had been shattered.

The Israeli Air Force has been able to use its jets and helicopters – as well as missiles – in campaigns against Hizbollah in southern Lebanon, and against Palestinian fighters in the West Bank and, still more, in the Gaza Strip. The territories in question do not have significant air defences. Nor are Arab air forces coordinated sufficiently to risk coming to the defence of the Lebanese or Palestinians. With Syria keen to avoid direct confrontation with Israel, and Egypt no longer a military player, Israel has the freedom of the skies. Only the acquisition of more sophisticated surface-to-air missiles by Hizbollah would present a challenge to Israeli pilots.

If, for differing reasons, the air forces of Egypt and Syria are constrained by issues relating to Israel's military might, the same cannot be said for the Iraqi Air Force, the oldest in the Middle East. The constraints it has faced since 1980 relate to questionable decisions taken first by President Saddam Hussein and secondly by President George W Bush. In 1980, relations between Iraq and Iran deteriorated, leading Saddam Hussein to abrogate a joint agreement on the shared status of the Shatt al-Arab waterway leading into the northern Gulf. The Iraqi leader saw what he thought was an opportunity to seize control of the waterway and territory to the east of it, while at the same time stopping the spread of the Iranian revolution that had toppled the shah the previous year. With political turmoil continuing in Iran, his assumption was that a quick and decisive victory could be achieved. His opening shot was not unlike that of Israel in 1967: he ordered his air force to launch pre-emptive attacks on airbases throughout Iran, with the aim of disabling its air power on the ground. At the same time, the Iraqi army launched a ground offensive. Iraqi pilots carried out their mission, but not with the success that Iraqi commanders had counted on. Only a few Iranian planes were knocked out and the damage to runways and airbase facilities was not sufficient to prevent Iranian fighters taking off. The Iranian Air Force under the shah had been equipped with Phantoms and other American jets and these were soon in the skies over Iraq. So began the long slog of the First Gulf War, an eight-year conflict that resulted in the deaths of around half a million Iraqis and Iranians. In the opening months, the Iranian Air Force was superior in both the number of operational aircraft and in the level of pilots' skills. But as the war progressed, Iraq acquired new Russian and French planes, while Iran was prevented by sanctions from acquiring spares for its fleets of American jets. By the time the conflict ended, in August 1988, the Iranian Air Force had relatively few operational aircraft left.

Iraq's military pilots saw action again in August 1990 when Saddam Hussein, in a moment of grand folly, ordered his forces to invade Kuwait. Helicopters ferried Iraqi commandos across the border, while Russian and French fighters attacked military and civilian airports. The Kuwaiti Air Force was no match for the Iraqis. But the subsequent American-led war to remove the Iraqis from Kuwait and the 2003 American-led invasion, triggered for spurious reasons by George W Bush, destroyed whatever was left of the Iraqi Air Force. Once again, skilled Arab pilots and support teams – in this case descendants of the first pioneering air wing in the region – were let down by crass leadership, and one of the few air forces of substance there was annihilated.

So, Israel remains the dominant air power, in a position to watch and, if true to past form, take unilateral military action should another country in the region appear to be able to challenge it. On paper, Saudi Arabia might be the one Middle Eastern country to start coming close to matching Israel in amassing new aircraft. In 2010, in a $60 billion deal, the United States agreed to supply the kingdom with 84 new Boeing F-15 fighters and to upgrade 70 existing ones. Saudi Arabia would also receive 106 helicopters. Yet despite attempts to develop an air force in the 1930s, when air wings were formed in Iraq and Egypt, the kingdom did not start to build a modern force until the mid-1960s when it perceived a threat to its oil interests from Egypt (through Yemen). Despite huge government-to-government deals between Saudi Arabia and the United Kingdom, and an extensive training programme, the Saudi Air Force is not rated as one of the best in the region. Furthermore, the purpose of its expansion is more to defend than attack – with Iran (or possibly Iraq) the most likely sources of potential danger. Challenging Israel's air superiority over Lebanon or any other Arab country is not on Saudi Arabia's agenda. Meanwhile, the dream of a pan-Arab air force – one that might come close to matching Israeli air power – remains as elusive as ever. The creation of such a force would require collective political will – something that so far has been absent, as the bickering and boycotts at summit meetings called by the Arab League testify. Article 5 of the league's charter states: "The recourse to force for the settlement of disputes between two or more member States shall not be allowed." Nevertheless, the prospect of inter-Arab conflicts remains a source of instability in the region. The final outcome of popular uprisings and regime changes across the region that began in 2011 will not be known for some time. But there are likely to be as many diversities of interest in the new Middle East as in the old one. So there seems precious little chance – no matter how much the next generation of Arab leaders may desire it – that the accumulated fleets of war planes, costing billions of dollars, will be organized in such a way even to challenge Israel's air superiority.

eleven

Opportunities Missed

A century after the 1910 week of flying at Heliopolis in Egypt, Arab aviation finally became a giant player on the world stage – but not the way that might have been imagined in earlier decades. Throughout the 100 years of flying in the Middle East there have been three successive centres of aviation: Cairo, Beirut and the Gulf. By 1990, when the 15-year-long war in Lebanon ended, the aviation scene had changed, and Beirut found that its role had been largely superseded. Bigger and faster airliners had been developed that could fly from northern Europe to the Far East without needing a refuelling stop in the Eastern Mediterranean. The Gulf was a more logical choice for a stopover, since the oil boom had turned this corner of the region into the business and trading centre of the Middle East. Beirut, while gradually regaining its role as an attractive destination in itself in the post-civil-war years, was no longer a natural stop on intercontinental routes. Dubai, on the other hand, was becoming exactly that.

The expectation in the last two decades of the 20th century was that Gulf Air, owned by Abu Dhabi, Bahrain, Oman and Qatar, would develop from a strong regional airline into a major world-class carrier. What happened was almost the complete opposite: three world-class airlines emerged from the Gulf, as the regional carrier fragmented. The first step towards the Gulf becoming a global aviation hub was the creation of Emirates airline in Dubai in the mid-1980s. Dubai had never become a partner in Gulf Air, reflecting the independent-mindedness of the ruling Maktoum family who had developed the emirate over centuries into a thriving centre of commerce decades before the discovery of oil. Sensing that Bahrain-focused Gulf Air was not giving Dubai the service it deserved, the ruling family backed the creation of its own airline. The effects were soon felt: Gulf Air found itself challenged on its own turf and in services further afield. Aided by slick marketing, Dubai airport started to grow into a major centre, attracting business away from Bahrain, the other magnet for air transport in the Gulf (Sharjah had long been surpassed as a Gulf stopover). Dubai also offered, for the first time in the region, mass tourism.

Three of the Gulf Air partners, meanwhile, growing richer by the day through rising oil and gas prices, clearly felt that they could emulate Emirates' success. Between the end of 2002 and mid-2007, Qatar, Abu Dhabi and Oman successively withdrew from Gulf Air, leaving Bahrain as the sole owner (at a time, ironically, when the Gulf Cooperation Council was working harder than ever to integrate the currencies and economies of its member states). The Qatari authorities concentrated their efforts on turning Qatar Airways into a world giant, while, with more modest revenue from hydrocarbon sales, Oman Air developed in a less flamboyant way. With Emirates and Qatar Airways expanding fast and carrying huge numbers of passengers each year, it seemed that the Gulf could not sustain another major carrier. But it did. Etihad Airways was established in 2003 by an emiri decree which pointedly designated the new airline as "the flag carrier of the United Arab Emirates" – sending a clear message to Emirates, 93 miles away up the road in Dubai, that it could no longer upstage the richest and most powerful emirate in the confederation, and the seat of the UAE's capital. Given its name and the large red, green and black stripes of the UAE flag on its tail, Emirates had given the impression of being the country's state airline.

So, with three giants (Emirates, Etihad and Qatar Airways), a handful of medium-sized airlines (Gulf Air, Oman Air, Saudi

Airlines, Kuwait Airways) and a string of low-budget airlines (including Air Arabia, Dubai Air, Bahrain Air, Jazeera Airways), the Gulf became a powerhouse of Arab aviation. During the economic recession of the early years of the 21st century, these carriers did much to keep the major European and US aircraft manufacturers in business. Increasingly at international aerospace trade shows, such as that in Farnborough in southern England, civilian and military aircraft makers display wares specifically designed and developed to tempt the Gulf customers, offering everything from the very top-of-the-range long-haul luxury models to the most basic utilitarian aircraft for short-haul budget travel. During the 2010 Farnborough Air Show, *Flight International* observed that "the Middle East – its big three Arabian Gulf carriers in attendance – retains its huge appetite for the West's aerospace products: civil and military."[1] On this appetite depended the success or failure of, for example, the Airbus A380, the double-decker super-jumbo. In mid-2010, Emirates took the aviation world by surprise when it announced an order for an extra 32 A380s, which would eventually bring its total up to 80. This "staggering" new order meant that, in one move, the A380 – sales of which had been stuttering for two years – had been "given a huge boost to its credibility and towards its supposed break-even of 300 units. Emirates, already the biggest A380 customer by some margin, will dominate the type's fleet..."[2]

This appetite for the West's products can be satisfied because the Gulf countries in question, major exporters of oil and natural gas, have the necessary financial resources. But after a century's exposure to flying, when aviation has played a defining part in shaping the Middle East it is strange – disappointing, one might say – that Arab countries as a whole have not been more active in establishing a 'home-grown' culture of aviation by designing and manufacturing aircraft of their own.

As far back as the Heliopolis aviation week, less than a decade after the Wright brothers' first flight, some Arab analysts were already concerned at the way the region was lagging behind the West in embracing science and technology. "This week," a commentator in the Cairo newspaper *al-Mu'ayyad* wrote in 1910, "Egyptians are hastening to Heliopolis to observe this Western discovery, which has surpassed all Oriental work with respect to the difference between the striving of Easterners and Westerners in their activities and life. The Orientals have been indolent. They have slept and have become submissive, while the Westerners have gone to the opposite condition to the extent that they are starting to take control of the sky... Europe and America have the most abundant share of science and the scientific method and have left us behind so that we can hardly distinguish between them in their accomplishments... In the Week of Aviation, the position of the Oriental before these Europeans who are passing through the strata of the sky is a melancholy one, because it is the position of the ignorant before the learned, the position of the weak next to the strong, the position of the defenceless in the hands of those bristling with arms."[3] The essence of that Egyptian columnist's argument was that the modern world was leaving the Arabs behind. Nearly a century later, in 2003, a report written by a group of Arab social scientists, commissioned by the United Nations Development Programme (UNDP), concluded: "Successive waves of change bypassed an inward-looking Arab scientific and technological establishment, leaving it isolated from the dynamic global mainstream."[4] The gist of these two statements, nearly 100 years apart, is identical. In the 21st century, the Arab world is still lagging far behind the West – explaining in part why the Arabs' early opportunities to be among the innovators in aviation were not taken.

The three Gulf airline giants were forced to turn to Europeans and Americans for their aerospace needs because Arab countries have not developed their own industries. The Middle East never experienced an industrial revolution, so in order to enter an industrial age it would need to rapidly acquire skills and knowledge – which in turn would require a revolution in the way society was ordered. In short, far-reaching and fundamental political and social reforms – not least in the education system – would have to be introduced to allow people to ingest the ideas and intellectual process needed to acquire knowledge from the modern world. For several hundred years before the 19th and 20th centuries, Arabs had

had minimal contact with Western ideas or the fruits of Western science and technology. Bringing about the changes that would be required to acquire these presented problems. An influential group of Arab intellectuals grappled with the problem of how a society steeped in the traditions of Islam should introduce religious and political reforms. Many of these intellectuals were disciples of Jamal al-Din al-Afghani, whose thoughts acted as a catalyst for movements seeking change in the opening decades of the 20th century – the earliest pioneering era of flight. Afghani (who came from Iran, not Afghanistan as his name suggests) believed that Muslim society should return to the fundamentals of Islam and, by doing so, should stand up to the encroachments of the West in the Middle East. He started a debate that has continued ever since. Should Arabs return totally to Islam and turn their backs on the West? Should they compromise, adhering to the principles of religion, but making necessary adjustments to accommodate the modern world? Or should they seek a purely secular way forward, leaving the door open to Western ideas and influence?

The need to grapple with such questions slowed, at the very least, the reform process. In some areas, such as public education, while the curriculum was changed to incorporate the teaching of science, modern history and so on, the methods of instruction remained untouched. Learning was still largely by rote; questioning, analysis and debate were proscribed. This did not provide a productive learning environment for young Arabs who might aspire to be scientists – or pilots or aircraft designers. While it is true that under colonial rule, encouraging the development of education was not a high priority, once Arab states achieved independence they had opportunities to provide their young people with the means to acquire the knowledge and skills that would have enabled them to compete with their peers in the West. To receive the necessary education, Arabs who could afford the fees sent their sons and daughters to study overseas. In many instances, those who graduated never returned, while those who did go back to their home countries could not find institutions of a sufficient standard to work where they could pass on their skills to others.

In the same way, there were attempts to acquire manufacturing and other skills from the West with a view to implanting them in the Middle East. This worked to an extent – but not to the degree that was originally envisaged. Too often the technology was imported but not the skills. The UNDP report quoted above noted that "with few exceptions, the experience of individual Arab countries in technology transfer, management and adaptation has not met initial expectations, although technology transfer has always been a top national priority. Arab countries recognised, at an early stage, that their socio-economic development required moving towards industrial and export-based economies. This perception, in principle, was correct, yet it was not translated into effective policies. Industrialisation policies, in particular, centred merely on the acquisition of factories and production technology (purchase contracts), and on the training of local labour to produce goods acquired in factories using acquired means of production."[5]

Egypt's attempts to set up an aerospace industry illustrate the failings outlined above. At the beginning of the 1950s, the country had practically no manufacturing industry, and very limited resources of skilled manpower. Nevertheless, the Military Factories Directorate in 1951 set up a State Aircraft Factory at Heliopolis. Assisted by Czech technicians, the factory produced a series of two-seater basic training aircraft based on the German Bücker Bü181D Bestmann, an aircraft designed just before the Second World War. The Egyptian-made model was called a 'Gomhouria' (Arabic for 'republic'). Around 300 were delivered to the air forces of Egypt, Jordan, Saudi Arabia and Sudan.[6] The plane was by no means a state-of-the-art product, but its successful manufacture in Heliopolis represented a promising start to an industry that, it seemed, might develop into a significant aircraft supplier for the region.

In 1960, President Nasser's government embarked on a project that was far more ambitious than that of the Gomhouria: the aim was to produce an all-Egyptian-made supersonic jet fighter. But to gain experience it was decided to start by adopting a foreign design to make a simple jet trainer. The Egyptians opted for a Spanish aircraft, the La Hispano-Aviacion HA-200 Saeta, which had been designed by a German team led by Willy Messerschmitt, the creator of the famous World War Two German fighter aircraft. These trainers were built under licence in Helwan south of Cairo and given the name 'al-Qahira' (Cairo). The first off the production line was displayed before Nasser and the Egyptian leadership at the Revolution Day parade in Cairo in July 1962.

All the while, Messerschmitt was supervising the design of a supersonic jet fighter in Spain, the HA-300. During the design process the Spanish government decided that the project was too expensive, and Egypt agreed to take it over. Design and development equipment, including tooling, was transferred *en masse* to Helwan – along with a team of Spanish and other European engineers and technicians. The initial idea was that the HA-300 would be powered by a British-built engine. But Egypt wanted the plane to have one that had been made locally, so approached Ferdinand Brandner, an Austrian who had held a senior position in the engines division of the German aircraft firm Junkers during World War Two. He recruited a team of Austrians, Germans and Swiss to work on the new engine in Helwan. The work was slow and costly, with Brandner complaining later that the project became bogged down by bureaucracy and the fact that "the whole concept of inspection and quality control was foreign to the Egyptians, so that particularly detailed directives were essential." In the early 1960s, India responded to a request from Egypt and sent pilots and a maintenance crew to Helwan, and an Indian pilot was at the controls when the HA-300, powered by a British engine, made its first flight in March 1964. The following year India supplied an aircraft on which the new Brandner-designed engine could be tested. The Indian personnel also trained two Egyptian test pilots. The trials of the HA-300 and its engine were interrupted by the June 1967 Arab-Israeli war, when both test pilots were transferred to operational duties during the build-up to the conflict. Miraculously, when the mass Israeli air strikes ended it was discovered that the production facilities were undamaged. Nevertheless, the frustrations felt by the team of Europeans and Indians involved in the project at the volume of paperwork demanded by the government caused relations between the two sides to become increasingly strained. The Indian government subsequently recalled its personnel, causing yet another interruption to trials, and on 25 May 1969, Egyptian Minister for Military Factories Aziz Sidky decreed that the German-led team was not to enter the factory after 1 June – just six weeks before the first HA-300 powered by the new Egyptian-made engine was to make its maiden flight. The Egyptian authorities, it seemed, felt that tackling the challenges of developing the country's own aircraft manufacturing industry – and dealing with the demands of the foreign managers – was not worth the effort involved. Overnight, the nine-year project that had cost £52 million was dropped. Brandner recalled with evident bitterness that the Egyptian Air Force, equipped with Russian aircraft, was "no longer interested" in a national project.[7] The two completed HA-300s were put into storage.

Brandner and his team were in Egypt at a time of widespread nationalisation, when the imposition of socialist-style state control was increasing the level of bureaucracy in industry as a whole. The Austrian complained that while the factory was well organised along European lines and had excellent equipment, progress on the aircraft and engine projects was impaired by an unnecessarily huge and inefficient administrative department. Then there was the problem that "few Egyptians have been educated to take responsibility, and even the simplest decision is automatically passed to the next man up in the hierarchy until it reaches the top. Social legislation also made it virtually impossible ever to sack an employee for any reason... A further handicap to efficient operation was the fact that all pay was based on time-rates only, thus offering no incentive to quality work. We arrived in Egypt full of enthusiasm for our task, completely free of prejudices and confident that we should one day be able to leave behind us a well-trained and efficient development crew. That we failed in this, to our great disappointment, is due to Arab socialism in its present form and to the country's political dependence."[8]

Brandner's account presents a bleak picture. The difficulties he identified were to prove even more damaging for the development of Egyptian aviation than the much more dramatic and high profile blow dealt by the Israelis in 1967. Despite the experience of developing the Gomhouria, the al-Qahira and the HA-300, Egyptians had failed to acquire the skills necessary to indigenise technology. They had merely transplanted factories and production technology, and learned how to reproduce the goods. Whether the vital step towards indigenisation of technological skill would have been taken if the HA-300 had gone into production one will never know. But even if production had gone ahead, without the creation of an indigenous skilled workforce, new foreign licences and new production lines would inevitably have been needed before long. For such factories can meet, to quote the UNDP report again, "all or some of the local market's needs for a period of time. But these simple acquisition policies, which did not recognise the importance of managing and adapting these technologies, left the production sector highly vulnerable since the technology it depended on became obsolete over a short period of time."[9]

The optimism surrounding the production of the Gomhouria in the 1950s arose, in part, from the prospect of the country becoming both a successful manufacturer and a regional supplier. Nasser, in a Revolution Day speech in the early 1960s, predicted that Egypt's aircraft industry would produce a sufficient number of planes not only for Egypt but also for the entire Arab world. This, of course, would have been the perfect outcome. However, given the fragile state of the industry at the time, that particular Revolution Day declaration must rate among the most extravagantly over-optimistic of any Nasser made. A more realistic prospect would have been the formalisation of regional support for – if not participation in – Egypt's aircraft industry. This was an idea that finally took shape just over a decade later, in 1975. Egypt, Qatar, Saudi Arabia and the UAE formed the Arab Organisation for Industrialisation (AOI). This Cairo-based institution, with capital of more than $1 billion, was intended to marry Egypt's industrial skills with oil revenue from the three Gulf states – oil prices having soared in the wake of the 1973 Arab-Israeli war. If successful, AOI would have had a huge impact on the region, reducing its overwhelming dependence on foreign aircraft and arms producers. AOI had the potential to change the political landscape. Instead, politics killed it off before it had achieved anything. President Sadat's visit to Israel and the subsequent Camp David peace agreements resulted in Egypt being expelled from the Arab League in 1979. Saudi Arabia announced that it and the other two Gulf partners were withdrawing from AOI, adding that "the signing of a peace treaty between Egypt and Israel clashes with the purpose of establishing the company."[10] Although Egypt was readmitted to the Arab League in 1989, the Gulf partners never returned to AOI, and it has remained an Egyptian company ever since.

The AOI was not the only body that might have fostered an Arab aviation industry to be killed off by regional politics. In 1976, plans were drawn up for the creation of an Arab Fund for Science and Technology, one of its aims being to "encourage the appropriate transfer of scientific and technological knowledge from abroad and set the terms and conditions upon which such transfer will be based." Ample funds were available in Gulf states in the late 1970s and a prevailing belief at that time "in the importance of joint Arab action". But despite the declared commitment of these countries to contribute to the Fund's capital, "political differences over the management of the Fund's operations and its headquarters prevented its establishment at that time." As the region's development prospects began to change at the beginning of the 1980s, and with diminishing financial resources accruing from oil exports and "the fatigue that afflicted joint Arab action", enthusiasm for the Fund diminished and the project was abandoned.[11]

The obstacles in the way of joint Arab action are, at first sight, not easy for foreigners to understand. Arabs, from Morocco in the west to Oman in the east, share a common language, culture, religion and history. Arabs have always dreamt of unity, but have never come close to achieving it – or even significant regional co-operation. It is true that Britain and France promised the Arabs independence in the lands that would be liberated from Ottoman control in the First World War. Instead, they connived to establish nation states under European patronage. But one by one these states gained their independence. Unity was still a possibility. A leading and influential proponent of Arab nationalism in the decades after the First World

War, Sati' al-Husri, insisted that "the Arab nation consists of all who speak Arabic as their mother tongue, no more, no less." Writing in the 1950s, he said that the Arabs "rose up against the English, we revolted against the French... We revolted against those who requisitioned our land and tried to drive us out." Arabs suffered in this process and many were killed or tortured. Despite all this, "when we freed ourselves from the yoke of the foreigners we began to sanctify the borders which they had established in our lands after they had broken the links between us."[12] In short, the regimes that took power when the colonial rulers left were more interested in protecting their own interests than in working for the good of the region. Staying in power at all cost became the chief occupation of Arab leaders, and this meant suppressing any potential opposition, from inside or outside the country's borders. Regional rivalry replaced the dream of regional co-operation. Dictatorship replaced the vision of democracy. Dictators, by definition, do not want to share power or make political compromises that might diminish their own authority, so they are never likely to view with favour the concept of shared power and responsibility. Lebanese historian Kamal Salibi, in an interview in 2010, said "democracy opens the door to unity or co-operation, or something akin to this. But when you have people or states hating each other, competing in a negative way, it's a bad state of affairs. The merger of undemocratic regimes would be a fabrication and a bad move."[13]

The 1950s and 60s, when Egypt's aircraft industry appeared to have a future, was the period when Arab unity still seemed attainable. Nasser, more than any other Arab head of state, encouraged Arabs to believe this. Yet when he was talked reluctantly into uniting Egypt with Syria – his only attempt to put his theory into practice – the resulting United Arab Republic was a short-lived failure. There were no further ventures of this kind, and it is unlikely that any would have been successful. For not only was Nasser considered a dictator, he was also the embodiment of revolutionary Egypt, a giant personality who would never have accepted sharing power and responsibility. A near contemporary of Nasser's, who served as an officer in the Syrian army, concluded in his memoirs that this was precisely why Nasser failed. "Unity was the aim of every Arab," Muhammad Ma'arouf wrote, "and along came Abdel-Nasser to crown this dream. No other Arab leader enjoyed the love and admiration of the Arab masses as Nasser did... With the co-operation of his loyal supporters he had the potential to become the hoped for leader of the whole Arab world." But Nasser knew little about conditions in other Arab countries, and his focus remained on Egypt: "As far as he was concerned history began with the [1952] revolution in Egypt. Nasser monopolised the leadership and opinion forming, not allowing anyone to share in his decision-making, and removing his colleagues one by one."[14]

So the conditions in the middle of the last century were not ripe either for the indigenisation of aircraft design and construction skills, or for regional co-operation to develop a joint Arab aerospace firm. While Egypt has since built other planes under licence and Abu Dhabi in the opening decades of the 21st century was expanding its aerospace industry centred on al-Ain (initially manufacturing aircraft parts – for Airbus airliners and other models), Arab countries continue to lack the structure necessary either to create their own aircraft or work jointly to achieve that goal. The net result is that many young Arabs with the abilities and ambitions to work in an advanced aerospace industry look for jobs in Europe, the United State, Russia and elsewhere. According to a UNDP report, "arguably, emigration of highly qualified Arabs to the West has been one of the most serious factors undermining knowledge acquisition in Arab countries. It is no exaggeration to characterise this outflow as a haemorrhage. The trend is large-scale and is steadily accelerating." It is estimated that by the year 1976, 23 per cent of Arab engineers, 50 per cent of Arab doctors and 15 per cent of Arab BSc holders had emigrated.[15] The subsequent failures of AOI and the Arab Fund for Science and Technology will have done nothing to stem the outflow of talent.

In their defence, Arabs point to the decades in the 20th century lived under colonial rule, when the education systems were under foreign supervision and when their own focus on achieving independence was all-consuming, to explain why they have lagged behind the West in scientific and technological fields. They also cite the creation of Israel as another major distraction, with the issue of how to face up to its existence sapping energy and resources that might otherwise have been channelled into more fruitful enterprises. In the view of the Arab authors of the UNDP report, "the occupation of Palestine constitutes a severe impediment to human development. This occupation distorts policy priorities, retards human development and freezes opportunities for growth, prosperity and freedom across the region, and not in the Occupied Palestinian Territories alone. The harsh indignities arising from occupation extend to all the Arab people... The threat of Israeli domination also creates a pretext for deferring political and economic reforms in Arab countries in the name of national solidarity against a formidably armed external aggressor."16 Arabs point out, too, that Israel enjoys the unquestioning support of the United States and access to American technology to keep it on its feet and superior in arms and technology to its neighbours.

Even so, from the middle of the 20th century onwards, Israel for its part and independent Arab countries for theirs had an opportunity – from a standing start – to develop aerospace industries. Israel could call on Jews with experience acquired outside Israel. The Arabs, with their roots in aviation going back to 1910, could call on Europeans for assistance. The results show that it was Israel, rather than one Arab country or a group of them that was able to acquire and fashion the necessary aerospace industry skills. In 1976, with Egypt's HA-300 scrapped before ever going into service, *Flight International* reported that Israel was "unique in the Middle East in having itself designed, developed, manufactured and successfully used in action both aircraft and missiles."17 In April the previous year, Israel's Kfir fighter, an extensively redesigned version of a French Mirage, made its first flight. *Air International* described the new plane as a "mélange of French aerodynamic design and US technology stirred with a good measure of Jewish *chochem* or astuteness."18

Arabs needed and lacked similar astuteness. They knew well from as far back as the First World War, when fragile British biplanes monitored the progress of the Ottoman army towards the poorly defended Suez Canal, how important mastery of the air could be. As they saw the nascent Jewish state rapidly developing and expanding its aerial capability there could, surely, have been no greater incentive for Arab governments to make the foundation of a modern and efficient aerospace industry a priority and to work collectively in doing this. But, with or without such an incentive, conditions in the region contrived to rule out this possibility. In the post-independence era, the new states were proud to decorate their stamps with images of aircraft of their nascent national airlines. But all through this period of history, when the roots of an indigenous aerospace industry could have been established, the Middle East was beset by intra-regional tension: a revolution in Egypt – in 1952; a series of coups in Syria (a military aircraft had the dubious distinction of dropping leaflets over Damascus to announce the first of them in March 1949[19]); mutual hostility between Saudi Arabia on the one side and the Hashemite regimes in Iraq and Jordan on the other; a desire on the part of Jordan, Iraq and Lebanon to create a fertile crescent alliance against Syria and Egypt; the divisiveness of the Baghdad Pact; the bloody military coup that toppled the monarchy in Iraq in 1958; the brief civil war in Lebanon the same year; and so on. The list of intra-Arab antagonisms is startling. The atmosphere in the region was not certainly conducive to the allocation of money and the expending of effort on scientific and technological research and development – or indeed even on reforming the education system to produce students who would be qualified to undertake such work.

Blame for these failures must be laid at the feet of Arab leaders. Not only were they bent on staying in power at all costs, but they were also, more often than not, corrupt. Money that might have been allocated to improve the education system or for scientific or technological research and development found its way into the pockets of the ruling clique. Armies and air forces were also victims of these failings. Arab troops and pilots were often sent into battle with inadequate, poorly maintained equipment. On top of this, they were given orders by commanders who were frequently shown to be incompetent. The Royal Iraqi Air Force, defeated by the RAF during the Rashid Ali coup in 1941, might have put up a creditable performance if it had been ordered into action in time. Israel's ultimate victory in the 1948 war would not have been assured if Egypt's air force had been used to the full in the opening hours. When Israel invaded Sinai in 1956, Egyptian pilots were never even ordered to take off. Then, in the biggest fiasco of all, the Egyptian Air Force was wiped out on the ground in 1967, even though war was expected and Israeli attacks on airbases in the first wave of the conflict had been predicted. In later years, two disastrous decisions by Saddam Hussein resulted in Iraq's air force being wiped out yet again. All such setbacks contributed to the malaise affecting the Arab people and the deep cynicism felt towards those in power in the second half of the 20th century. Conversely, had those abject failures been even partial successes, then the morale and self-esteem of the Arab people would have received a boost. Arab aviation – civil and military – had an opportunity to shape the region's history, to be an instrument for change and a source of Arab pride. Instead, in the hands of egocentric and often ruthless leaders, flying became a victim of the region's politics.

Perhaps all this will change. The popular revolutions that began in 2011 swept aside in a matter of weeks President Ben Ali of Tunisia and President Mubarak of Egypt, ruthless dictators who between them had been in power for decades. The talk from Morocco in the west to the Gulf states in the east was of Arabs, at long last, starting to regain their pride. But before the new, revolutionary Middle East was more than a few months old, Arabs faced an uncomfortable reminder of the century of wasted opportunity. In response to a popular uprising that began in Benghazi in eastern Libya in February 2011, Colonel Muammar Qadhafi ordered his air force, as well as ground forces, into action against his own people. Within weeks, the Arab League had met in Cairo and backed the imposition of a no-fly zone over Libya. The UN Security Council endorsed the decision. But despite the many decades of flying experience and the many billions of dollar spent on buying military aircraft from abroad, the Arabs looked to European and north American air forces to impose the measure – with just token support from some Gulf states. The Arabs' latest failure to act revealed the degree to which governments, largely through political differences, had squandered the experience gained by their pilots since the 1930s. It was another moment of humiliation, just when Arab self-esteem appeared to be recovering. "Where are the Arabs in the confrontation between Muammar Qadhafi and his people?" asked an Arab commentator, Jihad el-Khazen. "They have disappeared, as if the matter does not concern them. France and Britain seem more concerned with the tragedy of the Libyan people at the hand of Qadhafi and his sons than the Arab states that could act, if they wished." The Egyptians and the Saudis, Khazen added, had received huge military assistance from the United States for many years. Co-operation and coordination between them should have been possible.[20]

Yet again in 2011, as was consistently the case over the previous century, co-operation and coordination between Arab states were not possible. Nor had all Arab leaders learned from the blunders of others before them. In another echo of the past, one more Arab air force – this time Libyan – was annihilated because of reckless decisions taken by the country's leadership. Within days of the no-fly operation beginning, a senior RAF officer said that "the Libyan Air Force no longer exists as a fighting force" – his announcement sounding uncannily similar to that RAF statement in Iraq back in 1941: "Iraq's air force was largely destroyed."

At the time of writing it is not clear what kind of new regimes will emerge to take the place of the old ones. The cries are for democracy, with open and fair societies. If these goals are realised, then the Arab countries will at last be on a path to foster and develop new systems of education and training that would benefit the aviation sector as much as many others.

As the Libya no-fly experience showed, at least until the ultimate outcome of the revolutions is clear, the region will continue largely to reap the harvest of the past. Indeed, it is hard to look back over the century of the Arabs' association with aviation without a touch of melancholy – a tinge of regret at wasted opportunities. The Heliopolis aviation week raised huge expectations, some of them hopelessly over-optimistic. One Egyptian columnist predicted at the time that flying would bring about international harmony because aeroplanes would cause borders to disappear: "They will scoff at them from above. Friendly relations will increase among peoples and so will the binding of their technological, commercial, and social relations. In short, the world will see a new golden age."[21] Two years later a street in Cairo was named after Wilbur Wright[22] and pioneering flights down the Nile to Sudan were under way. A golden age still seemed possible. But soon after that, hopes evaporated as aircraft were flown in a war for the first time – in Egypt, Iraq and Palestine. The region then witnessed the great transcontinental pioneering flights and the establishment of commercial air routes. By the 1930s, professional Arab pilots were taking to the skies of the Middle East.

The potential was enormous. Not only could the Arabs have been successful in developing an aerospace industry of their own, but flying could also have had a positive impact on the development of an integrated Middle East. Instead, the region has had to rely on the skills and technology from abroad. Air superiority, too, has almost always been enjoyed by foreigners – the British, French and (latterly) the Americans; and the Israelis. At the same time, foreign powers have used their domination of the skies to tighten their hold on their colonial possessions, and to come to the support of their Arab friends and allies.

Long after the end of the colonial era Arabs at last have an aviation achievement of which they can be proud – one that has nothing to do with military prowess. The success of Gulf-based airlines in the opening years of the 21st century and their international reputation for comfort and efficiency also provide a fitting legacy of the important role played by Bahrain and Sharjah in the establishment of air routes to India and Australia in the 1930s. But this achievement, while considerable in itself, is no substitute for the more influential role the Arab world could have played in civil and military aviation. As a UNDP report in 2009 pointed out, "building skyscrapers and state-of-the-art airports and owning luxury cars are the external shell of economic modernity, not its

231

beating heart, which lies in science, knowledge, and technological innovation."[23] These are the vital ingredients that the Arabs must acquire, if flying is eventually to have a positive impact on the Middle East of the future. The new generation of younger Arab leaders, it is hoped, will be sufficiently perspicacious to steer the region away from entering another long period of missed opportunities.

A right royal occasion: Heliopolis Aviation Week, February 1910. Crowds in Egypt watched displays of flying, only months after Louis Blériot had made history by crossing from France to Britain by air. (*Courtesy of George Eastman House*)

A Blériot monoplane, on display in Alexandria in 1909 in the build-up to the Heliopolis Aviation Week, was an object of public fascination – the model here is part of the Shuttleworth Collection in Britain. (*The author*)

Frank McClean's Short biplane on the Nile during his epic flight from Cairo to Khartoum and back in 1914. (*Courtesy of the Royal Aeronautical Society*)

Frank McClean and Roland Garros were among the early pioneers of flight who began to attract increasing media attention.

FLIES 558 MILES ACROSS THE SEA

Garros Reaches Tunis from France, Crossing the Mediterranean in 7 Hours 45 Minutes.

ATLANTIC FLIGHT NEARER

From Ireland to Newfoundland About 3 1-2 Times the Distance Garros Went Yesterday.

By Marconi Transatlantic Wireless Telegraph to The New York Times.

PARIS, Sept. 23.—The aviator Roland G. Garros to-day crossed the Mediterranean from Frejus, near Cannes, to Bizerta, near Tunis, adding another record to the list of French aerial achievements.

Garros had contemplated the flight for some time, despite the efforts of his friends to persuade him to abandon the idea. He disdained the offer

ROLAND G. GARROS.

of the French Admiralty to assist him with a chain of torpedo boats, and, without saying anything to any one but a few friends, arranged to make the attempt.

At 6 o'clock this morning in a Morane-Saulnier monoplane fitted with a Gnome engine, he flew south on his 558-mile journey over the sea. The weather was fine.

For some time after Garros had disappeared his friends were without news. Then, between 7 and 8 o'clock, a wireless message from Ajaccio, Corsica, announced that the monoplane had passed there, heading for Tunis. Ajaccio is about 112 miles from the French coast.

Shortly afterward Garros was reported over the coast of Sardinia, and at 1:45 P. M. a message from Bizerta announced that he had landed there, having made a no-stop flight.

Garros's flight ranks as one of the most notable feats in aviation. He did not actually fly 558 miles without passing land, but two stages, one of 112 miles and the other of 125 miles, were over the sea, without the possibility of rescue had he fallen. His actual flying time was 7 hours 45 minutes.

There were scenes of wild enthusiasm in Bizerta when Garros landed. The crews of the warships in the roads joined the townspeople in giving him a magnificent ovation.

The author's uncle, who served with the Royal Flying Corps and later in the Royal Air Force, was stationed in Iraq for several years and sent this postcard showing his flying colleagues to his family in Britain. (*Courtesy of the Butt family*)

Not sleek, but effective for carrying troops: a line-up of Vickers Vernons at RAF Hinaidi near Baghdad after World War One. (*Courtesy of the National Archives, Kew, UK*)

The RAF camp at Mosul in northern Iraq during World War One. (*Courtesy of the National Archives, Kew, UK*)

An RAF Dh9a biplane over the Sulaimaniya Valley in northern Iraq – this type of aircraft was in service throughout the Middle East. (*Courtesy of the National Archives, Kew, UK*)

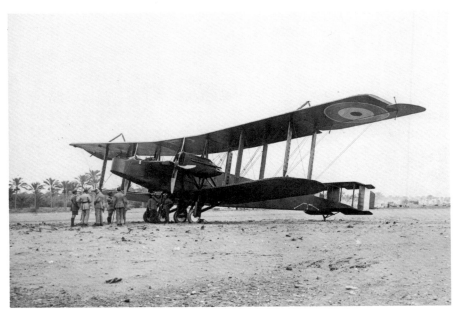

The second Handley Page 0/400 bomber to reach Egypt in December 1918 – en route via the Gulf to India. (*Courtesy of the National Archives, Kew, UK*)

A senior British officer climbs aboard a biplane in Cairo for an inspection flight along the Suez Canal. (*Courtesy of the National Archives, Kew, UK*)

Some of the first Arabs to be trained as pilots pose on a grass field in England before flying their Gypsy Moth biplanes in formation to Iraq where they received a royal welcome. (*Courtesy of Flight*)

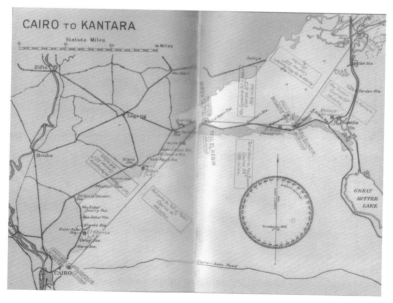

A part of one of the detailed maps showing the air route from Cairo to Baghdad that was contained in a pilot's handbook published in the 1920s. The handbook contained a range of information – including how to draw signals in the desert sand after forced landings. (*Courtesy of the British Airways Heritage Centre*)

الحكومة البريطانيــة   **BRITISH GOVERNMENT**

الى كل عربى كريم

السلام عليكم ورحمة الله وبركاته وبعد ، فحامل هذا الكتاب ض بط بالجيش البريطاني وهو صديق
وفي لكافه الشعوب العربية فنرجو أن تعامله بالعطف والاكرام . وأن تحافظوا على حياته من كل
طارىء ، ونأمل عند الاضطرار أن تقدموا له مايحتاج اليه من طعام وشراب . وأن ترشدوه الى
أقرب معسكر بريطاني . وسنكافئكم مالياً بسخاء على ماتسدونه اليه من خدمات .
والسلام عليكم ورحمة الله وبركاته ؟   القيادة البريطانية العامة فى الشرق الاوسط

To All Arab Peoples—Greetings and Peace be upon you. The bearer of this letter is
an Officer of the British Government and a friend of all Arabs. Treat him well, guard him from
harm, give him food and drink, help him to return to the nearest British soldiers and you will
be rewarded. Peace and the Mercy of God upon you. *The British High Command in the East.*

SOME POINTS ON CONDUCT WHEN MEETING THE ARABS IN THE DESERT

Remove footwear on entering their tents. Completely ignore their women. If thirsty drink
the water they offer, but DO NOT fill your waterbottle from their personal supply. Go to their
well and fetch what you want. Never neglect any puddle or other water supply for topping up
your bottle. Use the Halazone included in your Aid Box. Do not expect breakfast if you
sleep the night. Arabs will give you a mid-day or evening meal.

REMEMBER, NEVER TRY TO HURRY IN THE DESERT, SLOW AND SURE DOES IT

A FEW USEFUL WORDS					
English		**Arabic**	**English**		**Arabic**
English ..	.. ..	Ingleezi	Day ..	.. ..	Nahaar or Yom
Friend ..	.. ..	Sa-hib, Sa-deck	Night ..	.. ..	Layl
Water ..	.. ..	Moya	Half ..	.. ..	Nuss
Food ..	.. ..	Akl or Mungareh	Half a day ..	.. ..	Nuss il Nahaar
Village ..	.. ..	Balaad	Near ..	.. ..	Gareeb
Tired ..	.. ..	Ta-eban	Far ..	.. ..	Baeed

English	**Arabic**
Take me to the English and you will be rewarded	Hud nee eind el Ingelez wa lahud Mu-ka-fa
English Flying Officer	Za-bit Ingleezi Tye-yara
How far (how many kilos?)	Kam kilo?
Enemy	Germani, Taliani, Siziliani

Distance and time: Remember, Slow and Sure does it

The older Arabs cannot read, write or tell the time. They measure distance by the number
of days' journey. " Near " may mean 10 minutes or 10 hours. Far more probably means over a
day's journey. A day's journey is probably about 30 miles. The younger Arabs are more accurate.

GOOD LUCK

1

A message in Arabic and English, plus a few useful Arabic words that a pilot was
advised to learn in case of a forced landing in the desert – in a handbook covering
the air route from Cairo to Karachi, published in the 1940s. (*Courtesy of the British
Airways Heritage Centre*)

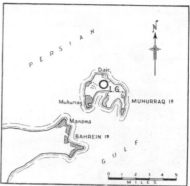

Maps and an aerial photograph of the landing ground in Bahrain – one of the most modern and best equipped in the Middle East in the 1930s and 40s. (*Courtesy of the British Airways Heritage Centre*)

A Dh66 Hercules of Imperial Airways that was used on the first passenger service linking Britain with the Middle East – seen here refuelling at Cairo. (*Courtesy of the British Airways Heritage Centre*)

From Cairo, Imperial Airways opened up a route to South Africa, with Khartoum one of the first stops for the Armstrong Whitworth Argosies. (*Courtesy of the British Airways Heritage Centre*)

'City of Jerusalem' was the name given to this Hercules, making a stop at a desert landing strip. The aircraft crashed in 1929 at Jask in Iran. (*Courtesy of the British Airways Heritage Centre*)

An imperial roll-call – a timetable indicating the range of destinations, with Egypt at the hub, for Imperial Airways' eastern and southern routes. (*Courtesy of the British Airways Heritage Centre*)

The Handley Page HP42 (named Hanno) became stuck in the desert when it first landed in Bahrain in 1932. After it had been pulled clear it took off again and landed on Muharraq Island, where Bahrain's airport has been ever since. (*Courtesy of the Imperial War Museum, London*)

Rutbah Wells seen from the air, a castle in the desert where Imperial Airways passengers spent a night on flights to and from India. (*Courtesy of the Library of Congress*)

Gaza was another refuelling stop for the HP42 en route from Cairo to the Gulf and India. (*Courtesy of the Library of Congress*)

The HP42 was a familiar sight in Egypt and the Gulf – but also flew for a time on routes through Khartoum. (*Courtesy of the British Airways Heritage Centre*)

Luxury was the name of the game for passengers on the HP42s, with lavish meals served as the plane flew slowly but majestically from Cairo to India and back in the 1930s. (*Courtesy of the British Airways Heritage Centre*)

Bahrain airport was one of the most sophisticated in the Gulf in the 1930s, even though not all the buildings were modern. (*Courtesy of the British Airways Heritage Centre*)

The Sea of Galilee was a refuelling stop for Imperial Airways' Short Kent flying boat service between the Mediterranean and the Gulf. (*Courtesy of the British Airways Heritage Centre*)

The romance of reaching the 'exotic' east by air is captured in this early Imperial Airways poster. (*Courtesy of the British Airways Heritage Centre*)

The Imperial Airways staff magazine, as much as any other publication of the day, liked to reinforce the stereotypical image of the Arab world, into which the civilising force of Western technology had been injected. (*Courtesy of the British Airways Heritage Centre*)

Many aviation pioneers who criss-crossed the Middle East wrote accounts of their flights – including Jean Batten, posing here in front of her Gypsy Moth at Nicosia in Cyprus before heading for Lebanon on her record-breaking flight from Britain to Australia in 1934. (*Courtesy of the Der Avedissian family*)

Arrival of an Imperial Airways HP42 at Haifa, Palestine in the 1930s. (*Courtesy of the Library of Congress*)

The River Nile in Egypt was the point of arrival and departure for Imperial Airways'
seaplane services in the late 1930s. (Top: *Courtesy of the Imperial War Museum*;
bottom: *Courtesy of the British Airways Heritage Centre*)

This carefully constructed scene was photographed by Imperial Airways as part of its advertising drive to attract passengers to flying boat services. (*Courtesy of the British Airways Heritage Centre*)

A Lockheed Lodestar over Cairo during World War Two descending towards Heliopolis. (*Courtesy of the Imperial War Museum*)

Arab Legion soldiers guard an RAF landing ground in the Jordanian desert close to the Iraqi border, at the time of the Rashid Ali coup in May 1941. (*Courtesy of the Imperial War Museum*)

An RAF Lysander off the coast of Beirut after the Allies had defeated the German-backed Vichy forces in July 1941. (*Courtesy of the Imperial War Museum*)

The de Havilland Rapide became the workhorse of the Middle East oil industry in the 1930s and 40s – this one in the service of the Iraq Petroleum Company. (*Courtesy of the Library of Congress*)

KLM was one of a handful of airlines tha began to challenge Imperial Airways' grip o commercial services between Europe and th Middle East – here a DC3 Dakota is refuelle at Lydda in Palestine. (*Courtesy of the Librar of Congress*)

A 1950s BOAC ticket issued to the author (aged four) for a flight from London to Amman. (*The author*)

Date of Flight	Aircraft and Registration	From	To	Hrs. Mins.	Statute Miles	Captain's Signature
		Brought Forward.	36:50		10,439	
3/4/62	COMET 4 G·APDL	LONDON	BAHRAIN	8·20	3,590	J H Waterfield
1 MAY 1962	RR 707 G·APFL	BAHRAIN	LONDON.	8·40	3·627	KM Carey
17/1/63	VISCOUNT G-APOW	BAHREIN	DOHA.	:30	93	R L Greenacre
20/1/63	COMET IV G-APDN	BAHRAIN	LONDON	9·20 ~~8·900~~	35·6 ~~3·900~~	J Martin p/o CAPT. BELL
30/7/63	Comet iv G·APDB	London	Bahrain	8·55	3·343	J H Gorway p/o Capt Bell
		Accumulative Totals	71·15		24,613	

A page from the author's Junior Jet Club log book, signed by the captain on every BOAC flight. (*The author*)

أتستطيع بحث المسألة فى الأسبوع القادم ؟

" Easily — I'll fly at once! "

Competition in today's rapidly changing markets waits for no man.
Buyers and sellers with overseas interests know that a decision made
today outside their territory may well mean a flying trip tomorrow.
They know, too, that 175,000 miles of Speedbird routes to 51
countries on *all six continents* enable them to fly without delay, swiftly
and in comfort—on *one ticket* all the way. Complimentary meals
are served en route. No tips or extras for prompt, courteous
attention. It's part of B.O.A.C.'s 31-year-old tradition
of Speedbird service and experience.

*Book Now! No charge for advice, information or bookings by Speedbird to all six continents at your local
B.O.A.C. Appointed Agent or B.O.A.C., Airways Terminal, Buckingham Palace Road, London, S.W.1.*

B.O.A.C. TAKES GOOD CARE OF YOU

FLY · BY · B·O·A·C

BRITISH OVERSEAS AIRWAYS CORPORATION IN ASSOCIATION WITH QANTAS EMPIRE AIRWAYS
LIMITED, SOUTH AFRICAN AIRWAYS & TASMAN EMPIRE AIRWAYS LIMITED

Attracting business travellers in the 1950s, BOAC's marketing department opted for
caricature figures of a cigarette-smoking Egyptian and a stiff-upper-lip Englishman.
(*Courtesy of the British Airways Heritage Centre*)

Aviation was a common theme on postage stamps as national airlines in the Arab
world expanded in the 1950s and 60s. (*The author*)

Brash and confident: publicity material and an in-flight drinks menu from Middle East Airlines in the late 1950s, during Beirut's golden era. (*The author*)

الخطوط الجوّيّة العراقيّة

بخط سكة الحكومة العراقيّة

IRAQI

AIRWAYS

TIMETABLE AND FARES

Effective 1st February, 1952.

IRAQI STATE RAILWAYS

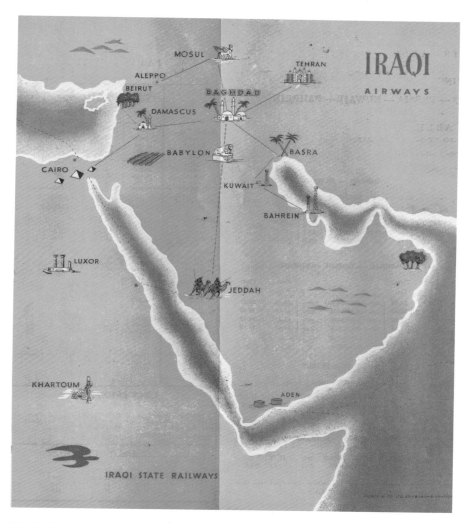

Newly formed Iraqi Airways in the 1950s connected Baghdad with nine cities in the region. (*The author*)

Luggage being carried from a Gulf Aviation de Havilland Heron at Dubai airport in the late 1950s. (*Courtesy of the Butt family*)

Muharraq airport, Bahrain: a BOAC Bristol Britannia in the foreground and Lockheed Constellation in the background. (*Courtesy of the Butt family*)

Family snapshots. *Top*: The author (second on the right) at Amman airport in the early 1950s with his siblings before their return on a BOAC Canadair Argonaut to boarding school in Britain. *Centre*: The author's mother by the wingtip of a Gulf Aviation Heron at Abu Dhabi in 1963. *Bottom*: The author (in centre of picture, left arm raised) arriving in Bahrain for school holidays in 1963. (*Courtesy of the Butt family*)

A Kuwait Airways Vickers Viscount on the sandy tarmac at Dubai in the early 1960s. (*Courtesy of the Butt family*)

View of Dubai terminal and control tower taken from inside the Viscount. (*Courtesy of the Butt family*)

When three airliners hijacked by Palestinian gunmen were blown up on a desert airfield in Jordan in September, aviation had already become a pawn in the violent politics of the Middle East, a grim association that reached its nadir in the terrorist attacks on New York and Washington in September 2001. (*Courtesy of the Al-Safir, Beirut*)

The three airlines that finally made Arab aviation a giant player on the world stage: Emirates, Qatar Airways and Etihad.
(Top: *courtesy of Emirates*; Centre & Bottom: *The author*)

Endnotes

Introduction

1. Grant R G, *Flight: 100 Years of Aviation*, Dorling Kindersley, London, 2004, p 10.

2. Mearles V E, (Editor), *Highways of the Air*, Michael Mason, London, 1946, p 87.

Chapter 1

1. *Egyptian Gazette*, 12 October 1909.
2. *Egyptian Gazette*, 13 October 1909.
3. *Flight*, 15 May 1909.
4. *Flight*, 4 December 1909.
5. *Egyptian Gazette*, 30 November 1909.
6. *Egyptian Gazette*, 14 December 1909.
7. *Egyptian Gazette*, 16 December 1909.
8. *Egyptian Gazette*, 21 December 1909.
9 *Egyptian Gazette*, 12 January 1910.
10 *Egyptian Gazette*, 1 February 1910.
11 *Flight*, 5 February 1910.
12. *Egyptian Gazette*, 28 January 1910.
13. Quoted by *Egyptian Gazette*, 19 January 1910.
14. Quoted by Gary Leiser, "The First Flight Above Egypt: The Great Week of Aviation at Heliopolis, 1910", *Journal of the Royal Asiatic Society* (2010), Third Series, 20:267-294, Cambridge University Press. All other quotations from the Arabic press in Egypt in this chapter are sourced from this article.
15. Gary Leiser, "The First Flight Above Egypt: The Great Week of Aviation at Heliopolis, 1910".
16. *Egyptian Gazette*, 7 February 1910.
17. Quoted in *International Herald Tribune*, 10 February 2010.
18. *Egyptian Gazette*, 11 February.
19. Gary Leiser, "The First Flight Above Egypt: The Great Week of Aviation at Heliopolis, 1910".
20. *The New York Times*, 17 July 1910.
21. *Flight*, 15 April 1911.
22. *Flight*, 22 April 1911.
23. *Flight*, 6 July 1912.
24. *Flight*, 3 February 1912.
25. *Flight*, 17 February 1912.
26. *Flight*, 27 September 1913.

27. *The New York Times*, 24 September 1913.
28. Grant R G, *Flight: 100 Years of Aviation*, p 43.
29. *Flight*, 10 September 1910.
30. *Flight*, 23 September 1911.
31. *Flight*, 5 October 1912.
32. *Flight*, 22 November 1913.
33. *Flight*, 6 December 1913.
34. *Flight*, 27 December 1913.
35. Jadayel, Oussama C, *Aviation in Lebanon 1913-1944: It Happened in our Skies*, Editions Dar An-Nahar/Publications of the University of Balamand, 2005, p 27.
36. *Flight*, 3 January 1914.
37. *Flight*, 10 January 1914.
38. *Flight*, 27 December 1913.
39. *The Times*, 4 February 1914.
40. Quoted in an exhibition at the British Royal Naval Air Station Museum at Yeovilton, Somerset.
41. *The Times*, 5 January 1914.
42. Jadayel, Oussama C, *Aviation in Lebanon 1913-1944*, p 35.
43. Jadayel, Oussama C, *Aviation in Lebanon 1913-1944*, p 49.
44. *Flight*, 12 November 1910.
45. Vandewalle, Dirk, *A History of Modern Libya*, Cambridge University Press, 2006, p 24.
46. *Flight*, 6 January 1912.
47. *Flight*, 17 February 1912.
48. *BBC News Online*, 10 May 2011 (http://www.bbc.co.uk/news/world-europe-13294524).
49. *Flight*, 27 January 1912.
50. *Flight*, 21 September 1912.

Chapter 2
1. Strachan, Hew, *The First World War: A New Illustrated History*, Pocket Books, London 2003, p 168.
2. Lawrence, T E, *Seven Pillars of Wisdom*, Penguin, 1978, p 59.
3. The Royal Flying Corps (RFC) was established in April 1912. The Royal Air Force was created in April 1918, bringing together the RFC and the Royal Naval Air Service (RNAS).
4. Tennant, Lt Col John E, *Baghdad: the Air War in Mesopotamia 1916-1918*, reprinted by the Battery Press, Nashville, 1992, p 8.
5. *History of No. 30 Squadron: Egypt and Mesopotamia 1914 to 1919*, Naval & Military Press in association with the Imperial War Museum, London, (Mesopotamia Section), p 2.

6. Strachan, Hew, *The First World War: A New Illustrated History*, p 169.

7. *History of No. 30 Squadron*, (Mesopotamia Section), p 2.

8. *History of No. 30 Squadron*, (Mesopotamia Section), p 5.

9. Cited by *History of No. 30 Squadron*, (Mesopotamia Section), p 5.

10. Strachan, Hew, T*he First World War: A New Illustrated History*, p 169.

11. Lawrence, T E, *Seven Pillars of Wisdom*, Penguin, p 59.

12. Quoted by *Flight*, 18 May 1916.

13. *History of No. 30 Squadron*, (Mesopotamia Section), p 7.

14. Jadayel, Oussama C, *Aviation in Lebanon 1913-1944*, p 57.

15. *History of No. 30 Squadron*, (Mesopotamia Section), p 9.

16. *History of No. 30 Squadron*, (Mesopotamia Section), p 10.

17. Strachan, Hew, *The First World War: A New Illustrated History*, p 169.

18. Lawrence, T E, *Seven Pillars of Wisdom*, pp 59-60.

19. *History of No. 30 Squadron*, (Mesopotamia Section), p 11.

20. Lewis, Cecil, *Sagittarius Rising*, Greenhill Books, London; Stackpole Books, Pennsylvania, 2003, p 65.

21. *Flight*, 29 June 1916.

22. *Flight*, 15 January 1915.

23. *The Times*, 28 January 1915.

24. *The Times*, 8 February 1915.

25. *Flight*, 5 March 1915.

26. *Flight*, 23 April 1915.

27. *Flight*, 17 September 1915.

28. *The Times*, 28 March 1916.

29. *Flight*, 25 May 1916.

30. *The Times*, 19 June 1916.

31. *Flight*, 7 December 1916.

32. Mansfield, Peter, *The British in Egypt*, Holt, Rinehart and Winston, New York, Chicago, San Francisco, 1971, p 215.

33. *Flight*, 16 November 1916.

34. For a detailed account of the battles for Gaza in the First World War, see Gerald Butt's *Life at the Crossroads: A History of Gaza*, Rimal Publications, Nicosia, new edition 2009.

35. Hughes, C E, *Above and Beyond Palestine: An Account of the Work of the East Indies and Egypt Seaplane Squadron 1916-1918*, Ernest Benn Ltd, London, 1930, p 213.

36. Hughes, C E, *Above and Beyond Palestine: An Account of the Work of the East Indies and Egypt Seaplane Squadron 1916-1918*, p 72.

37. Hughes, C E, *Above and Beyond Palestine: An Account of the Work of the East Indies and Egypt Seaplane Squadron 1916-1918*, pp 197-200.

38. al-Shawwa, Rushdi Sa'id, unpublished memoirs, quoted by kind permission of the Shawwa family.

39. Lawrence, T E, *Seven Pillars of Wisdom*, p 561.
40. Lawrence, T E, *Seven Pillars of Wisdom*, p 350.
41. Lawrence, T E, *Seven Pillars of Wisdom*, p 616.
42. Lawrence, T E, *Seven Pillars of Wisdom*, p 636.
43. *Flight*, 13 October 1921.
44. Tennant, Lt-Col J E, *In the Clouds Above Baghdad*, 1992.
45. Grant, R G, *Flight: 100 Years of Aviation*, p 67.
46. McMinnies, W G, *Practical Flying: Complete Course of Flying Instruction*, Temple Press Limited, London, 1918, pp 3-4.

Chapter 3

1. *The New York Times*, 1 June 1917.
2. *Flight*, 8 March 1917.
3. *Flight*, 28 June 1917.
4. *The Times*, 6 February 1919.
5. *The Times*, 13 December 1918.
6. *The Times*, 8 January 1919.
7. *Flight*, 25 September 1919.
8. Ross Smith referred to this in a diary entry during his stopover in India: "Great interest shown in machine [Vimy], especially in the parts that flew the Atlantic with Alcock" *Flight*, 18 December 1919.
9. *The Times*, 15 December 1919; *Flight,* 18 December 1919.
10. *Flight*, 18 December 1919.
11. *Flight*, 27 February 1919.
12. *Flight*, 12 June 1919.
13. *The Times*, 6 and 7 February 1920.
14. *Flight*, 11 December 1919.
15. Quoted by Penrose, Harald, *Wings Across the World: An Illustrated History of British Airways*, Cassell, London, 1980, p 27.
16. Penrose, Harald, *Wings Across the World*, p 27.
17. *Pilots' Handbook of the Cairo-Baghdad Route.*
18. McGregor, Alan, "Flying the Furrow", *Saudi Aramco World*, March/April 2001, pp 24-31.
19. Mearles, V E (Editor), *Highways of the Air*, Michael Mason, London, 1946, p 30.
20. *Cook's Traveller's Handbook: Palestine and Syria*, London, 1925, p 419.
21. *Flight*, 30 June 1921.
22. *Flight*, 18 August 1921.
23. McGregor, Alan, "Flying the Furrow", *Saudi Aramco World*, March/April 2001, pp 24-31.
24. *The Times*, 18 January 1922.
25. *Flight*, 2 January 1919.

26. *The Times*, 4 February 1920.
27. *The Times*, 5 February 1920.
28. *The Times*, 7 February 1920.
29. *Flight*, 25 March 1920.
30. *The Times*, 16 February 1920.
31. Mansfield, Peter, *A History of the Middle East*, Penguin, London, 1992, p 96.
32. Cobham, Sir Alan, *Twenty-thousand Miles in a Flying Boat*, Tempus Publishing Ltd, Stroud, 2007, p 189.
33. Taylor, Michael J H, and Mondey, David, *Milestones of Flight*, pp 64 and 69.
34. Grant, R G, *Flight: 100 Years of Aviation*, p 132.
35. Taylor, Michael J H, and Mondey, David, *Milestones of Flight*, p 69.
36. *Flight*, 17 February 1921.
37. *The Times*, 31 August 1921.
38. Jadayel, Oussama C, *Aviation in Lebanon 1913-1944*, p 79.

Chapter 4

1. Quoted by Penrose, Harald, *Wings Across the World*, p 38.
2. *The Times*, 12 March 1925.
3. Quoted by Penrose, Harald, *Wings Across the World*, p 44.
4. *Flight*, 17 September 1925.
5. British Airways Heritage Centre.
6. *The Times*, 8 September 1926.
7. Cobham, Sir Alan, *To the Ends of the Earth: Memoirs of a Pioneering Aviator*, Tempus, UK, 2007, pp 92-107.
8. *The Times*, 16 December 1926.
9. Penrose, Harald, *Wings Across the World*, p 51.
10. *Flight*, 13 January 1927.
11. The following paragraphs quote extensively from this handbook which was published in the 1920s.
12. Almost certainly the work of Dr John Ball, a member of the Survey of Egypt team and compiler of *Military Notes on Western Egypt 1915-16*.
13. British Airways Heritage Centre.
14. *Flight*, 5 May 1927.
15. *Flight*, 5 January 1928.
16. *Flight*, 22 August 1930.
17. Mackey, Sandra, *The Iranians: Persia, Islam and the Soul of a Nation*, Dutton, New York, 1996, p 158.
18. *Flight*, 7 April 1927.
19. Mackey, Sandra, *The Iranians*, p 161.
20. *The Times*, 30 March 1927.
21. *Memorandum to the Secretary of State for Air – Concerning the position of Imperial Airways in relation to the Persian Gulf Section of the England-India*

Air Service, 15 March 1932, British Airways Heritage Centre.

22. Quoted by Penrose, Harald, *Wings Across the World*, p 65.

Chapter 5

1. Burchall, Lieut-Colonel H, DSO, *The Political Aspects of Commercial Air Routes* (Lecture), Imperial Airways, 1932, p 4.

2. *The Times*, 1 February 1929.

3. *The Times*, 30 March 1929.

4. *Daily Telegraph*, 15 April 1929.

5. *Imperial Gazette*, August 1929.

6. *Imperial Gazette*, September 1929.

7. Penrose, Harald, *Wings Across the World*, p 60.

8. British Library, India Office Records, IOR/POS/12/1954.

9. *Flight*, 30 October 1931.

10. *Flight*, 19 February 1932.

11. *Memorandum to the Secretary of State for Air – Concerning the position of Imperial Airways in relation to The Persian Gulf Section of the England-India Air Service*, 15 March 1932, British Airways Heritage Centre.

12. This quote and subsequent ones until the next endnote are from: British Library, India Office Records, IOR/L/PS/12/1954.

13. Until 1947, the political resident was based in Bushehr in Iran and reported to the British government in India. Lower ranking diplomats (political agents) were based in Bahrain, Qatar, Dubai and Abu Dhabi. In 1947, after India gained independence, the political agent was based in Bahrain. The post was scrapped in 1971 when Britain withdrew from the Gulf.

14. The Indian rupee was the standard currency in the Gulf until the mid-1960s – until 1970 in the case of Oman.

15. *Agreement between Shaikh Sultan bin Saqar, Ruler of Shargah, and the British Government for the Establishment of an Air Station at Shargah*, British Airways Heritage Centre.

16. Burchall, Lieut-Colonel H, DSO, *The Political Aspects of Commercial Air Routes* (Lecture), Imperial Airways, 1932, pp 21-22.

17. British Library, India Office Records, IOR/POS/12/1954.

Chapter 6

1. Mearles, V E, (editor) *Highways of the Air*, p 31.

2. Penrose, Harald, *Wings Across the World*, p 73.

3. Frater, Alexander, *Beyond the Blue Horizon: On the Track of Imperial Airways*, Picador, London, 2005, p 11.

4. *Imperial Gazette*, October 1932.

5. Quoted by Penrose, Harald, *Wings Across the World*, p 59.

6. *Flight*, 19 February 1932.

7. Britain recognised the Kingdom of Hejaz and Nejd in 1927. The two regions were united to become the Kingdom of Saudi Arabia in September 1932.

8. *Flight*, 30 September 1932.

9. Watts, David, *The Story of Aviation in the Kingdom of Bahrain*, Bahrain Aerospace in association with Key Books, UK, 2010, p 55.

10. Watts, David, *The Story of Aviation in the Kingdom of Bahrain*, p 62.

11. Frater, Alexander, *Beyond the Blue Horizon*, p 102.

12. *Air Route Book: Cairo to Karachi via North Arabia and Persian Gulf*, RAF Transport Command, 1943.

13. The forerunner of today's Saudi Aramco, the state oil company of Saudi Arabia.

14. A flag introduced in Britain in 1931 to be flown at United Kingdom airports and by UK aircraft landing overseas. It consisted of a dark blue cross on a light blue background, with a union flag in the top quarter close to the flagpole.

15. A flag flown by British aircraft when landing overseas during the 1930s – a gold crown and bugle on a navy blue background.

16. *Air Outpost*, Directed by John Taylor and Ralph Keen, 1937, British Airways Heritage Centre.

17. Quoted by Frater, Alexander, *Beyond the Blue Horizon*, pp 112-113.

18. *Imperial Gazette*, January 1933.

19. Tuson, Penelope, *Playing the Game: Western Women in Arabia*, I B Tauris, London, 2003, p 209.

20. Quoted by Frater, Alexander, *Beyond the Blue Horizon*, pp 85-86.

21. *Imperial Gazette*, February 1937.

22. *Aeroplane Monthly*, October 2010, p 20.

23. Hudson, Kenneth and Pettifer, Julian, *Diamonds in the Sky: A Social History of Air Travel*, Bodley Head/BBC Publications, London, 1979, p 80.

24. *Imperial Airways Staff News*, 10 January 1933.

25. *Imperial Gazette*, September 1933.

26. Frater, Alexander, *Beyond the Blue Horizon*, p 79.

27. *Imperial Gazette*, August and September 1933.

28. *The Times*, 30 April 1929.

29. *Imperial Gazette*, August 1933.

30. *Imperial Gazette*, February 1932.

31. Penrose, Harald, *Wings Across the World*, p 76.

32. *Flight*, 8 April 1932.

33. *Imperial Gazette*, June 1930.

34. *Flight*, 5 September 1930.

35. Batten, Jean, *My Life*, George G Harrap & Co Ltd, London, 1938 pp 45-46.

36. St Exupéry, Antoine de, *Wind, Sand and Stars*, Picador, London, 1987, pp 87-114.

37. *The Times*, 17 November 1934.

38. *Imperial Gazette*, October 1929.

Chapter 7

1. Grant, R G, *Flight: 100 Years of Aviation*, p 136.
2. Hudson, Kenneth and Pettifer, Julian, *Diamonds in the Sky*, p 79.
3. Watts, David, *The Story of Aviation in the Kingdom of Bahrain*, p 62.
4. *Imperial Airways Staff News*, 21 February 1933.
5. British Library, India Office Records, IOR L/POS/12/1971.
6. *Imperial Airways Monthly Bulletin*, June 1927.
7. *Imperial Gazette*, July 1933.
8. *Flight*, 17 April 1931; *The Times*, 24 April 1931.
9. *Egyptian Gazette*, 1 April 1932.
10. *Egyptian Gazette*, 11 April 1932.
11. *Egyptian Gazette*, 3 June 1932.
12. Fromkin, David, *A Peace to End All Peace: Creating the Modern Middle East 1914-1922*, Andre Deutsch, London, 1989, p 503.
13. Mansfield, Peter, *A History of the Middle East*, p 197.
14. Head of the RAF's bomber command in World War Two, and an advocate of 'saturation' and 'area' bombing of German cities.
15. McDowall, David, *A Modern History of the Kurds*, IB Tauris, London, 2005, p 180.
16. Omissi, David, *Air Power and Colonial Control: The RAF 1919-1939*, Manchester, 1991, p 37 – quoted by McDowall, David, *A Modern History of the Kurds*, p 160.
17. Mansfield, Peter, *A History of the Middle East*, p 197.
18. *The Times,* 14 April 1925.
19. *Flight*, 21 March 1930.
20. Dickson, H R P, *The Arab of the Desert: A Glimpse into Badawin Life in Kuwait and Sau'di Arabia*, George Allen & Unwin Ltd, London, 1949, p 346.
21. Green, William and Fricker, John, *Air Forces of the World: Their History, Development and Present Strength*, Macdonald, London, 1958, p 237.
22. *Flight*, 12 September 1930.
23. British Library, India Office Records, IOR Ps/12/1950.
24. *Flight*, 28 February 1930.
25. *Egyptian Gazette*, 30 April 1932.
26. *Egyptian Gazette*, 18 June 1932.
27. National Archives, FO 141/727/3.
28. *Egyptian Gazette*, 13 January 1931.
29. *Egyptian Gazette*, 8 June 1932.
30. *The Times*, 14 March 1935.
31. *Egyptian Gazette*, 13 January 1931.

32. *The Times*, 16 June 1930.
33. Stegner, Wallace, *Saudi Aramco World*, July/August 1968.
34. Yergin, Daniel, *The Prize: The Epic Quest for Oil, Money & Power*, Free Press, New York, 1992, p 300.
35. *The Times*, 16 June 1930.
36. *Flight*, 10 January 1935.

Chapter 8

1. Lyman, Robert, *Iraq 1941: The battles for Basra, Habbaniya, Fallujah and Baghdad*, Osprey Publishing, UK, p 9.
2. Tripp, Charles, *A History of Iraq* (New Edition), Cambridge University Press, 2002, p 99.
3. Tripp, Charles, *A History of Iraq* (New Edition), pp 101-102.
4. Lyman, Robert, *Iraq 1941*, p 29.
5. After the fall of France in 1940, Syria (a French mandate) sided with the Vichy French government that, while officially neutral, collaborated with the German Nazis. For a detailed and comprehensive account of the Allied campaign against the Vichy forces, see Colin Smith's *England's Last War Against France: Fighting Vichy 1940-1942*, Weidenfeld & Nicolson, London, 2009.
6. Lyman, Robert, *Iraq 1941*, pp 38-39.
7. Lyman, Robert, *Iraq 1941*, p 41.
8. Lyman, Robert, *Iraq 1941*, p 27.
9. Lyman, Robert, *Iraq 1941*, p 52.
10. Quoted by Smith, Colin, *England's Last War Against France: Fighting Vichy 1940-1942*, Weidenfeld & Nicolson, London, 2009, p 177.
11. *The Times*, 5 May 1941.
12. *The Times*, 6 May 1941.
13. Lyman, Robert, *Iraq 1941*, p 52.
14. *The Times*, 16 May 1941.
15. *The Times*, 17 May 1941.
16. *Flight*, 20 November 1941.
17. *Flight*, 4 December 1941.
18. Grant, R G, *Flight: 100 Years of Aviation*, p 191.
19. Jadayel, Oussama C, *Aviation in Lebanon 1913-1944*, p 159.
20. *The Times*, 26 June 1941.
21. *Flight*, 17 July 1941.
22. *Air International* magazine, May 1982. Most of the subsequent information about the development of the REAF up to 1948 comes from this source.
23. Green, William and Fricker, John, *The Air Forces of the World*, p 283.
24. *Air International* magazine, May 1982.
25. Green, William and Fricker, John, *The Air Forces of the World*, p 284.
26. *Flight*, 15 March 1945.
27. *Flight*, 27 January 1944.

Chapter 9

1. *Time Magazine*, 24 November 1958.
2. Interviewed by the author, 2009.
3. Quoted by Grant, R G, *Flight: 100 Years of Aviation*, p 378.
4. Davies, R E G, *A History of the World's Airlines*, Oxford University Press, 1967, p 399
5. Established by the US Congress in 1938 to regulate civil aviation and air routes.
6. *Flight*, 23 August 1945.
7. Davies, R E G, *A History of the World's Airlines*, p 399.
8. Aburish, Said K, *Nasser: The Last Arab*, Duckworth, London, 2005, p 24.
9. *The Middle East: A Political and Economic Survey*, Royal Institute of International Affairs, London & New York, 1954, p 486.
10. Alamuddin, Najib, *The Flying Sheikh*, Quartet Books, London, 1987, p 38.
11. Alamuddin, Najib, *The Flying Sheikh*, p 39.
12. *Flight*, 12 August 1955.
13. *Flight*, 1 November 1957.
14. For a fascinating and comprehensive history of Aden Airways, see Watson, Dacre, *Red Sea Caravan: The Aden Airways Story*, Air-Britain (Historians) Ltd, 2008.
15. Alamuddin, Najib, *The Flying Sheikh*, p 97-98.
16. Alamuddin, Najib, *The Flying Sheikh*, p 60.
17. *Flight*, 16 April 1964.
18. *Flight*, 16 January 1969.
19. Grant, R G, *Flight: 100 Years of Aviation*, p 409.
20. Interviewed by the author, 2010.
21. Alamuddin, Najib, *The Flying Sheikh*, pp 204-205.
22. *Flight*, 13 November 1976.
23. Shute, Nevil, *Round the Bend*, Pan Books, 1968, p 47.
24. Frater, Alexander, *Beyond the Blue Horizon*, pp 107-108.
25. *Flight*, 16 May 1952.
26. *Flight*, 26 September 1952.
27. *The Times*, 16 September 1995.

Chapter 10

1. Green, William and Fricker, John, *The Air Forces of the World*, p 167.
2. Aloni, Shlomo, "The Knives of Israel", *Aeroplane* magazine, June 2008.
3. Green, William and Fricker, John, *The Air Forces of the World*, p 167.
4. Green, William and Fricker, John, *The Air Forces of the World*, p 167.
5. Ovendale, Ritchie, *The Origins of the Arab-Israeli Wars*, Longman, London and New York, 1984, p 121.
6. Mansfield, Peter, *A History of the Middle East*, p 236.
7. Mansfield, Peter, *A History of the Middle East*, p 241.

8. Green, William and Fricker, John, *The Air Forces of the World*, p 284.
9. Green, William and Fricker, John, *The Air Forces of the World*, p 285.
10. *Air International*, April 1982.
11. Sharaf, Sami, *Sanawaat wa Ayaam ma' Gemal Abdel-Nasser (Years and Days with Gemal Abdel-Nasser)*, Dar al-Farasan, Cairo, 2005, p 440.
12. *Flight International*, 29 February 1968.
13. *Air International*, April 1982.
14. Ovendale, Ritchie, *The Origins of the Arab-Israeli Wars*, pp 191-192.
15. Mansfield, Peter, *A History of the Middle East*, p 294.
16. Mansfield, Peter, *A History of the Middle East*, p 296.
17. *Air International*, April 1982.
18. *Flight*, 29 September 1979.

Chapter 11
1. *Flight International*, 27 July 2010.
2. *Flight International*, 15 June 2010.
3. Quoted by Gary Leiser, "The First Flight Above Egypt: The Great Week of Aviation at Heliopolis, 1910".
4. *Arab Human Development Report 2003: Building a Knowledge Society*, United Nations Development Programme, p 104.
5. *Arab Human Development Report 2003*, pp 97-98.
6. *Flight*, 26 March 1964.
7. *Flight*, 19 February 1970.
8. *Flight*, 19 February 1970.
9. *Arab Human Development Report 2003*, p 98.
10. *Flight*, 26 May 1079.
11. *Arab Human Development Report 2003*, p 106.
12. Al-Husri, Sati', *Difa'a 'an il-uruba (Defence of Arabism)*, Baghdad, Dar al-Ilm, Beirut, 1956, p 17.
13. *Al-Mustaqbal al-Arabi*, August 2010.
14. Ma'arouf, Muhammad, *Ayaam 'ishtuha (Days that I lived through 1949-1969)*, Riad El-Rayyes Books, Beirut, 2003, p 282.
15. *Arab Human Development Report 2003*, p 144.
16. *Arab Human Development Report 2003*, p 23.
17. *Flight International*, 19 June 1976.
18. *Air International*, June 1975.
19. Ma'arouf, Muhammad, *Ayaam 'ishtuha*, p 109.
20. El-Khazen, Jihad, *al-Hayat*, 21 March 2011.
21. Quoted by Gary Leiser, "The First Flight Above Egypt: The Great Week of Aviation at Heliopolis, 1910".
22. *Flight*, 18 August 1912.
23. *Arab Human Development Report 2009: Challenges to Human Security in the Arab Countries*, UNDP, p 198.

Index